Psychoanalysis and Theism

Psychoanalysis and Theism

Critical Reflections on the Grünbaum Thesis

Edited by Benjamin Beit-Hallahmi, PhD

JASON ARONSON
Lanham • Boulder • New York • Toronto • Plymouth, UK

Published by Jason Aronson
An imprint of Rowman & Littlefield Publishers, Inc.
A wholly owned subsidiary of The Rowman & Littlefield Publishing Group, Inc.
4501 Forbes Boulevard, Suite 200, Lanham, Maryland 20706
http://www.rowmanlittlefield.com

Estover Road, Plymouth PL6 7PY, United Kingdom

British Library Cataloguing in Publication Information Available

Library of Congress Cataloging-in-Publication Data
Psychoanalysis and theism : critical reflections on the Grünbaum thesis / edited by Benjamin Beit-Hallahmi.
p. ; cm.
Includes bibliographical references and index.
ISBN 978-0-7657-0722-2 (cloth : alk. paper)
1. Psychoanalysis and religion. I. Beit-Hallahmi, Benjamin.
[DNLM: 1. Freud, Sigmund, 1856–1939. 2. Grünbaum, Adolf. 3. Freudian Theory. 4. Religion and Psychology. WM 460.5.F9 P974 2010]
BF175.4.R44P79 2010
201'.6150195—dc22

2010014170

The paper used in this publication meets the minimum requirements of American National Standard for Information Sciences-Permanence of Paper for Printed Library Materials, ANSI/NISO Z39.48-1992.

Printed in the United States of America

Contents

Part II: Interpretation and Meaning

Preface

This volume constitutes part of the ongoing debate on the legacy of classical psychoanalysis within the context of the academic study of religion. How should we approach the psychological study of religion, and how relevant to its theorizing is classical psychoanalysis, identified with the writings of Sigmund Freud? Freud's writings of religion continue to attract attention and debate. Psychoanalysis has had more to say about religious matters than any of the various traditions in academic psychology and it has had a major effect on the study of religion in all the human sciences. It has been among the few psychological approaches which offer an explanation of religion as part of a comprehensive theory of human behavior, and in which religion is presented as an instance of general psychological forces in action.

Adolf Grünbaum's voice has been heard in the debate over the uses of psychoanalytic theory. Grünbaum has been known for decades as a leading philosopher of science, and since 1984, as a leading critic of psychoanalysis (Grünbaum 1984, 1993). He is also known as a secular humanist, and has devoted much time and effort to dissecting religious claims, especially those attempting to rely on theories and findings in physics. What Grünbaum makes clear in his "Autobiographical-Philosophical Narrative" (Jokic, 2009) is that his life's work is all of a piece, inspired by Enlightenment ideals and demanding equality not only when it comes to individual rights, but when judging and evaluating ideas. Claims should be backed by evidence, whether in physics, psychology, or in culture, and that includes religion, of course.

Grünbaum's "Psychoanalysis and Theism," which appeared in his *Validation in the Clinical Theory of Psychoanalysis* (1993), has been quoted, reprinted, criticized, and praised. It looks at Freud's general claims about the psychological mechanisms involved in religion and finds them lacking. Then, in a surprising turn, Grünbaum judges some of Freud's interpretations of concrete religious ideas and practices to be not only cogent, but indispensible. When it comes to the case of the belief in Virgin Birth, Grünbaum finds an Oedipal interpretation to be our only choice.

This remarkable essay is the stimulus for a symposium with seven scholars, coming from the fields of philosophy, psychology, and sociology, presenting their critical reflections on how we should study religion, how we should treat Freud's ideas, and what should be some of the future directions in psychological research on concrete religious behavior. Of special interest are essays which deal with the Virgin Birth doctrine and its possible psychological sources, and with the potential for future psychoanalytic studies of faith and ritual. Other essays focus on Freud's conscious and unconscious motivations for studying religion, as well as the hidden biases and lacunae in the social science literature on religious practices.

We need a theoretical framework capable of explaining both religion as a phenomenon and its specific historical manifestations as well. What the audience of educated readers is expecting of us are explanations of specific religious ideas and their underlying meanings. Classical psychoanalysis turns out to be one source of useful and usable ideas for mapping the imagination.

References

Grünbaum, A. (1984). *The Foundations of Psychoanalysis: A Philosophical Critique.* Berkeley, CA: University of California Press.

Grünbaum, A. (1993). *Validation in the Clinical Theory of Psychoanalysis: A Study in the Philosophy of Psychoanalysis.* Madison, CT: International Universities Press.

Jokic, A. (ed.) (2009). *Philosophy of Religion, Physics, and Psychology: Essays in Honor of Adolf Grünbaum.* Amherst, NY: Prometheus Books.

Acknowledgments

The preparation of this volume has been possible only because of the encouragement and good advice of good friends and the generous support of the University of Haifa.

David Livingstone Smith offered encouragement at an early stage, when the idea for the book was just a vague fantasy. Adolf Grünbaum has been supportive and patient ever since I first approached him about the project in 2007. Moreover, he also agreed to read some of the chapters and offered invaluable editorial advice, which really made a difference.

But it was my dear friend Gabriel Bar-Haim, who made the book a reality by alerting me to publication possibilities, when the project had been lying dormant in my computer for a while.

Jerry S. Piven, Emanuel Berman, Warren S. Goldstein, Gustavo S. Mesch, Jacob Ben-Cnaan, and Arie Grumet provided encouragement, ideas, and practical help. Genoveba Breitstein took care of preparing the manuscript.

Aharon Ben-Zeev, the president of the University of Haifa, offered both encouragement and vital financial help. The dean of social science at the University, Avi Sagi-Schwartz, has offered generous support.

The University of Haifa Research Authority, the Department of Psychology, and the University of Haifa Library made the work involved much easier. The computer support team proved its worth more than once when I got into trouble with the equipment.

Last but not least, all contributors to this volume have been a wonderful group to work with. Both their intellects and their collective generosity and reliability have made this project exciting and enjoyable. This has been a totally pleasing learning experience.

Part I: Methods and Motives

Chapter 1
Psychoanalysis and Theism

Adolf Grünbaum

The topic of "Psychoanalysis and Theism" suggests two distinct questions. First, what is the import, if any, of psychoanalytic theory for the truth or falsity of theism? And furthermore, what was the attitude of Freud, the man, toward belief in God? It must be borne in mind that *psychological* explanations of any sort as to why people believe in God are subject to an important *caveat.* Even if they are true, such explanations are not entitled to beg the following *different* question: Is religious belief *justified* by pertinent evidence or argument, whatever its motivational inspiration? Freud's usage, as well as stylistic reasons of my own, prompt me to use the terms "religion" and "theism" more or less interchangeably, although in other contexts the notion of religion is, of course, more inclusive.

Freud declared himself to be an atheist. But I submit that when he offered his psychological account of religious allegiances, he did *not* succumb to the temptation of arguing for atheism by begging the question. He understood all too well that a purely psychological explanation—however unflattering—of why people embrace Judaism, Christianity, or Islam does not itself suffice to discredit theism. Therefore, I claim, he did *not* fall prey to the well-known genetic fallacy, which is often called "the reductionism of nothing but." As he himself pointed out, those who commit this error overlook that the validity or invalidity of a doctrine as well as its truth or falsity are still left open by the psychological causes of its espousal. Thus, in a section on "The Philosophical Interest of Psychoanalysis," Freud wrote:

> psycho-analysis can indicate the subjective and individual motives behind philosophical theories which have ostensibly sprung from impartial logical work. . . . It is not the business of psychoanalysis [itself]; however, to undertake . . . criticism [of these theories] . . . for . . . the fact that [the acceptance of] a theory is psychologically determined does not in the least invalidate its scientific truth (1913b, p. 179).

Like Nietzsche before him, Freud had become an atheist in his student days. As a young student in Vienna, Freud took a course on the existence of God from Franz Brentano (McGrath, 1986).

Then, in 1901, at the age of 45, he offered his first published psychiatric diagnosis of religion as an obsessional neurosis. He did so in order to illustrate his psychological account of superstition (1901, pp. 258-259). As for the credibility of theism, he had reached a dismal verdict: "it is precisely the elements . . . which have the task of solving the riddles of the universe and of reconciling us to the sufferings of life—it is precisely those elements that are the least well authenticated of any" (1927, p. 27). But note how careful he was to stress the logical priority of his atheism *vis-à-vis* his psychology of theism:

> Nothing that I have said here against the truth-value of religions needed the support of psycho-analysis; it had been said by others long before analysis came into existence. If the application of the psycho-analytic method makes it possible to find a new argument against the truths of religion, *tant pis* [so much the worse] for religion; but defenders of religion will by the same right make use of psycho-analysis in order to give full value to the affective significance of religious doctrines (1927, p. 37).

In the same vein, he declared: "All I have done—and this is the only thing that is new in my exposition—is to add some psychological foundation to the [evidential] criticisms of my great predecessors" (1927, p. 35).

Apparently, Freud will be walking a tightrope. As we saw, he was very much aware that it is one thing to provide a *psychogenesis* of religious belief, and quite another to appraise that belief epistemologically, with a view to estimating its truth value. Yet, as he just told us, he also claimed that, after all, the *psychogenesis* of theism can have a *supplementary* philosophical bearing on the question of the truth or falsity of religion. And he sees his own contribution to the debate as being one of elucidating precisely that supplementary import. Hence, if we are to examine the philosophical case that Freud tries to make for atheism, we must first consider the evidential merit of the explanatory psychological hypotheses on which his psychogenetic portrait of religion relies.

My first task will be to develop the purely psychological content of Freud's theory of religion, but with a view to passing an epistemological judgment on its major psychological assumptions. These pivotal hypotheses are of three main sorts. Yet, only *two* of these sorts are *psychoanalytic* in the technical sense. Thus, only two-thirds of Freud's psychology of religion depends on the epistemic fortunes of his psychoanalytic enterprise. Later, I shall endeavor to articulate *and* appraise his sophisticated effort to harness his psychogenetic account of theism in the service of his irreligious philosophical agenda.

Freud's Psychogenesis of Religion

A short book entitled *The Future of an Illusion* (1927) is one of Freud's several major writings on religion. Just what claims did he make about belief in God by characterizing it as an "illusion"? As he tells us, "we call a belief an illusion when a wish-fulfillment is a prominent factor in its motivation, and in doing so we disregard its relation to reality, just as the illusion itself sets no store by verification" (p. 31). Thus, this sense of the term "illusion" is both psychogenetic and epistemological. It requires that the wish-fulfilling character of the belief content be an important motivating factor in its acceptance, whereas the availability of supporting evidence played no such psychogenetic role. In brief, Freud calls a belief an illusion, just when it is inspired by wishes *rather than* by awareness of some evidential warrant for it. Hence, as he uses the label, it is psychologically descriptive but epistemologically derogatory.

Yet clearly, it is then still an empirical question of actual fact whether any given illusion, thus defined, is true or false. Someone's wish-inspired belief to have bought a winning ticket to the Pennsylvania lottery may well be pathetically ill-founded, but just may turn out to be true after all. Christopher Columbus's conviction that he had discovered a new, shorter sea route to the orient was at once wish-inspired and false. In the vast majority of cases, middle-class girls who have believed that a prince charming will come and marry them were concocting mere fantasies. Yet, in a few instances, this hope was not dashed. Hence Freud points out (pp. 30-31) that an illusion is not necessarily false. Nor is a false belief necessarily illusory. For example, the belief that the earth is flat may be induced mainly by inadequate observations, rather than by wishes. To qualify as an illusion, even a false belief needs to have been prompted mainly by a wish, rather than by known evidence.

There is an important subclass of false illusions whose generating wishes are complex enough to include unconscious desires. For example, according to Freud's theory of paranoia, the false notions of persecution entertained by a paranoiac are held to be inspired by repressed homosexual wishes, and by the operation of two unconscious defense mechanisms. Freud uses the term "delusion" to refer to such psychogenetically complex false illusions (1927, pp. 31-81; 1911, pp. 59-65; 1915a; 1922). Thus, he also speaks of delusions of jealousy, delusions of grandeur, and the delusions associated with heterosexual erotomania (Laplanche and Pontalis, 1973, p. 296). In brief, every delusion is a false illusion, generated by requisitely complex wishes. Thus, a false illusion can fail to qualify as a delusion, if the desires that inspire it lack the stated psychogenetic complexity. But how do both illusions and delusions matter in Freud's philosophy of religion? They do, because the nub of his own philosophical argument for atheism will turn out to be the attempt to demonstrate the following: The theistic religions are delusions, rather than just illusions; in fact, they are mass delusions in important parts of the world.

It is to be borne in mind that these two technical notions differ importantly from the senses of "illusion" and "delusion" encountered in the *Psychiatric Dictionary* published by the Oxford University Press in 1981 (pp. 307-308). By contrast to Freud's wish-laden notion of "illusion," the Oxford *Psychiatric Dictionary* uses the same term to denote a false sense perception produced by a real external stimulus, as in the case of some mirages. Thus, when a straight pencil or glass tube is partially immersed in water, we have the so-called visual illusion that the submerged portion has bent and forms an angle with its free upper part, though it is actually still straight. In virtue of thus being induced by a real stimulus, an illusion in Oxford parlance differs from a *hallucinatory* sensation, which has no source in the subject's environment, but is produced endogenously.

Evidently, the Oxford sense of "illusion" requires that the perceptually induced belief be false, whereas Freud's wish-laden notion does not insist on a generic attribution of falsity. And instead of requiring a particular external physical object to be the eliciting cause, his concept calls for a psychological state. Later, when we address Freud's philosophical aim, we shall see just how the definition of "delusion" in the Oxford *Psychiatric Dictionary* (p. 157) seriously diverges from his, no less than its notion of illusion does. In Oxford parlance, it is a matter of definition that there cannot be any mass delusions, but only idiosyncratic ones.

By saying that Freud's psychogenetic portrait of theism depicts it as a collection of "illusions," we have so far merely scratched its surface. That portrayal has at least two other major features.

1. The relevant illusions pertain to the fulfillment of those time-honored and widely shared human yearnings that the theologian Paul Tillich dubbed "ultimate concerns." Thus, in this context, Freud's accent was not on illusions—however strong—that are entertained only temporarily, or by only a relatively small number of people, let alone on more or less idiosyncratic ones. A purely wish-inspired belief that your favorite team will win the Super Bowl does qualify as an illusion in the Freudian sense. But this illusion is both demographically and temporally parochial. By contrast, his theory of religion claims importance for evidentially ill-founded beliefs that envision actual "fulfillments of the oldest, strongest and most urgent wishes of mankind" (1927, p. 30). As he tells us, these beliefs, though still widespread today, were already held by "our wretched, ignorant, and downtrodden ancestors" (p. 33). These forebears, we know, did not have the joys of American football. Therefore, we can refer to the sort of illusion already entertained by our ignorant, primitive ancestors as "archaic," if not as venerable.

2. A further, even more important psychological earmark of theism, in Freud's view, is that this doctrine is engendered by the cooperation or synergism of three significantly different sorts of powerful, relentless wishes. And for each of this trio of wishes, he offers a distinct scenario that specifies their content and mode of operation. Hence let us consider the relevant triad of hypotheses in turn. As he points out (p. 33), the first set of these psychogenetic assumptions features wish motives that are largely conscious or *"manifest,"* instead of being the re-

pressed wishes postulated by psychoanalytic theory. Accordingly, this component of Freud's triadic psychology of religion does not rely on any of his technical psychoanalytic teachings. But what are the relevant archaic conscious wishes? He explains eloquently:

> the terrifying impression of helplessness in childhood aroused the need for protection—for protection through love—which was provided by the father; and the recognition that this helplessness lasts throughout life made it necessary to cling to the existence of a father, but this time a more powerful one. Thus the benevolent rule of a divine Providence allays our fear of the dangers of life; the establishment of a moral world-order ensures the fulfillment of the demands of justice, which have so often remained unfulfilled in human civilization; and the prolongation of earthly existence in a future life provides the local and temporal framework in which these wish-fulfillments shall take place. Answers to the riddles that tempt the curiosity of man, such as how the universe began or what the relation is between body and mind, are developed in conformity with the underlying assumptions of this system (p. 30).

Understandably, therefore, the protector, creator, *and* lawgiver are all rolled into one. No wonder, says Freud (1933, pp. 163-164), that, in one and the same breath, Immanuel Kant coupled the starry heavens above, and the moral law within as both being awe-inspiring. After all, Freud asks rhetorically, "what have the heavenly bodies to do with the question of whether one human creature loves another or kills him?" And he answers: "The same father (or parental agency) which gave the child life and guarded him against its perils, taught him as well what he might do and what he must leave undone" (p. 164).

Therefore, Freud deems it to be quite natural that man is receptive to the psychological subordination inherent in compliance with authority, especially authority that is claimed to derive from God. In this vein, Freud would presumably say that the Roman Catholic clergy astutely potentiates the religious fealty of its faithful by requiring them to call its priests "Father," to refer to the Pope as "the Holy Father," and to the Church itself as "Holy Mother Church." Again, Freud might adduce that when parents are asked by their children to give a reason for their commands, many an exasperated, if not authoritarian, mother or father will answer with finality: "Because!" No wonder, then, that religious systems too can secure the acquiescence of their believers, if they teach that the will of God is mysterious or inscrutable, and that some of their tenets transcend human understanding. In sum, it is one of Freud's recurrent psychological contentions that theism *infantilizes* adults by reinforcing the childish residues in their minds (1927, p. 49; 1930, p. 85).

But even the liberal Catholic theologian Hans Küng goes so far as to say: "All religions have in common the periodical *childlike* surrender to a Provider or providers who dispense earthly fortune as well as spiritual health" (1979, p. 120, my italics; for a critique of Hans Küng's theological views, see Albert, 1979).

The motivational account cited from Freud thus far is not predicated on psychoanalytic theory. Small wonder, therefore, that it was largely anticipated by earlier thinkers. At about age 18, Freud studied philosophy with Franz Brentano.

Thereby he was exposed to the ideas of the early nineteenth-century German atheist-theologian Ludwig Feuerbach, whose writings made a lasting impression on him (Stepansky, 1986, pp. 231-232). According to Feuerbach's psychological projection theory, it was man who created God in his own image, rather than conversely. Being dependent on external nature, and beset by the slings and arrows of outrageous fortune, man projects his cravings and fantasies outward onto the cosmos into a figment of his own imagination.

Feuerbach took it to be the task of his atheistic theology 'to *demystify* religious beliefs by showing in detail how God was an object "of the heart's necessity, not of the mind's freedom" (quoted in Stepansky, 1986, p. 223). Freud (1927, pp. 35, 37) used psychoanalysis to yield a further demystification by specifying additional, repressed feelings of human dependency on a father figure that would enhance the substance and credibility of Feuerbach's psychological reconstruction of religious history.

Likewise strongly influenced by Feuerbach, Karl Marx wrote: "Religion . . . is . . . the *protest* against real distress. Religion is the sigh of the oppressed creature, the heart of a heartless world, just as it is the spirit of an unspiritual situation. It is the *opium* of the people (in Feuer, 1959, p. 523). In Marx's time, opium was the most available painkiller and could be bought without any prescription. As he uses the name of this drug, its meaning is largely descriptive rather than pejorative. But Marx appreciated insufficiently that an impoverished nineteenth-century industrial proletariat and peasantry are not the only groups in society that crave supernatural consolation for the trials and tribulations of life. Freud took into account, much more than Marx did, that a good many of the rich and privileged in society also seek religious refuge from the blows of existence. At least to this extent, Freud was closer to Feuerbach's view than Marx was. Recently, Sidney Hook (1985) drew a germane comparison between Feuerbach and Marx, declaring Feuerbach to have been "more profound":

> when Marx says, "Religion is the opium of the people," he is really echoing Feuerbach. In Feuerbach's day it wasn't a disgrace to take opium. It was a medicine, an anodyne. It was the only thing people had to relieve their pain. Feuerbach was really implying that under any system there will be tragedy, heartache, failure, and frustration. Religion, for him (he regarded humanism and even atheism as a religion), serves that function [of relieving distress] in every society. Marx ridiculed this view because he was more optimistic than Feuerbach. He believed that science would solve not only the problem of economic scarcity but all human problems that arise from it. He ignored other human problems. Feuerbach seems to me to be more realistic about most human beings (p. 33).

Insofar as Freud's psychogenetic portrayal of religion depicts it as the product of *conscious* wishes, his account draws, I submit, not only on Feuerbach, but also on commonsense psychology. After all, at least *prima facie,* it is rather a commonplace that people seek to avoid anxiety, and that they therefore tend to welcome the replacement of threatening beliefs by reassuring ones. Hence, for brevity, we can refer to this component of Freud's triadic psychology of religion as "the commonsense hypothesis," which is not to say, however, that it is obviously true. Each of the other two components of his trinity is a set of *psychoanalytic* claims, asserting the operation of repressed motives. And yet they differ from each other, because one of them relies on Freud's theory of the psychosexual development of the human individual, while the other consists of *ethnopsychological* and psychohistorical averments pertaining to the evolution of our species as a whole. Accordingly, we shall label the psychoanalytic assumptions relating to the individual as "ontogenetic," but will refer to the ethnopsychological ones as "phylogenetic."

As previously emphasized, the legitimacy of any psychogenetic portrait of religious creeds depends on the *evidential merit* of the explanatory psychological hypotheses adduced by it. Even the commonsense component of Freud's triad is subject to this *caveat.* Invoking the criticisms of his great predecessors, he took it for granted that there is no cogency in any of the arguments for the existence of God offered by believers. But he coupled this philosophical judgment with the daring motivational claim that the faithful who nonetheless adduce such proofs had not, in fact, themselves been decisively moved by them, when giving assent to theism. Instead, he maintained, psychologically this assent is emotional or affective in origin:

> Where questions of religion are concerned, people are guilty of every possible sort of dishonesty and intellectual misdemeanour. Philosophers stretch the meaning of words until they retain scarcely anything of their original sense. They give the name of 'God' to some vague abstraction which they have created for themselves; having done so . . . they can even boast that they have recognized a higher, purer concept of God, notwithstanding that their God is now nothing more than an insubstantial shadow and no longer the mighty personality of religious doctrines (1927, p. 32).

In brief, he is telling us that motivationally, the dialectical excogitations offered as existence proofs are *post hoc* rationalizations in which an elaborate intellectual facade takes the place of the deep-seated wishes that actually persuaded the theologians. Speaking epigrammatically in another context, Freud quotes Falstaff as saying that reasons are "as plenty as blackberries" (1914, p. 24). Hence, Freud could not have disagreed more with Edward Gibbon, who reversed the order of motivational priority as follows, though perhaps only tongue-in-cheek:

> Our curiosity is naturally prompted to inquire by what means the Christian faith obtained so remarkable a victory over the established religions of the earth. To this inquiry an obvious but satisfactory answer may be returned; that it was owing to the convincing evidence of the doctrine itself, and to the ruling providence of its great Author. But as truth and reason seldom find so favourable a reception in the world, and as the wisdom of Providence frequently condescends to use the passions of the human heart, and the general circumstances of mankind, as instruments to execute its purpose, we may still be permitted, though with becoming submission, to ask, not indeed what were the first, but

> what were the secondary causes of the rapid growth of the Christian church? (1899, p. 523).

It would seem to be basically a matter of empirical psychological fact whether the commonsense constituent of Freud's psychogenetic portrait of religion is sound. Yet, it is not clear how to design a cogent test even of this hypothesis. Note that the required design needs to have two epistemic capabilities as follows: (1) It needs to yield evidence bearing on the validity of the functional explanation of religious belief as being anxiety reducing; presumably this explanation postulates some kind of stabilizing psychic servomechanism that reacts homeostatically to psychological threat. Furthermore, (2) the required test needs to be at least able to rank-order the intensity of the wish to escape from anxiety, as compared to the motivational persuasiveness of the theological existence proofs. Perhaps oscillating anxieties of believers who went through cycles of doubt and belief have already gone some way toward meeting the first condition by Mill's method of concomitant variations. In any case, it would seem that an explicitly *fideist* belief in the existence of God—which avowedly is *not* based on any arguments—calls for *psychological* explanation in terms of wish motives! The second requirement, however, seems to be a tall order indeed, although it does not warrant putting a cap on the ingenuity of potential empirical investigators. It too must be met, because of Freud's bold claim that even the best of the arguments for the existence of God would not have convinced the great minds who advanced them, unless stronger tacit wishes had carried the day, or had prompted these intellects to prevaricate. But note that, so far, Freud's portrayal of the motives for religious belief has studiously refrained from claiming that this belief is false.

Hence whatever the empirical difficulties of validating his psychogenetic portrait, they are hardly tantamount to his commission of the hackneyed genetic fallacy, a mode of inference that he explicitly rejected by means of disclaimers and qualifications, as we saw. Yet this state of affairs is completely overlooked in Philip Rieff's very influential book (1959). There Rieff offers a combination of intellectual history, sociology of knowledge, and philosophy of culture. As he would have it, Freud's psychology of religion refurbishes the inveterate genetic fallacy (p. 292) "by which animus is sanctified as science," with the aid of some "scientistic name calling" (p. 268). Moreover, as indicated by the title of Rieff's book, he sees the entire monumental psychoanalytic corpus as a thinly veiled system of moralisms.

To be sure, as we shall see, Freud deemed religion an undesirably arrestive childish fixation. And avowedly, he did *advocate* (1927, p. 48)—as an "experiment" worth making—that children be given an irreligious education. But he took pains to say at once: "Should the experiment prove unsatisfactory I am ready to give up the reform and to return to my earlier; purely descriptive judgment that man is a creature of weak intelligence who is ruled by his instinctual wishes" (pp. 48-49). How then does Rieff reason that, throughout his theoretical system, Freud "can always get from description to judgment in a single step" (p. 293) such that *all* of psychoanalytic theory is moralistic? Rieff explains, "because in his case histories Freud never *reported* the facts but *interpreted* them, what passes for description in the Freudian method is already judgment" (p. 293).

But when Freud spoke of possibly having to retract his plea for an atheistic education in favor of returning to his "earlier, purely descriptive judgement" of human nature, he was using the term "descriptive" in contrast to "normative" to characterize a claim as being devoid of *moral* advocacy. And he was fully alert to the truism that the psychoanalytic method generated theory-laden interpretations. Indeed, Freud had emphasized, in a Kantian vein, that even a purportedly observational description of phenomena is already theory-laden (1915b, p. 117). Yet when Rieff uses the term 'judgment" to refer to an interpretation, he slides from the fact that the latter is theory-laden to its also necessarily being *value-laden.* Thus, he reckons speciously that all psychoanalytic interpretations are tantamount to moral judgments, simply because they are theory-laden.

Apparently, Freud's psychology of religion is exonerated from Rieff's reproach that it incurred the genetic fallacy and was part of a *globally* moralistic theoretical enterprise (pp. 257, 263, 265). Ironically, it is Rieff himself who begs the question in regard to the evidence against theism (p. 269). For example, he diagnoses the appeal of atheism during the Enlightenment as depending on religious illiteracy, such as unfamiliarity "with the lines of self-criticism laid down by the theologians themselves" (p. 272). Thus Rieff endeavors to garner support for religion by offering a psychological discreditation of atheism.

Yet the imperative to avoid the genetic fallacy cuts both ways. Just as the psychogenesis of religious belief cannot itself refute theism, so also the emotional gratifications it affords cannot support it *epistemically.* The dissident psychoanalysts Carl Jung and Alfred Adler appreciated this point, although they did claim *psychological* value or even emotional necessity for belief in God (Küng, pp. 62-63). Jung saw God as man's projection, manufactured from human emotions and from archetypes that he believed to have excavated psychoanalytically from an untamed collective unconscious. But, as a therapist, he thought that we court psychological disaster, if we do not give conscious expression to unconscious religious feelings. All the same, he stressed that the purportedly necessary psychological function of the idea of God has "nothing whatever to do with the question of God's existence" (quoted in Stepansky, 1986, p. 227).

Let us turn to the two psychoanalytic ingredients of Freud's triad, consisting of his ontogeny and phylogeny of theism. In their case, we must ask, I claim, even whether there is good evidence for the existence of the repressed wishes postulated by them. Insofar as even the very existence of these hidden desires is questionable, one remains less than convinced, when told that they contributed significantly to the initial genesis and later persistence of religious creeds.

It is a major tenet of Freudian theory that psychopathology is rooted in the psychic conflict created by unsuccessfully repressed desires. Guided by this model of mental disorder, his ontogeny and phylogeny diagnose religion as a mixture of syndromes, featuring oedipal, paranoid, and obsessional elements. Yet he explicitly allowed that there are several interesting differences between, say, the illusions of a paranoiac and religious beliefs. For example, the specifics of the former are idiosyncratic, while the latter are usually shared, sometimes even widely (1907, pp. 119-120; 1927, p. 44). Let us now consider, in turn, some of the highlights of the ontogeny and the phylogeny.

In 1901, in his *Psychopathology of Everyday Life,* Freud traced superstitions to unconscious causes (pp. 258-260). The psychological mechanism operative here, we are told (1913a, p. 92), is that of transmuting feelings and impulses into external agencies by *projection* or displacement.

> Psycho-analysis can also say something new about the *quality* of the unconscious motives that find expression in superstition. It can be recognized most clearly in neurotics suffering from obsessional thinking or obsessional states—people who are often of high intelligence—that superstition derives from suppressed hostile and cruel impulses. Superstition is in large part the expectation of trouble; and a person who has harboured frequent evil wishes against others, but has been brought up to be good and has therefore repressed such wishes into the unconscious, will be especially ready to expect punishment for his unconscious wickedness in the form of trouble threatening him from without (1901, p. 260).

Obsessional neurosis features relentlessly intrusive, anxiety producing thoughts, rumination, doubt, and scruples as well as *repetitive* impulses to perform such acts as ceremonials, counting, hand washing, checking, etc. One might include here perhaps the reported practice of a world-famous logician to cover his handwritten address on envelopes with transparent nail polish as prophylaxis against moisture. The hypothesized causes of a disorder X are said to be the "etiology" of X. Derivatively, the term "etiology" is also used to refer to the pertinent causal *hypothesis,* rather than to the presumed causes themselves.

In Freud's 1907 paper "Obsessive Actions and Religious Practices," he employed his etiology of obsessional neurosis to diagnose religious *rituals,* no less than obsessive-compulsive secular acts. According to his etiologic hypothesis, these repetitive acts result from the conflict between a repressed forbidden instinct and the repressing forces of consciousness. *Qua* being a species of obsessive-compulsive acts, the religious rites are seen etiologically as *exorcistic defenses* against evil wishes, and against the disasters that such forbidden desires are feared to engender by sheer magic. Precisely by fearing that *mere* desires or thoughts can magically produce calamities, the obsessive's overvaluation of the power of mental processes betrays the mind-set of savages, who believe in just such an omnipotence of thoughts (see Freud's case history of the Rat-Man; 1909b, pp. 229ff.; 1913a, p. 86). And by performing the supposedly protective rituals, the obsessive wards off a crescendo of anxiety, the qualms of conscience brought on by their neglect (1907, p. 119). Here then, Freud's psychogenetic accent is on religious ceremonials or sacramental *acts,* rather than on theoretical religious doctrine.

But what of the important differences between religious practices or doctrine, on the one hand, and obsessive-compulsive acts or thoughts, on the other? He addresses these differences head on, only to proceed to neutralize them diagnostically by psychoanalytic argument. Speaking of the "obvious" differences, he declares:

> a few of them are so glaring that they make the comparison a sacrilege: the greater individual variability of [neurotic] ceremonial actions in contrast to the stereotyped character of rituals (prayer, turning to the East, etc.), their private nature as opposed to the public and communal character of religious observances, above all, however, the fact that, while the minutiae of religious ceremonial are full of significance and have a symbolic meaning, those of neurotics seem foolish and senseless. In this respect an obsessional neurosis presents a travesty, half comic and half tragic, of a private religion. But it is precisely this sharpest difference between neurotic and religious ceremonial which disappears when, with the help of the psycho-analytic technique of investigation, one penetrates to the true meaning of obsessive actions.
>
> Those who are familiar with the findings of psycho-analytic investigation into the psychoneuroses will not be surprised to learn that what is being represented in obsessive actions or in ceremonials is derived from the most intimate, and for the most part from the sexual, experiences of the patient (1907, pp. 119-120).

Diagnostically, therefore, Freud rejects the objection that he has ridden roughshod over the differences between neurosis and religion, when he "psychopathologized" religion. This charge was leveled in 1983 by the psychoanalyst E. R. Wallace (For his most recent account, see Wallace, 1985). According to Wallace, Freud "overlooked an important distinction between symptom and ritual: the *ego-dystonic* nature of the former versus the *ego-syntonic* [nature] of the latter" (p. 277). This means that, subjectively, the compulsive hand washer finds his repetitive need disagreeable, whereas the religious worshipper finds his observances congenial. It is less than clear, however, that—for example—Roman Catholics typically find it ego-syntonic, when they are asked to say so many "Hail Marys" or Lord's Prayers for penance. To be sure, these repetitive acts may relieve the anxiety induced by the priest's admonition. But let us grant Wallace that all religious observances are ego-syntonic. Even then, according to standard psychoanalytic theory, which Wallace accepts (p. 276), the ego-syntonic character of feelings and behavior does not necessarily militate against their etiologic status as a neurotic manifestation: The so-called "character neuroses" are distinguished, within the theory, from the "symptom neuroses" by precisely the fact that the former are ego-syntonic, while the latter are not (Laplanche and Pontalis, 1973, pp. 67-68). Thus, having the narcissistic personality syndrome need not militate against the self-satisfaction of its exemplar, and the paranoiac afflicted by delusions of grandeur need not find them ego-dystonic.

Qua neurotic manifestations, Freud sees religious rituals as typically conducing to psychological intimidation, uniformity and dependence, if not to outright infantilization. Hans Küng, the liberal Roman Catholic theologian, is a vigorous champion of psychoanalysis as a scientific theory (pp. 93, 95, 98, and esp. 102-109). Yet, in this 1979 book, he claims, *contra* Freud, that "religious rites . . . foster man's individuation and self-discovery . . . and [can] . . . contribute to creativity" (p. 119). Freud himself does emphasize, however, that sharing in the glorified, enlarged obsessional neurosis of religion with other people can obviate an idiosyncratic one: "Devout believers are safeguarded in a high degree against the risk of certain neurotic illnesses; their acceptance of the universal neurosis spares them the task of constructing a personal one" (1927b, p. 44). This sort of trade-off is a theme that Freud strikes time and again, starting in 1907 and ending with his *Moses and Monotheism,* which appeared in 1939, the year of his death (see 1907; 1910, pp. 123, 146; 1921, p. 142; 1930, pp. 84-85, 144; 1939, pp. 72-80).

It would seem that within the ranks of religious psychoanalysts, Wallace's critique of Freud's psychopathology of religion has failed to carry conviction. A notable case in point is the Roman Catholic Jesuit priest William Meissner, who is a practicing psychoanalyst and professor of psychiatry at Harvard. In his 1984 book, he paints a sobering psychological picture of religion. True, Meissner tells us that religious experience can occur at different levels of development, and can include at its apex, "mature, integrated, and adaptive levels of psychic functioning." And, if so, then "Freud was able to envision only a segment of the broader developmental spectrum" (p. 14). But, unlike Wallace, Meissner does make a major concession as follows: "the psychology of religious experience . . . overlaps, and to a significant degree is intertwined with mental processes that, from a clinical perspective, can be described as pathological" (pp. 9-10). Referring to one of Freud's famous case histories, Meissner says: "the Wolf Man's obsessive religiosity was a vehicle for his instinctual pathology" (p. 60). Indeed, Meissner's verdict is rather dismal:

> A caricature of [ideal] religion, which Freud himself employed as an analogy to obsessional states, is not infrequently found among religious people in whom blind adherence to ritual and scrupulous conscientiousness, as well as conscience, dominate religious life. In fact, we can safely say that the great mass of believers lend credence to Freud's formulations.
>
> More mature and integrated forms of religious experience are modestly distributed among the people of God. Those who reach the highest level of religious experience and achieve the maximum expression of religious ideals are very rare indeed. . . . Unfortunately, to study the religious experience of those more advanced and saintly souls who have gained a high level of religious maturity, we must rely on the secondhand historical accounts that leave many questions unanswered and unapproachable. . . . The theologian directs his attention to a more or less idealized, rarely attained level of religious maturity (p. 15).

Freud's psychopathological ontogeny of theism is not confined to obsessional neurosis. He thought that the Oedipus "complex constitutes the nucleus of all neuroses" (1913a, pp. 129, 157). Thus, we learn, the pathogens of obsessional neurosis are interwoven with those of the Oedipus complex. In its so-called "complete" form of ambivalence toward *each* parent, that complex is produced by the conflict between affectionate sexual feelings, on the one hand, and hostile aggressive feelings of rivalry, on the other, which are entertained toward both parents in the psyche of all children between the ages of three and six (Laplanche and Pontalis, 1973, pp. 282-286). The special focus of these affects is the powerful, protective, and yet threatening father, who has replaced the mother in her initial role of providing food and protection (1927, p. 24). Being too disturbing to be entertained consciously, these emotions are repressed (Fenichel, 1945, pp. 91-98). It may be asked at once how the oedipal conflict can be deemed pathogenically relevant, if *all* people experience it in childhood, while only *some* become strikingly neurotic. The Freudian answer is that people do differ in regard to their success in *resolving* the infantile Oedipus complex (1925, pp. 55-56). But some ambivalence toward the father figure lingers on into adulthood.

Hence the cosmic projection and exaltation of this authority figure as a Deity in publicly approved fashion has an enormous appeal. As Freud (l927b) puts it: "It is an enormous relief to the individual psyche if the conflicts of its childhood arising from the father-complex—conflicts which it has never wholly overcome—are removed from it and brought to a solution which is universally accepted" (p. 30). By the same token, a true child-father relationship is achieved, once polytheism yields to monotheism after man "creates for himself the gods whom he dreads, whom he seeks to propitiate, and whom he nevertheless entrusts with his own protection" (p. 24).

Indeed, the psychoanalytically fathomed, unconscious wishes of the adult's residual Oedipus complex are held to combine *synergistically* with the urgent desire for relief from the *conscious* fears of enduring vulnerability, fears which are lifelong intensifications of the child's dread of helplessness (1927, pp. 23-24). The product is the belief in an omnipotent God, who is thought to love any of us, even if no one else does.

Apparently, the apotheosis of the father does fit Judaism, Christianity, and Islam. But Freud seems to have neglected Hinduism, Buddhism, and Taoism. And at least one writer (Erdelyi, 1985, p. 207) has claimed that as between the two parents, the mother seems to be the more important figure in these religions. Yet Freud did say: "the creator is usually a man, though there is far from being a lack of female deities; and some mythologies actually make the creation begin with a male God getting rid of a female deity, who is degraded into being a monster" (1933, p. 162).

It is a measure of the current influence of psychoanalytic oedipal theory that Hans Küng peremptorily takes this hypothesis to be an empirically well-established body of knowledge. Nay, he vigorously champions it in the face of criticisms (pp. 93, 98, and esp. 102-109). Indeed, Küng (p. 95), no less than Meissner (pp. 213, 216), explicitly endorses the method of psychoanalytic investigation as a *natural science* mode of inquiry. True, both of these two Roman Catholic writers repeatedly contend that the *full dimensions* of religious experience elude capture by Freud's theory of psychopathology. Yet, despite their denial of such complete explanatory subsumption, they regard psychoanalytic *ontogeny* as a viable and illuminating part of the psychology of religious belief. More generally, the Protestant theologian Paul Tillich opted for the use of psychoanalysis, along with Marxism, to offer unflattering motivational explanations of what he regarded as much false consciousness in Western society (see Shinn, 1986).

But what are the actual empirical credentials of Freud's sexual etiology of obsessional neurosis, and of his oedipal *ontogeny* of theism? In the context of the conjugal family, this oedipal plot calls for not only an erotic love-hate triangle prior to the age of 6, but also a redemptive denouement of the guilt-laden parricidal wish by projective exaltation of the father into God. It is a clear moral of my recent book (1984) that, far from having good empirical support, at best these obsessional and oedipal hypotheses have yet to be adequately tested, even prior to their use in a psychology of religion. *A fortiori,* the psychoanalytic ontogeny of theism still lacks evidential warrant, with the possible exception of the psychogenesis of the doctrine of the Virgin Birth of Jesus, as we shall see below. Until and unless there is more warrant for the ontogeny, it is surely at least the better part of wisdom to place little explanatory reliance on it, brilliantly suggestive though it may be.

But Freud was not content to confine himself to explanatory reliance on the conscious quest for anxiety reduction, and on his ontogeny of theism. Rather, he went on to develop a psychoanalytic *phylogeny* of theism (1913c, essay IV). In his view, this historical ethnopsychology is a valid extension of psychoanalysis. He reasoned as follows:

> The obscure sense of guilt to which mankind has been subject since prehistoric times, and which in some religions has been condensed into the doctrine of primal guilt, or original sin, is probably the outcome of a blood-guilt incurred by prehistoric man. In my book *Totem and Taboo* (1912-13) I have, following clues given by Robertson Smith, Atkinson and Charles Darwin, tried to guess the nature of this primal guilt, and to believe, too, that the Christian doctrine of today enables us to deduce it. If the Son of God was obliged to sacrifice his life to redeem mankind from original sin, then by the [Mosaic] law of talion, the requital of like by like, that sin must have been a killing, a murder. Nothing else could call for the sacrifice of a life for its expiation. And if the original sin was an offence against God the Father, the primal crime of mankind must have been a parricide, the killing of the primal father of the primitive human horde, whose mnemic image was later transfigured into a deity (1915b, pp. 292-293; see also 1939, pp. 130-131).

Yet there is still the question of how Freud conjectured the *motive* for the inferred parricide. As he tells us: "Darwin deduced from the habits of the higher apes that men, too, originally lived in comparatively small groups or hordes within which the jealousy of the oldest and strongest male prevented sexual promiscuity" (1913c, p. 125). In each of these hordes or families, the dominant male imposed such erotic restraint on his younger and subordinate male rivals by controlling their sexual access to the women of the clan. But this prohibition did not sit well with these rivals. Freud speculates that, driven by their ensuing hostility, and being cannibals, they banded together into a brother clan to *kill and eat* their own father (1913c, pp. 141-142). Yet they soon began to quarrel over the sexual spoils of his harem. Thus, they became highly ambivalent about their parricidal achievement. The memory of the homicide itself was repressed, and thereby generated guilt.

The resulting filial remorse, in turn, issued in two major developments: (1)

The delayed enforcement of the father's original edict against incestuous sex within the clan made exogamy mandatory, thereby generating the incest taboo (1913c, pp. 5-6); and (2) the prohibition of parricide turned into the expiatory *deification* of the slain parent. As Freud put it: "the primal father, at once feared and hated, revered and envied, became the prototype of God himself" (1925, p. 68).

Freud assumed that over the millennia, our primitive ancestors reenacted the parricidal scenario countless times (1939, p. 81). And, as a convinced Lamarckian, he believed that racial memories of it, cumulatively registered by our primitive ancestors—but subsequently repressed by them—were transmitted to us by the inheritance of acquired characteristics (Sulloway, 1977, pp. 274-275, 439-442). Thus, at least each male has supposedly stored this phylogenetic legacy in his unconscious, including the resulting sense of collective guilt over the primal crime (1939, p. 132). Hence, shortly before Freud's death, he confidently announced that "men have always known (in this special [Lamarckian] way) that they once possessed a primal father and killed him" (1939, p. 101). He explicitly credits the Scottish biblical scholar Robertson Smith and the anthropologist G. Frazer with the recognition that Christian Communion is a residue of the eating of the sacred totem animal, which in turn appeared to Freud to hark back to the eating of the slain primal father (1925, p. 68).

As he sees it, by combining ethnography with psychoanalysis, he has discerned a third set of strong wishes that unite synergistically with the other two classes of his triad, and make the psychogenesis of belief in God the Father the more imperative. Therefore he proclaimed: "We now observe that the store of religious ideas includes not only wish-fulfillments but important historical recollections. This concurrent influence of past and present must give religion a truly incomparable wealth of power" (1927, p. 42).

Moreover, the *ontogeny* of the Oedipus complex is, at least in its earlier stages, developmentally similar to its conjectured *phylogeny.* And this psychogenetic parallelism seemed all the more credible to Freud because he saw it as the psychological counterpart of Ernst Haeckel's biogenetic law. According to Haeckel, the embryonic ontogeny of each animal, including man, *recapitulates* the morphological changes undergone by the successive ancestors of the species during its phylogeny. No wonder that Freud felt entitled to regard the early *ontogenetic* development of moral dispositions like remorse and guilt in each of us as both a replica and a phylogenetic residue of the primal father complex of early man (1923a, p. 37).

At this point, standing at the portal of death in 1939, Freud is ready to deploy his repression etiology of neurosis, together with his ethnopsychological retrodictions. And he joins them to explain the characteristic irrationality of traditional theism as follows:

> A tradition that was based only on communication could not lead to the compulsive character that attaches to religious phenomena. It would be listened to, judged, and perhaps dismissed, like any other piece of information from outside; it would never attain the privilege of being liberated from the constraint of logical thought. It must have undergone the fate of being repressed, the condi-

> tion of lingering in the unconscious, before it is able to display such powerful effects on its return, to bring the masses under its spell, as we have seen with astonishment and hitherto without comprehension in the case of religious tradition (1939, p. 101).

As we learn on the same page, the "return" of the religious tradition refers to the *reawakening* of the repressed memory of ancestral totemistic parricide. And this reanimation was supposedly effected by two epoch-making episodes, each of which Freud claimed to be historically authentic: First, the murder of Moses by the ancient Hebrews, who rebelled against his tyrannical imposition of the intolerable prescriptions of monotheism; thereafter, "the supposed judicial murder of Christ."

Daring and ingenious though it is, Freud's psychoanalytic phylogeny of theism is dubious, if only because it assumes a Lamarckian inheritance of repressed racial memories. Furthermore, contrary to the uniform evolution of religions required by his account, more recent historical scholarship seems to call for developmental pluriformity (Küng, p. 67). And if there are such differences of religious history, it becomes more difficult to sustain the historical authenticity of the common parricidal scenario postulated by Freud's phylogeny. Overall, Küng (1979, pp. 70-71) emphasizes that hitherto no primordial religion has been found. Indeed, "the sources necessary for a historical explanation of the origin of religion are simply not available." Meissner devotes chapter 5 to the scrutiny of Freud's psychoanalytic phylogeny of Mosaic monotheism. Writing from the standpoint of biblical archeology, exegesis, and anthropology, Meissner reaches the following verdict: "Subsequent years have subjected the whole area of biblical studies and criticism to a radical revision that makes it clear that the fundamental points of view on which Freud based his synthetic reconstruction were themselves faulty and misleading" (p. ix).

Freud's Argument for Atheism

Having maintained that, psychogenetically, theistic beliefs are illusions, Freud deploys the following dialectical strategy on behalf of atheism: He aims to show that religious illusions, in particular, are very probably *false*. For that purpose, he deems it relevant—rather than *ad hominem*—to point out that religious illusions, though still widespread, were already commonly held by our ignorant, primitive ancestors. We shall designate *any* beliefs of such primitive vintage as "archaic," for brevity.

Freud makes only very cursory mention of the dread of the "evil eye" (1919, p. 240). But this belief is presumably archaic and still rampant. According to its adherents, the covetous glances of some persons have the malignant power to injure or kill people and animals, even involuntarily. Among the Greeks and Romans, as well as in the musical *Fiddler on the Roof,* spitting was used as a supposed antidote to the poison of the evil eye. Other gestures too—often intentionally obscene ones—were regarded as prophylactics on meeting the dreaded poisonous individual. By extension, praise for one's possessions or good fortune was thought to be an omen of bad luck. Thus, when I was a boy in Germany, even educated people who reported being in good health would *protectively* hasten to add the German word "unberufen," which literally means "uncalled for" or "unauthorized." Not to be outdone by Germans, Americans say "knock on wood" with equal prophylactic efficacy. Presumably, no one has ever run a controlled study to determine whether envious glances have the pernicious effects envisaged in the evil eye doctrine. But it is safe to say that if there were any such dire effects, the wealthy and successful of this world, who have been known to dread evil eyes, would not fare nearly as well as they actually do. Hence we may conclude that the archaic belief in the evil eye doctrine is false.

How then does Freud invoke the *archaic* character of theism as a means of discrediting religious belief? He puts it as follows:

> To assess the truth-value of religious doctrines does not lie within the scope of the present enquiry. It is enough for us that we have recognized them as being, in their psychological nature, illusions. But we do not have to conceal the fact that this discovery also strongly influences our attitude to the question [of truth-value] which must appear to many to be the most important of all. We know approximately at what periods and by what kind of men religious doctrines were created. If in addition we discover the motives which led to this, our attitude to the problem of [the truth of] religion will undergo a marked displacement. We shall tell ourselves that it would be very nice if there were a God who created the world and was a benevolent Providence, and if there were a moral order in the universe and an after-life; but it is a very striking fact that all this is exactly as we are bound to wish it to be. And it would be more remarkable still if our wretched, ignorant and downtrodden ancestors had succeeded in solving all these difficult riddles of the universe (1927, p. 33).

In context, the opening disclaimer in this statement as to the scope of his inquiry is an ellipsis for his aforecited tribute to his atheistic predecessors. Presumably, by "religious doctrines," Freud means here beliefs, including totemism and polytheism, that *eventuated* in theism. And, in view of the phylogenetic history he postulated for theism, that religious belief qualifies as "archaic." Though the *word* "theism" was apparently coined in a book by Cudworth as recently as 1678, the belief itself antedates the birth of Christ by nearly a millennium, at least among the Jews. In its traditional form, it asserts the existence of an omnipotent, omniscient, and omnibenevolent paternal creator—at once immanent and transcendent—who is accessible to personal communion with us. This divine being is to be respected, loved, and feared. In fact, normally, compliance with His ethical demands holds out the promise of heaven, though there have been theists who disbelieved in personal immortality. On this construal, at least some forms of Buddhism and Taoism do not teach belief in the existence of God, as was noted by Supreme Court Justice Hugo L. Black in a decision he wrote in 1961 (see Safire, 1986).

To reconstruct the logical framework of Freud's own case for atheism, we can encapsulate his argument in the following syllogism (1933, p. 168; 1927, p. 33):

Premise 1: All archaic, evidentially ill-supported illusions are very probably false.
Premise 2: Anyone's belief in theism is an archaic, evidentially ill-supported illusion.

Conclusion: Anyone's belief in theism is very probably false.

Note that since Freudian illusions are, by definition, evidentially unwarranted, the modifying adjective "evidentially ill-supported" in the two premises is redundant. But it is there for the sake of emphasis. Furthermore, observe that by talking about the belief states of all theists, both the second premise and the conclusion are, in effect, making claims about *all known versions* of theism, except those that no one ever took seriously enough to believe them. Formally speaking, this syllogism is deductively valid, if we can regard probable falsity as a property of some beliefs. Hence the warrant for presuming its conclusion to be true depends, of course, on the epistemic merits of the two premises. In effect, the first premise says that the world being what it is, archaic illusions are, so to speak, too good to be true. The second premise, however, is a terse assertion of Freud's psychogenetic and epistemological thesis that religious beliefs are indeed archaic illusions: it states that these creeds were prompted not by cogent evidence, but by the need to fulfill a trio of "the oldest, strongest, and most urgent wishes of mankind" (1927, p. 30). Freud is making use of the fact that a belief state can be characterized motivationally, while its content can be appraised as to the evidence for it, if any, and also as to its truth value.

Consider the first premise. It would seem that he took it to be a legitimate induction from the discreditation of various archaic illusions by scientific advances. But *prima facie,* one might think that an example of his own from the history of alchemy furnishes evidence against the universal claim of Premise 1, which is that all archaic illusions are probably false: As he points out: "Examples of illusions which have proved true are not easy to find, but the illusion of the alchemists that all metals can be turned into gold might be one of them" (1927, p. 31). When Freud allowed that the wish-inspired guess of the alchemists might perhaps be redeemed after all, he was presumably referring to the transmutation of elements known from the radioactive decay of metals of high atomic weight, such as uranium and thorium. Though relevant, let us ignore questions of practical and economic feasibility, and suppose that all base metals can be turned into noble ones, as desired by the alchemists. Then this state of affairs would not refute Freud's first premise, which claims only that any archaic illusion is very likely to be false, rather than that it is categorically false. Besides, even the Greek and Egyptian alchemists of old probably towered in intellectual sophistication over the members of Darwin's primal hordes. Hence even these early alchemists presumably do not qualify as primitive and wretched ancestors by

Freud's standards. And if not, then the belief in alchemy—though psychogenetically and evidentially an "illusion" for centuries—does not count as an "archaic" illusion.

Anyone who is still inclined to quarrel with Premise One will find it sobering to bear in mind how very difficult even science finds it to come up with true theories. Indeed, the history of science—both ancient and modern—is largely the history of discarded theories. Hence even for scientific theories that are now well-supported by evidence, it is a reasonable induction from the past that they, too, will be found wanting in due course. Moreover, success has eluded Karl Popper and others who have tried to develop a technical notion of relative proximity to the truth or comparative verisimilitude, so that consecutive scientific theories would demonstrably get ever closer to being true. As we know, these bleak results have bedeviled the so-called "realist" philosophies of science. Thus, even the Australian aborigines of 12,000 years ago, if now alive, could be looking at Premise One undauntedly and say to Freud: *"Tu quoque."* Therefore, the discreditation of archaic illusions by scientific advances, which presumably legitimates Premise 1, seems to pose a paradox: If the great scientific theories themselves eventually turn out to be false, by what right can Freud, or anyone, rely on *them* to scorn archaic illusory beliefs as sheer superstitions?

We have reason to think that Newtonian physics, and perhaps even general relativity theory, are partly wrong. But that does not prevent either from yielding otherwise unavailable, often stunningly accurate predictions of, say, the trajectory of the interplanetary Voyager 2, and of Halley's Comet. Again, the current theories of neurotransmitters may well turn out to be wrong in some respects. Yet, the fact remains that dopamine and related medications—though of limited efficacy—control the symptoms of Parkinson's disease far more reliably than exorcistic rituals based on archaic illusions, such as shamanism, sorcery, occult art, thamaturgy, demonology, voodoo, hoodoo, incantation, mumbo-jumbo, hocus-pocus, and abracadabra. More often than not, the manifestly true *predictions* made by scientific theories—as distinct from their more speculative hypotheses—suffice to discredit archaic beliefs, such as that of the evil eye, which claims small amounts of visible light to be injurious, if not lethal. Thus, such discreditation does *not* stand or fall with the truth of the major scientific hypotheses themselves. Indeed, in striking contrast to the tenacity with which people cling to illusory beliefs, the methods of the scientific enterprise seem to have the following distinction: They are the only means of choosing theoretical beliefs that allow observational evidence to override, sooner or later, the appeal to wish fulfillment.

It emerges after all that, though the history of science is the history of abandoned theories, scientific advances redound to the credibility of Premise 1, instead of leaving it devoid of support. Therefore, we can permit that premise to stand.

As for Premise 2, however, we need to recall our earlier hesitations and doubts. Let us grant Freud that theists have produced no proofs for the existence of God that are cogent, either severally or even collectively. Then there still remains the motivational question whether some of the faithful, when giving assent to theism, had not, in fact, been decisively moved by supposed proofs, rather than by deep-seated wishes. To be sure, the existence of a conscious wish for anxiety reduction by reassuring beliefs is well attested. Yet it is not clear empirically that every case of religious belief can be attributed psychogenetically either to this wish or to the more speculative unconscious oedipal craving, let alone to the questionable repressed desire to expiate the parricidal guilt of Freud's Lamarckian phylogeny. Note that this *caveat* in regard to repressed oedipal wishes and parricidal guilt is not a matter of *generic* doubts as to the psychic operation of a mechanism of repression; instead, the doubts pertain to the existence of the *specific* sorts of repressed wishes invoked here by Freud, and to their explanatory role as the actual causes of the belief phenomena he claims to explain. For his part, Freud thought that precisely by being so strong and urgent, his trio of wishes were psychologically theogenic. Anyway, the second premise seems to be the weak link in Freud's deductively valid syllogism.

Still, we can *allow* that all cases of belief in God may perhaps be inspired by conscious favoritism for consoling beliefs over ominous ones, combined with any repressed wishes that do turn out to have such psychogenetic credentials.

The Bridge from Illusion to Delusion

Recall that Freud labels as a "delusion" a *false* illusion produced by wishes that are complex enough to include repressed desires or defense mechanisms. And suppose that one were to grant him both of the premises in his syllogism, including his triadic construal of the wishes that engender the illusions of the second premise. Then it would follow that theistic beliefs are indeed *very probably* delusions, rather than just illusions. As he reminds us: "In the case of delusions, we emphasize as essential their being in contradiction with reality," i.e., their falsity, whereas "Illusions need not necessarily be false" (1927b, p. 31). Moreover, Freud's psychogenetic, epistemological, and semantic concept of delusion allows that delusional beliefs be either idiosyncratic or socially shared. In fact, as he explains in *Civilization and Its Discontents,* he sees religion as an infantilizing mass delusion:

> one can try to re-create the world, to build up in its stead another world in which its most unbearable features are eliminated and replaced by others that are in conformity with one's own wishes. But whoever, in desperate defiance, sets out upon this path to happiness will as a rule attain nothing. Reality is too strong for him. . . . A special importance attaches to the case in which this attempt to procure a certainty of happiness and a protection against suffering through a delusional remoulding of reality is made by a considerable number of people in common. The religions of mankind must be classed among the mass-delusions of this kind. No one, needless to say, who shares a delusion ever recognizes it as such (1930, p. 81).
>
> . . . by forcibly fixing them in a state of psychical infantilism and by drawing them into a mass-delusion, religion succeeds in sparing many people an in-

dividual neurosis (1930, pp. 84-85).

But Freud's concept of a *mass* delusion is strongly at odds with the notion of delusion encountered in the 1970 and 1981 editions of the Oxford *Psychiatric Dictionary.* First let us note the points of agreement between them. In its 4th edition of 1970, the Oxford *Dictionary* says, under the rubric of "hallucination," that the belief associated with a hallucinatory sensation is a "delusion" in the sense of being "obviously contrary to demonstrable fact." And the stated reason is that a hallucination is defined there as "a *sense perception* to which there is no external stimulus" (p. 333).

Thus, the 4th edition speaks of a delusion as "a belief engendered without appropriate external stimulation and maintained by one in spite of what to normal beings constitutes incontrovertible and 'plain-as-day' proof or evidence to the contrary." So far, there is no conflict with Freud's concept of delusion. But then comes the sociological demurrer: "Further, the belief held is not one which is ordinarily accepted by other members of the patient's culture or subculture (i.e., it is not a commonly believed superstition)" (p. 191). The 5th Oxford edition repudiates Freud's supracultural notion of a "mass delusion" altogether in favor of an entirely intracultural concept of delusion. The later Oxford definition allows a false belief to qualify as a delusion *only* if it is held idiosyncratically, and it makes social consensus the *sole* arbiter of reality. It reads:

> **delusion** A false belief that is firmly maintained even though it is contradicted by social reality. While it is true that some superstitions and religious beliefs are held despite the lack of confirmatory evidence, such culturally engendered concepts are not considered delusions. What is characteristic of the delusion is that it is *not* shared by others; rather, it is an idiosyncratic and individual misconception or misinterpretation. Further, it is a thinking disorder of enough import to interfere with the subject's functioning, since in the area of his delusion he no longer shares a consensually validated reality with other people (p. 157).

Evidently, no matter how inordinately primitive, superstitious or anthropomorphic the belief, it does not earn the Oxford label "delusion," if it is *shared* in its cultural milieu. Thus, even the paranoid beliefs of a hysterical lynch mob cannot count as deluded. But we are not told how many others in a given society need to share an idea, if it is to be part of what that *Dictionary* calls "social reality." Does it have to be a majority? And, according to the definition, what counts as "social reality" in a highly pluralistic society such as the United States, in which there are subcultures holding radically different, incompatible beliefs? The secular humanists, who allegedly dominate the public schools, and the self-styled "moral majoritarians" extolled by President G.H.W. Bush are only two such subcultures. To avoid misunderstanding, let me emphasize that to object to social reality as the sole arbiter of warranted belief is *not* to deny that consensus among independent observers does play a role in evidential corroboration. After all, the chances that five or more experimental physicists will hallucinate *in unison* are smaller than that only one physicist will hallucinate.

Alas, the Oxford notion of socially deviant thought as being delusional seems to be akin to the view of some Soviet psychiatrists that individual political dissent should be seen as a psychiatric problem. Furthermore, like the psychoanalyst Wallace, the 1981 *Dictionary* limits the concept of delusion to idiosyncratic thinking disorders that are socially maladaptive *within* a culture. Thus, it makes no psychiatric allowance for shared beliefs that may turn out to be highly maladaptive for the group as a whole, even biologically, such as in Jonestown. And what of internecine religious wars, either civil or external, as between Hindu India and Moslem Pakistan? Finally, there is the Ayatollah Khomeini's theological diagnosis of President Carter as "Satan," which was undoubtedly shared by his mullahs and by some of the population in Iran. According to the Oxford definition, that belief is not delusional. By contrast, Freud depicted the belief in Satan as "nothing but a mass fantasy, constructed along the lines of a paranoid delusion" (quoted in Wallace, 1983, p. 271).

It is puzzling, therefore, that Philip Rieff (1959) has objected to Freud's notion of a mass delusion on the following grounds: "When large numbers of people share it, a delusion takes on a different meaning . . . He [Freud] inclined to treat a public emotion like religion . . . simply as a multiple of private emotions—ignoring the fact that a belief or act is not simply enlarged but fundamentally altered by being shared" (p. 289). But how, one must ask, does the sharing of an avowedly delusional belief "fundamentally alter" its content? If a Protestant in Northern Ireland whips up a frenzied group of his coreligionists to have a hysterical fear of Irish Catholics, how is the agitator's phobic belief basically changed thereby? And was it not Freud himself who pointed out that "religion succeeds in sparing many people an individual neurosis" (1930, p. 85)? Did he not thus recognize that the *effects* of shared beliefs can differ from those of idiosyncratic ones, even if the shared beliefs are, in his view, delusional?

As against the Oxford and Rieff views, Freud does *not* relativize his notion of delusion to social reality, but is prepared to make an independent epistemological and psychiatric assessment of belief systems held by a subculture or even by a majority. Thus, in a section devoted to "The Analogy" between Judaism and neurosis, he speaks of both as featuring "the characteristic of compulsion, which forces itself on the mind along with an overpowering of logical thought" (1939, p. 72). And he elaborates:

> the symptoms . . . have great psychical intensity and at the same time exhibit a far-reaching independence of the organization of the other mental processes, which are adjusted to the demands of the real external world and obey the laws of logical thinking . . . They [the symptoms] are, one might say, a State within a State, an inaccessible party, with which co-operation is impossible, but which may succeed in overcoming what is known as the normal party and forcing it into its service. If this happens, it implies a domination by an internal psychical reality over the reality of the external world and the path to a psychosis lies open (1939, p. 76).

Note Freud's stress here on the "far-reaching independence"—in one and the same person—of orthodox religious or neurotic thought processes from those of the individual's other modes of thought that, in Freud's view, are reality-oriented. What he seems to have in mind here is that just as true religious believers are often anything but credulous in their mundane pursuits in the business world, so also the paranoiac's intricate network of delusions are "typically isolated [thematically] from the rest of the personality and intellect" (Oxford *Psychiatric Dictionary*, 4th ed., p. 540).

For example, in the dual psychosis known as "*folie a deux*," there can be a transfer of a *circumscribed* delusion from a psychotic individual to a non-psychotic one within the framework of a close relationship, so that the previously non psychotic individual may well internalize only *one* of the delusions of the psychotic one. Similarly, I know of a very intelligent mental patient who is amiable, good-natured, delusionally suspicious of the state police in this country, and yet seems to regard all other people as normally benevolent or neutral. When he claimed that New Jersey state troopers had punitively implanted tiny metal strips in his head, his psychiatrist suggested a cat-scan of his brain. Predictably, when the X-ray turned out negative, the patient's response was that tomography had inadequate resolving power to detect the tiny metal strips.

As both a Jesuit priest and a psychoanalyst, William Meissner is all too aware of the striking similarity between the manner in which religious believers, on the one hand, and paranoiacs, on the other, dispose of evidence contrary to their claims. Hence in 1978 he was prompted to say: "we must ask what it is that distinguishes systems of religious belief from paranoid delusions" (p. 92). He adds poignancy to this question by reference to Freud's (1911) case study of the paranoiac Schreber, whose autobiography was heuristic for the psychoanalytic etiology of paranoia. As Meissner puts it:

> How, then, does one draw a line between the theocosmological delusions of Schreber and the belief system of religious men? Schreber's *Memoirs* read in part like an elaborate theological tract. His delusional system is a highly evolved and systematized attempt to organize and understand his experience in terms of a coherent theory. Organized [religious] doctrine represents a similar attempt to interpret human experience and give it meaning in terms of a divinely instituted plan and guidance. Both delusional and [religious] belief systems reach certain untestable conclusions which cannot be contradicted by available evidences. How in fact would one go about disproving Schreber's delusion that he was being transformed into a woman? How would one disprove the Christian assertion of the real presence in the Eucharistic sacrifice (p. 93)?

Let us consider, therefore, Meissner's example of Communion in the Roman Catholic Mass. The Eucharist sacrament is supposed to repeat the action of Jesus at his last supper with his disciples, when he reportedly gave them bread, saying, "This is my body," and wine, saying, "This is my blood" (Matt. 26; Mark 14; Luke 22; 1 Cor. 11). According to Roman Catholic doctrine, as I have read it, when the sacrament is performed, the bread and wine miraculously undergo literal transsubstantiation into the body and blood of the crucified savior. But the doctrine comes equipped with an immunizing strategy to deal with the following natural question: If the consumption of bread and wine at the sacrament is, in fact, ontologically a cannibalistic act, as claimed, how is it that no such chemical change into flesh and blood, let alone into the flesh and blood of Jesus of Nazareth in particular, is detectable by taste or otherwise?

To parry this question, a peculiar version of Aristotle's distinction between the essential and accidental properties of an object is called to the rescue. Familiarly, for Aristotle, being a rational animal was an essential property of being human, whereas being a shepherd or a Greek was an accidental one. What is peculiar, in the Eucharist doctrine, about the invocation of Aristotle's distinction is that, after the purported transsubstantiation, any and every bread-like and wine-like attribute of what is consumed is suddenly demoted to the status of being *only* "accidental." But the underlying substance purportedly bearing all the observation ally accessible properties is that of the body and blood of Jesus. Despite this supposed "real presence" of these biological attributes in, with, and under mere bread and wine, the biological ones mysteriously elude detection, whereas the ontologically demoted accidental properties stubbornly do not go away. In short, while all appearances remain the same, the words of consecration by a priest at Mass purportedly transform the entire substance of the bread and wine literally into Christ's body and blood. As will be recalled, the Freudian phylogeny of religion postulated that the primal father was cannibalized by his rebellious sons after they had killed him. Hence Freud sees Christian communion as one means of perpetuating guilt, which the faithful then expiate by bowing to religious authority, both intellectually and emotionally (see Rieff, p. 276). But even numerous disciples of the apostle John balked at his teaching of transsubstantiation. As we read in the Gospel of John (6: 60, 66), "Many of them said: 'This is a hard saying. Who can accept it?' . . . from that time many of His disciples went back and walked no more with him."

It was hard not to agree with Meissner, when he noted the epistemological similarity between the Eucharist doctrine of the real presence, on the one hand, and Schreber's delusional belief in his own sex change, on the other. Some traditional religious apologetics feature other examples of built-in devices for begging the question and evading refutation by contrary evidence. The attempt made by the influential twentieth-century Jewish theologian Martin Buber to reconcile the existence of evil with the omnibenevolence of God is another case in point. As I have noted on another occasion, *qua* proposed solution of the problem of evil, Buber's is perhaps one of the lamest in the history of theodicy. And I heed Richard Gale's admonition that it would therefore be misleading to regard the defects of Buber's account as typical for theodicies. Though indeed not representative in this respect, Buber's solution is, I claim, not atypical of both theological and paranoid stratagems for evading falsification (Grünbaum, 1992).

Buber apparently thought that the Nazi holocaust challenged the benevolence of God in particularly acute form. To deal with it, he decided that God temporarily goes into eclipse. And this eclipse-of-God doctrine has since been championed by the Jewish philosopher Emil Fackenheim. Just why a benevolent God would go into eclipse to accommodate the likes of Adolf Hitler is not explained. Yet going into eclipse would seem to be a case of morally irresponsible absenteeism on God's part. Indeed, if Buber is to be believed, and one looks at the history of the societies that have embraced theism in one form or another, then it is difficult to find any time at all when God was not at least partially in eclipse. It will suffice to give two further illustrations of religious reasoning that seem to be simply indistinguishable from paranoid processes. Take, for instance, the question-begging claim that the existence of God is not impugned by *prima facie* contrary evidence, because He is merely *testing* us by means of such misleading data. Doesn't the Book of Job suggest that one of Satan's tasks is to test us in this way? Furthermore, as the Old Testament tells us, barren women who prayed to God secured his active intervention to become mothers: Sarah, Rebecca, and Rachel were each blessed in this way ("to make fruitful the barren woman"). Presumably, the orthodox would not allow that fertility clinics nowadays are more efficacious than prayer. Yet over 350 years ago, Francis Bacon questioned the efficacy of petitionary prayer in his *Novum Organum* (I, Section 46). Francis Galton (1872) did so again by special reference to the enormous number of prayers that are said in monarchies for the health of members of the royal families. To such doubts, it has been replied that God does not always give the supplicant what he or she seeks, but rather what he or the prayed-for person "really needs." Thus, if a victim of arthritis prays for relief from this affliction, but contracts pancreatic cancer to boot, even then the petitioner's prayer has purportedly been "answered." Is this reasoning not clearly as immunized against contrary evidence as the mind-set of the paranoiac who interprets any conduct by others, however cordial, in accord with his persecutory delusion?

Meissner (1978) makes several additional observations concerning the similarities between paranoid delusions and religious belief systems:

> the degree of closedness and resistance to change by experience is a function of the degree to which the [religious] belief system serves a defensive function in preserving the believer from inner psychic insecurity and dread. Where the underlying anxiety is more intense [it] is reflected in an increased rigidity and dogmatism and a reluctance to even question any part of the complex of moral and speculative positions which compose the system (p. 93).

But turning in particular to the Roman Catholic rationale for communion, Meissner tries to snatch philosophical legitimacy from the jaws of psychopathological diagnosis:

> How would one disprove the Christian assertion of the real presence in the Eucharistic sacrifice? We can recognize that a delusional system is in conflict with reality as we interpret it, but how does one go about proving that our interpretation is sane and that the delusional one is insane and in contradiction to reality? Ultimately we cannot. We can resort to an appeal to consensus or to practical and adaptive exigencies that are consequent on our interpretation rather than the delusional one—but these are not matters of evidence (pp. 93-94).

Why—one must ask urgently—is it not a *matter of evidence* that the delusions of schizophrenics and paranoiacs are far less adaptive, even physically, than, say, belief in the principles of engineering accepted by the ancient Romans or

Greeks? Disappointingly, Meissner completely dodges and sidetracks the imperative to *justify* his *obiter dictum* that the distinction between sanity and insanity is just not a matter of evidence. Thus, he immediately switches to claiming a common emotional psychogenesis for both psychotic delusions and religious belief systems: "The delusional system as well as the [religious] belief system is maintained on the basis of a prior emotional commitment, not on the basis of evidences. The illusion sets no store by verification" (p. 94). Here Meissner is, of course, echoing Freud and indeed, his second sentence is taken verbatim from Freud (1927, p. 31).

But, unlike Meissner, Freud saw clearly that, though evidence may have played no role in the motivation of the believer, it is crucial for appraising the belief itself epistemically and semantically. How else can Meissner, the psychiatrist, ever reach the verdict of delusion, even if only fallibly? In the same vein, avowedly renouncing evidence for giving assent to the Bible, he says: "Apologetics must ultimately appeal to an acceptance through faith which lies beyond the reach of reason" (p. 94). But this characterization is an attempt to set such belief apart from a delusion. It does so by abandoning psychiatric vocabulary in favor of honorific language that gratuitously uses a spatial metaphor to elevate the illusion and to demote reason. Why not say instead that since the belief is avowedly ill-supported, it is *beneath* reason rather than beyond it? As for differences between religious tenets and psychotic delusions, Meissner lucidly elaborates on ideas that are vintage Freud (p. 94).

But in his most recent book (1984), Meissner does take issue with Freud by accusing him of misrepresenting the believer's own epistemic valuation of his faith:

> The believer does not regard his faith as a matter of wishful hallucination or of purely subjective implications. . . .
>
> The question we are addressing here is not that of the truth value of the believer's faith. The point, rather, is that to envision his faith solely in subjective terms, as essentially did Freud, is to do a disservice to the believer and actually to distort the substance of his belief (p. 178).

This complaint, however, seems misdirected. Freud never averred that his appraisal of the psychogenetic, epistemic, and semantic status of theism as both an illusion and a delusion (1930, pp. 81, 85; 1933, pp. 160-162, 166-168) is a *reconstruction* of the believer's own view of his creed. On the contrary, as he emphasized, "No one, needless to say, who shares a delusion ever recognizes it as such" (1930, p. 81). And Meissner is arguing at cross purposes with Freud, who was indeed addressing the question of truth value when he referred to Tertullian's declaration "Credo quia absurdum," and wrote: "But this *Credo* is only of interest as a self-confession. As an authoritative statement [vouching for the truth value of the faith] it has no binding force" (1927, p. 28).

Nor does it impugn any of Freud's theses on religion to adduce, as Meissner does, D.W. Winnicott's 1971 theory of child development. As the child makes its first attempts to relate to the world outside its mother, we learn, it creates so-called "transitional objects" that are "neither totally subjective nor totally objective" (p. 16). Instead, these objects share elements contributed from objective reality no less than from the child's subjective inner world, a view akin to John Locke's notion of primary and secondary qualities of material objects. And to the extent that the subjective component distorts the representation of an externally existing object, yet is *not* just hallucinatory, Winnicott's notion of transitional object can be assimilated to the *Oxford* sense of "illusion." According to that construal of the term, we recall, illusions are false sensory perceptions, but—unlike hallucinations—they do originate from a real external stimulus.

When Freud proclaimed that the consolations of religion are delusional, he had alluded, just in passing, to the germ of Winnicott's idea. Thus he declared: "It is asserted, however, that each one of us behaves in some one respect like a paranoic, corrects some aspect of the world which is unbearable to him by the construction of a wish and introduces this delusion into reality" (1930, p. 81). Examples that come to mind at once include the practice of what psychoanalysts call "denial," even by highly knowledgeable medical experts, who invent far-fetched diagnostic hypotheses to discount their own ominous symptoms of serious illness. Hence one may well grant Meissner the claim that none of us get through any stage of life without some reliance on Winnicott's transitional objects (pp. 165-171).

Yet the recognition of this state of affairs does not even begin to make a dent in Freud's case against theism. As Küng appreciates: "It does not follow—as some theologians have mistakenly concluded—from man's profound desire for God and eternal life that God exists and eternal life and happiness are real . . . It is true that the wish alone does not contain within itself its fulfillment" (p. 79; see also Ricoeur, 1966). Indeed, for any particular wish-inspired belief, it must be asked anew whether it is not just delusional, being a mere projection in the sense of Feuerbach and Freud. And clearly, in the context of religious experience, this key question can hardly be answered by the existence of *some* objects that do qualify as a kind of admixture of objective elements with subjective projections.

It would seem, therefore, that—interesting though it is in its own right—Meissner's extrapolation of Winnicott's notion of transitional object does not adequately come to grips with Freud's epistemological challenge, or even begs the question.

Unacknowledged Motives and Religious Belief

So far, our treatment of Freud's philosophy of religion has emphasized the important gaps in its evidential support. But there are also a number of considerations that either lend substance to some of his contentions, or pose important questions to which we have been alerted by his notion of belief in theism as psychopathology.

It is remarkable that neither Hans Küng nor William Meissner discussed the doctrine of the Virgin Birth of Jesus *vis-a-vis* psychoanalytic theory. Freud makes only incidental, passing reference to the ancient fable of virgin births among vultures, which the Church Fathers took up eagerly as a plausibility argument, drawn from the natural order (1910, p. 90). But it is an obvious psychological question to ask: Why is it thought to enhance Christ's moral or divine stature that he was supposedly born of a virgin? And what would Roman Catholic Maryology be without Mary's virginal status? She is venerated as the Mother of God by the Anglican, Eastern Orthodox, and Roman Catholic Churches. And the miracle of the Virgin Birth is reportedly that Christ was "conceived by the Holy Ghost and born of the Virgin Mary" (Luke 1:34-38). This asexual event is supposed to have occurred in response to her having asked the angel Gabriel how she, a virgin, should become the mother of the promised Messiah.

There are, of course, people in our culture who scoff at anthropological tales of asexual reproduction in humans, except for the Virgin Birth of Jesus. Yet they know very well that no one monitored Mary's encounters with Joseph, or with any other male. In fact, early Christian legends incorrectly described Joseph as an aged widower, presumably to discredit the idea that he was Jesus's biological father ("Joseph," *The World Book Encyclopedia, 11*, 132, 1966).

It is clear that anyone who believes in the divinity of Jesus may presume that his conception and birth were not tainted in any way. But the question is why his birth would have been less exalted if his conception had been sexual? If Mary's ovum itself is presumed to be unblemished, why then would Joseph's sperm or prostatic fluid be a pollutant? Is it not perhaps the pleasure incident upon sexual conception that is held to detract from divinity? And, if so, why? Does it not bespeak a strong desire to *dissociate* motherhood from sexuality, a desire that is normally deemed unrealizable, because people know better? Is it not precisely the opportunity to fulfill this wish that makes otherwise hard-headed, worldly, and even street-wise Christians eager to suspend all disbelief? And even if one is prepared to postulate that Mary's pregnancy was asexual, would it not be more reasonable to see it as a very rare case of *spontaneous* parthenogenesis among humans, rather than to attribute it to the action of the Holy Ghost? After all, in some kinds of lower species, the development of eggs without fertilization is the normal means of reproduction, as in the case of male ants, bees, and wasps. Yet according to current genetic theory, only *females* could develop *among humans* from an ovum that divides parthenogenetically. The Y chromosome that is needed to produce a male can come only from a sperm, since ova contain only X chromosomes. But Jesus was male.

It might be objected that this whole line of reasoning is unsound. Instead, it might be argued, a *sexual* conception is held to detract from the divinity of the offspring, because Jesus's conception would then no longer be *miraculous,* rather than because it would make Mary's motherhood pleasurably sexual. Yet this alternative rationale for the willingness to believe in the virgin birth does not seem to capture its psychological motivation adequately. In the first place, it is the *purity* of Mary's motherhood—rather than *just* its miraculousness—that is being steadily celebrated in the adulatory references to her as the Virgin. And the very notion that the ASEXUAL motherhood of a married woman is purer than the normal sexual sort—by being morally superior to the latter—seems to militate in favor of our original motivational conjecture: Psychologically, the doctrine of the virgin birth provides a golden, sublime opportunity to fulfill the wish to dissociate motherhood from sexuality. In the second place, if the hypothesized role of the Holy Ghost in Mary's pregnancy was only to render Jesus's conception miraculous, would it not be more credible that God the father created his own son directly *ex nihilo*—as he had done with photons, for example—rather than that the asexual story of the five Gospels is true? Hence let us proceed on the basis of our prior motivational interpretation.

But what accounts for the initial desire to dissociate sexuality from motherhood? Might it not be, after all, that this phenomenon is due to the existence of repressed oedipal conflicts? Let us assume with Freud that each child wishes to possess the parent of the opposite sex, and to eliminate the rival parent of the same sex. Then, at one stroke, the mother's supposed virginity fulfills the oedipal cravings of both boys and girls. The son has the satisfaction that the rival father did not possess the mother sexually; and the daughter gets her wish that the rival mother did not get her sexual tentacles on the father. If this is implausible, how much more implausible still is the belief in the virgin birth, whose ubiquity in Christendom cries out for psychological explanation, especially among those to whom you could never sell the Brooklyn Bridge. Again, if oedipal wishes are normally present, they might also be a contributory cause of the great frequency with which the Madonna and the Child are featured in the works of artists and musicians. Whatever the underlying psychological impetus, it seems very difficult to escape the conjecture that primarily a guilt-ridden, jaundiced view of sexuality inspires the strong feeling that Jesus's moral or theological stature is enhanced by his virgin birth.

The notion of an asexual reproduction in humans is intelligible, if implausible. But orthodox believers insist on making other religious utterances that are avowedly incomprehensible to themselves and to their fellows. To make this unintelligibility palatable, the pertinent linguistic pronouncements are sometimes said to express "mysteries." The renunciation of such mysteries and/or of their revelation is often a feature of eighteenth-century deism, insofar as it distances itself from theism. *Quà* being admittedly unintelligible, the so-called mysteries are not susceptible to evidential assessment in any ordinary sense, but are said to have the sanction of *special* revelation. Thus, Meissner (1984) strikes the theme of ultimate unintelligibility as follows: "faith is a response to revelation . . . and . . . revelation conveys a *content* that eludes human understanding" (p. 110; my italics). Yet, several considerations call for psychological explanation of why the faithful are eager to see themselves as giving creedal assent to beliefs whose very content is avowedly incomprehensible.

At least in our current state of biological evolution, our species may well be limited by intrinsic intellectual horizons of some sort, much as theoretical physics, for example, defies comprehension by dogs. Yet, whatever the extent of human inadequacy, the demand for creedal assent to an admittedly unintelligible declarative sentence seems to bespeak an altogether misplaced sense of intellectual humility. For, even if one is willing to accept such a claim on faith in the absence of evidence, it is impossible to do so, even with the best of intentions, since one can *believe* only a statement whose content one comprehends. Otherwise, what is it that is being believed? It would seem clear that assent, even on faith, requires prior understanding, if the assent is to be significant at all. But, if so, why do even the most highly intelligent among the faithful nevertheless affirm assent?

Recall that we allowed, in criticism of Freud, that arguments rather than mere wishes may have prompted *some* theists to believe in God. But spurious assent to avowedly incomprehensible utterances purely on faith is much more likely to be a matter of wish fulfillment. What else could motivate such would-be assent? What does it mean to say, as some have said, that God is transcendent to the point of being "wholly other"? And why does anyone want to say it?

In the same vein, if the very content of revelation does elude human understanding, how can it be conveyed in utterances? And why do the clergy not heed Wittgenstein's injunction: "Whereof one cannot speak, thereof one must be silent" in the wake of telling us about the intellectual horizons of our finite minds? How do ecclesiastics acquire greater expertise than others for discerning the limits of human cognition, say, in regard to so-called "ultimate causes"? As a further example, Yahweh, the god of Moses, was said to be even "above naming and beyond understanding" (Meissner, 1984, p. 119). How then can such an object be intelligibly loved, in addition to being feared and taken on faith? Indeed, how can love and fear of God be other than diffuse, if their very object eludes us? And why is this whole web of notions *not* a case of thought pathology?

Hans Küng's 1984 book on personal immortality unfortunately offers similar kinds of verbal fetish, which *evades* the substantial evidence against immortality. There he tells us in dozens of ways that eternal life is "beyond the dimension of space and time, in God's invisible, imperishable, *incomprehensible* domain" (p. 113; my italics). And, furthermore, that "The glory of eternal life is completely new, unsuspected and incomprehensible, unthinkable and unutterable" (p. 220). But, again, if the very domain of eternal life is avowedly "incomprehensible," what does it mean to *believe* in it? And how could Küng possibly take the "unutterable" on faith? In what sense does our personal identity survive in Küng's vision? Just what does the spatial metaphor "beyond" mean if the domain is "beyond spacetime"? Indeed, as Küng would have it, eternity is devoid of temporal succession and consists instead of an endless "now." But what is to be understood by an "endless now"? And how can the prospect of it be consoling to a person who is reflective, rather than just verbally conditioned? Why would a believer not pray to God for the oblivion of death as deliverance from such excruciating cosmic monotony? Moreover, this supposed eternal life is not even cold comfort as compensation for biological death. Is our fear of death not a matter of the impending loss of just those terrestrial joys that, we know, depend on the integrity of our physical brain? Would we not miss the embrace of someone we love, the fragrance of a rose, the satisfactions of work and friendship, the sounds of music, the panorama of a glorious sunrise or sunset, the biological pleasures of the body, and the delights of wit and humor? Hence, far from being blissful, the eternal beatitude held out by Küng, and by Pascal's wager, is at best stale, flat, and undeserving of our trust. Though well-intentioned, its vision of immortality seems to be largely an unintelligible myth. Yet none other than Martin Gardner (1986), the well-known science writer and debunker of pseudoscientific superstition, speaks *approvingly* of Reinhold Niebuhr's vision of a personal immortality that "will not destroy the essential unity of mind and body" (pp. 52-53). According to Gardner, Niebuhr took "Paul's symbol of the resurrection of the body as pointing to a transcendent realm, wholly beyond reason, where there would be no destruction of our essential nature, though in a manner about which we can know absolutely nothing." Alas, this is literally just nonsense!

One wonders, therefore, in what sense there can be a community of faith or belief, rather than of mere verbal utterance, in regard to those statements that are admittedly incomprehensible. And one is distressed by the intensity of the emotions engendered and the effort expended to secure from people an assent which, in the nature of the case, can be little more than parroting linguistic expressions. Man, it appears, is not only a symbol-using animal, but also a symbol-*abusing* being. To deplore the spurious assent orchestrated by linguistic regimentation is not to say, however, that it is ineffective as a means of securing the compliance of the faithful with concrete behavioral directives. On the contrary, precisely because the content of the purported mysteries is elusive, their utterance may enhance the psychological subordination needed for such compliance.

It has been said that these mysteries can perhaps be demystified, if they are seen as just allegorical expressions of the sense of awe felt by human beings in the face of the vastness and inexhaustible intricacy of the universe. But such awe can be and is felt by atheists too. As Freud observed: "what constitutes the essence of the religious attitude is not this feeling but only the next step after it, the reaction to it which seeks a remedy for it" (1927, p. 32) in religious belief.

We have considered the critical response to Freud's psychology of religion by the theological partisans Küng and Meissner. This focus on them seemed warranted, not only because their writings are psychoanalytically informed and recent, but also because they criticized Freud in a spirit of intellectual comradeship and human brotherhood. Both Küng and Meissner see themselves as having salvaged what is valid in his psychological critique of religion without fundamental detriment to the essential tenets of theism, or even of Roman Catholicism. For our part, we have claimed that Freud's syllogistic argument for atheism relies on a premise whose warrant is open to question. But, as we saw, Küng's and Meissner's own insistence that the content of some cardinal religious utterances is incomprehensible renders belief in them meaningless. Thus, it becomes imperative to explain *psychologically* what stake such theists have in paradoxically demanding credulous assent to those utterances. Unintelligible utterances are neither true nor false. Therefore, they cannot qualify technically as either delusions or illusions. Delusions are, by definition, false beliefs. And Freudian illusions are either true or false.

Though assent to incomprehensible utterances is spurious, the aura of mystery surrounding the elusive content of such would-be beliefs may perhaps furnish welcome release for the faithful from doubt as to the more intelligible beliefs that are wish-fulfilling. The dogma of the *bodily* assumption of Mary into heaven may thus facilitate credulous acceptance of her virginal motherhood. Any attrition of our critical faculty in a given domain seems to make it easier to suspend its use even more in that domain. Thus belief in personal immortality may be made more acceptable to some by the view that the angels now have the technology to read each person's DNA, and therefore they can clone each of us in heaven. But these psychological conjectures are only suggestions of mine, inspired by questions to which Freud's theory of religion as psychopathology has alerted us. In short, despite the major evidential lacunae in his philosophy of religion, it is probably not without some substantive merit, over and above its heuristic value.

In striking contrast to Küng and Meissner, the psychoanalyst Gregory Zilboorg, a one-time Russian Jew who became a convert to Roman Catholicism, characterized Freud's philosophy of religion as a case of "megalomanic scientism" (1962, p. 243). Yet Freud had fully acknowledged both the epistemic fallibility and substantive incompleteness of the scientific enterprise:

> I know how difficult it is to avoid illusions; perhaps the hopes I have confessed to for science are of an illusory nature, too. But I hold fast to one distinction. Apart from the fact that no penalty is imposed for not sharing them, my illusions are not, like religious ones, incapable of correction. They have not the character of a delusion. If experience should show—not to me, but to others after me, who think as I do—that we have been mistaken, we will give up our expectations (1927, p. 53).

And, in the wake of this concession, he says to the partisan of theism: "the weakness of my position does not imply any strengthening of yours." Thus, the capstone of these admonitions, which is the very last sentence of *The Future of an Illusion,* is the caveat: "But an illusion it would be to suppose that what science cannot give us we can get elsewhere" (1927, p. 56). This assertion hardly promises pie-in-the-sky from science.

The accusation of megalomania continues to be leveled against the irreligious humanism espoused by Freud. A notable, more recent example is furnished by Alexander Solzhenitsyn's 1978 Commencement Address at Harvard University. Entitled "A World Split Apart," it contains the following lament: "There is a disaster which is already very much with us. I am referring to the calamity of an autonomous [despiritualized] and irreligious, humanistic consciousness. It has made man the measure of all things on Earth—imperfect man, who is never free of pride, self-interest, envy, vanity, and dozens of other defects. . . . Is it true that man is above everything? Is there no Superior Spirit above him?"

Prima facie, this declaration may sound ingratiatingly modest. But, as it stands, it is morally hollow and theologically question-begging. Whose revelation, one must ask, is to supplant man as the measure of all things? That of the Czarist Russian Orthodox Church? Or the edicts of the Ayatollah Khomeini, as enforced by his mullahs? Those of the Dutch Reformed Church in apartheid

South Africa? Or the teachings of Pope John Paul II, who—amid starvation in Africa—is getting support from the native episcopate for the prohibition of "artificial" birth control? The moral prescriptions of the Church of England? Or yet those of the orthodox rabbinate in Israel, which prohibits autopsies, for example? And, of the latter, which of the two competing chief rabbis is to be believed, the Ashkenazi, or the Sephardic one? If the ethical perplexity of modern man is to be resolved by concrete moral injunctions, does Solzhenitsyn's jeremiad not simply replace secular man by *clergymen,* who become the moral touchstone of everything? Indeed, was the invocation of divine Providence not a regular feature of Hitler's speeches, illustrating anew that religion can also be the last refuge of the scoundrel?

After all, even if one has no problem with the very concept of divine omnibenevolence, this notion is itself altogether sterile in regard to specific moral imperatives. Assuming omnibenevolence, it presumably follows that all divinely ordained conduct is morally right. Yet we are left wholly in the dark as to whether to share or abhor, for example, the Reverend Falwell's and Rabbi Kahane's claim that a nuclear Armageddon is part of God's just and loving plan for us. From Rabbi Kahane we learn: "The Messiah will come. There will be a resurrection of the dead-all the things that Jews believed in before they got so damn sophisticated" (quoted in Friedman, 1986).

To an observer who is not already identified with one of the contending theological revelations, it appears that the moment a theology is to be used to yield ethical prescriptions, these rules of conduct are obtained by deliberations in whose outcome secular aims and thought are every bit as decisive as in the reflections of secular ethicists who deny theism. And the perplexity of moral problems is not lessened by the theological superstructure, which itself leaves us in an ethical quandary. That this superstructure is at best logically superfluous for ethics or simply unavailing emerges further from the failure of divine omnibenevolence to answer a key question, put by Socrates in Plato's *Euthyphro:* Is the conduct approved by the gods right because of *properties of its own,* or *merely* because it pleases the gods to command it? If God enjoins us to do what is desirable *in its own right,* then ethical rules do not depend for their validity on divine command, and they can then be independently adopted. But if conduct is good merely because God decrees it, then we are again faced with the cacophony of conflicting revelations as well as with the basic ethical disagreements existing even within the clergy of the same religious denomination.

No wonder that the Judaeo-Christian theology has been invoked as a sanction for such diverse ethical doctrines as the divine right of kings, the inalienable rights of life, liberty, and the pursuit of happiness, black slavery, "Deutschland über alles," the social Darwinism of Spencer, and socialism. Some religious sects in India would have us abstain from the surgical excision of cancerous growths in man, and Christian Scientists in the West reach somewhat similar conclusions from rather different premises. Roman Catholics, on the other hand, endorse the medical prevention of death but condemn interference with nature in the form of birth control, a position not shared by leading Protestant and Jewish clergymen. Indeed, both Mahatma Gandhi and Hitler saw themselves as serving

God. And divine Providence was as frequent a feature of Hitler's speeches as it is of Ronald Reagan's. One believer's will of God is another's will of Satan, as illustrated by the exchange between the Ayatollah Khomeini and President Carter, a born-again Christian.

Solzhenitsyn's charge of moral inadequacy against an irreligious humanistic consciousness is of a piece with the point of his rhetorical questions, "Is it true that man is above everything? Is there no Superior Spirit above him?" Surely the assumption that man may well *not* be above everything hardly requires belief in the existence of God. As we know, NASA has been scanning the skies for signals from extraterrestrial and indeed extrasolar humanoids, whose intelligence may indeed be suprahuman. Thus Voyager Two carries samples of our own intellectual productions to send a potential message from us. Yet theists and atheists alike know that if there are such mentally superior beings, they could be morally even worse than we are. For example, if they landed on earth, they might both bring the means and have the will to enslave our species beyond anything envisioned by George Orwell. By the same token, even if there were a disembodied spirit far superior to us intellectually, what is the evidence that it is not malevolent, allowing just enough good to exist to exacerbate the world's rampant evils (Russell, 1954, p. 590)?

Postscript (1992)

Meissner (1992) has just published an article on "The Pathology of Belief Systems," which is a sequel to his (1984) and to his earlier psychoanalytic treatment of religious beliefs (Meissner, 1978, pp. 92-95, 810-813). It behooves me to deal with those claims in his (1992) that pertain to the present chapter, which he cites (1992, pp. 107-109) from its original publication (Grünbaum, 1987).

Yet he took account of only my conceptual comparison of Freud's notion of delusion with the conflicting one offered in the Oxford *Psychiatric Dictionary* (Campbell, 1981, 1989). Besides, Meissner's statement of my view as to the relative merits of these rival notions is, alas, simply topsy turvy.

As the reader saw above, I sided explicitly with Freud's epistemologically and semantically derogatory construal of delusions, and I noted his claim that their psychogenetic status allows them to be socially shared as such. By the same token, I clearly opposed the recent Oxford socio-cultural relativization such that a "delusion" is idiosyncratic, which is politicized and precludes, by definition, that delusions be shared.

Thus, I commended Freud for allowing that there can be *mass* delusions or mass psychoses, and I rejected the Oxford notion as unacceptably restrictive. Yet Meissner saddles me with precisely the opposite view: "He [Grünbaum] takes issue with Freud's concept of mass delusion, insofar as it is not at all congruent with the notion of delusion found in common psychiatric usage" (1992, p. 107).

More disappointingly, Meissner (1992) is silent in regard to the principal arguments I offered in my (1987) against his (1978) and (1984) stance: He simply repeats (1992, pp. 123-124) almost verbatim contentions from his (1978) that I had clearly challenged. Indeed, his (1992) elaboration is even more vulnerable to my (1987) arguments than his earlier writings. Thus, now he tells us:

> Let us take one religious belief that is fairly widely accepted-in Christian religions, namely that there will be a final judgment by God when an ultimate disposition will be made of all men assigning them for all eternity to the beatitude of heaven or the torment of hell.
>
> . . . We have no empirical tests to satisfy our need for verification. We also have no means for demonstrating the falsity of these assertions. On what basis would we deny their validity? . . . If we accept the ideas, we accept them on the basis of faith. If we do not accept the ideas, we reject them on the basis of no faith. From the perspective of scientific or psychoanalytic understanding, we have no resource that would allow us to solve the matter. We can say no more than that we simply do not know (1992, p. 103).

Believing to have immunized religious belief systems in this way against any and all evidential scrutiny, Meissner claims nevertheless that they actually *explain* observable facts: "Religious belief systems are complex cognitive organizations which explain in a coherent fashion fundamental and existential questions involving the origin of the universe" (1992, p. 122).

As against these claims, I offer the following considerations.

1. Consider Meissner's example of the religious belief that, at the final judgment, men's souls will be assigned "for all eternity to the beatitude of heaven or the torment of hell." Insofar as the envisioned modes of the survival of personal identity are intelligible at all—rather than just gibberish—the given belief presupposes personal immortality.

But there is very strong evidence for the very dependence of consciousness—be it labeled "mind" or "soul"—on adequate brain function, and thus for the demise of personal identity upon the death of the brain (Edwards, 1992). For example, there are known mental and psychiatric effects of traumatic brain injury, brain tumors, Alzheimer's disease, degenerative dementias, toxic disorders (e.g., alcoholism), cerebro-vascular dysfunctions, and of endocrine disorders (Yudofsky and Hales, 1992, Part IV).

Just as personal immortality is discredited by adverse evidence, so also, contrary to Meissner, Schreber's belief that he was being transformed into a woman is gainsaid by refuting anatomical evidence. Of course, like other paranoiacs, Schreber might try to make his delusion irrefutable by tampering with its very content, such as modifying the criteria for being male or female. But such a gambit could hardly render his delusion of gender-transformation immune to evidential discreditation. Similarly, the belief in the purported efficacy of petitionary prayer to God by well-wishers of fatally ill people is statistically testable and thus disconfirmable by potential medical findings.

2. Both Pope John Paul II (Associated Press dispatch 5-24-1987) and Cardinal O'Connor of New York have endorsed exorcism, which is the therapeutic application of the demonic possession theory of insanity. This primitive animist theory has been adduced to "explain" hysteria, somnambulism and epilepsy. But

it is discredited by the aforecited dependence of at least some psychiatric disorders on known sorts of neuroanatomical or neurochemical brain dysfunctions. Besides, in the Roman Catholic exorcist ritual, the very existence of death in the world is attributed to Satanic activity, despite the overwhelming evidence for the physiological causation of our demise. Thus, even if Satan were to exist, he would be *causally irrelevant* to both psychosis and death, despite his useful allegorical role as Mephistopheles in Goethe's *Faust.*

Undaunted by such caveats, the current Pope has told us that Lucifer or Satan is "a cosmic liar and murderer . . . [who] has the skill in the world to induce people to deny his existence in the name of rationalism." Thus, John Paul II tries to render the purported Satanic activity immune to evidential discreditation by precisely the sorts of reasoning featured in the arguments characteristically employed by paranoiacs in defense of their delusions.

These animadversions alone undermine Meissner's allegation that "The problem in evaluating religious belief systems is that not only is there no evidence for them, but that there is also no evidence contradictory to them" (1992, p. 109). By the same token, the existence of cogent evidence against both personal immortality and demonic possession invalidates Meissner's charge that Freud "had no legitimate basis for declaring religious beliefs delusional, that is violating reality" (1992, p. 107). Having drawn that unsound conclusion, Meissner infers unjustifiably that Freud, *malgre lui,* had to base his assertion of the delusional character of religious beliefs *solely* on their wish-fulfilling character.

It appears that Meissner has fundamentally misportrayed the epistemology of religious doctrines by his wholesale declaration that "If we do not accept the ideas, we reject them on the basis of no faith. From the perspective of scientific or psychoanalytic understanding, we have no resource that would allow us to solve the matter" (1992, p. 103). Does Meissner himself really believe that his psychoanalytic account of the paranoid process is not evidentially superior to that offered by demonic possession? And is his preference for the psychoanalytic explanation merely a matter of his sheer lack of faith in the demonic one?

As he would have it, disbelievers can never have any grounds for rejecting religious doctrines other than the unavailability of supporting evidence. But, as I have argued, for at least a significant subclass of religious beliefs, there is telling evidence against them (Grünbaum, 1992).

Just as Popper erred seriously (see Chapter 2, Grünbaum, 1993) when he asserted the empirical untestability of psychoanalytic theory *tout court,* so also Meissner's sweeping fideist denial of the evidential scrutibility of religious beliefs is wide of the mark.

His claim that a religious belief, though eluding both evidential confirmation and disconfirmation, can "explain . . . the origin of the universe" (Meissner, 1992, p. 122) fares no better. In a famous 1951 address to the Pontifical Academy of Sciences, Pope Pius XII claimed that the "big bang" model of the origin of the universe, which has been in vogue among astrophysicists for three decades, vindicates the Christian doctrine of creation *ex nihilo,* which is familiar since the second century. In the fifth century, Augustine even taught that God created both matter *and time* out of nothing.

But, as I have contended in some of my cosmological writings (Grünbaum 1990b; 1991), in the big bang model based on Einstein's theory of general relativity, physical processes or states already existed in some form or other *at every actual past instant* of *time,* because there simply was no time at all during which the physical world did not already exist in some form or other.

Furthermore, Augustine's notion that *time itself* "was made" by God, along with matter, presupposes a fictitious super-time. And it literally makes no sense to treat time itself as being on a par with objects like stars or atoms that come into existence in the course of time. On the other hand, the concept of temporally simultaneous divine creation of time itself is either nonsensical or uselessly circular as an explanation.

As against Meissner's explanatory tribute to theological creationism, it emerges from the big bang cosmogony that Augustine's creation *ex nihilo* offers only a *pseudo-explanation* of the existence of the universe. Yet Meissner's observations on the role of psychopathology in rigid adherence to religious dogma and related behaviors are not impugned by these criticisms. On the other hand, I do not think that Meissner's (1990) elaborate critique of my (1984) really comes to grips with the problems I have posed, let alone offers a viable resolution of them.

References

Campbell, R.J., Ed. (1981). *Psychiatric Dictionary* (5th Ed.). New York: Oxford University Press. A sixth edition appeared in 1989.

Campbell, R.J. (1989). *Psychiatric Dictionary* (6th Ed.). New York: Oxford University Press.

Edwards, P. (1992). The dependence of consciousness on the brain. In P. Edwards (Ed.), *Immortality* (pp. 292-307). New York: Macmillan Publishing Co.

Erdelyi, M.H., (1985). *Psychoanalysis: Freud's Cognitive Psychology*. New York : W.H. Freeman and Company.

Fenichel, O. (1945). *The Psychoanalytic Theory of Neurosis.* New York: Norton.

Feuer, L. S. (Ed.) (1959). *Basic Writings on Politics and Philosophy, Karl Marx and Friedrich Engels.* Garden City, NY: Doubleday.

Freud, S. (1901). The psychopathology of everyday life. *The Standard Edition of the Complete Psychological Works of Sigmund Freud*, 6, 1-290. London: The Hogarth Press.

Freud, S. (1907). Obsessive actions and religious practices. *The Standard Edition of the Complete Psychological Works of Sigmund Freud*, 9, 15-27. London: The Hogarth Press.

Freud, S. (1909). Notes upon a case of obsessional neurosis. *The Standard Edition of the Complete Psychological Works of Sigmund Freud, 10*, 155-318. London: The Hogarth Press.

Freud, S. (1910). Leonardo Da Vinci and a memory of his childhood. *The Standard Edition of the Complete Psychological Works of Sigmund Freud, 11*, 63-137. London: The Hogarth Press.

Freud, S. (1911). Psycho-analytic notes on an autobiographical account of a case of paranoia (*dementia paranoides*). *The Standard Edition of the Complete Psychological Works of Sigmund Freud, 12*, 9-79. London: The Hogarth Press.

Freud, S. (1912). A note on the unconscious in psycho-analysis. *The Standard Edition of the Complete Psychological Works of Sigmund Freud, 12*, 260-266. London: The Hogarth Press.

Freud, S. (1913a). Animism, magic and the omnipotence of thought. *The Standard Edition of the Complete Psychological Works of Sigmund Freud, 13*, 75-99. London: The Hogarth Press.

Freud, S. (1913b). The claims of psycho-analysis to scientific interest. *The Standard Edition of the Complete Psychological Works of Sigmund Freud, 13*, 163-190. London: The Hogarth Press.

Freud, S. (1913c). Totem and taboo. *The Standard Edition of the Complete Psychological Works of Sigmund Freud, 13*, 1-162. London: The Hogarth Press.

Freud, S. (1914). On the history of the psycho-analytic movement. *The Standard Edition of the Complete Psychological Works of Sigmund Freud, 14*, 7-66. London: The Hogarth Press.

Freud, S. (1915a). A case of paranoia running counter to the psycho-analytic theory of the disease. *The Standard Edition of the Complete Psychological Works of Sigmund Freud, 14*, 263-272. London: The Hogarth Press.

Freud, S. (1915b). Thoughts for the times on war and death. *The Standard Edition of the Complete Psychological Works of Sigmund Freud, 14*, 271-302. London: The Hogarth Press.

Freud, S. (1919). The "uncanny." *The Standard Edition of the Complete Psychological Works of Sigmund Freud, 17*, 219-256. London: The Hogarth Press.

Freud, S. (1921). Group psychology and the analysis of the ego. *The Standard Edition of the Complete Psychological Works of Sigmund Freud, 18*, 65-143. London: The Hogarth Press.

Freud, S. (1922). Some neurotic mechanisms in jealousy, paranoia and homosexuality. *The Standard Edition of the Complete Psychological Works of Sigmund Freud, 18*, 223-232. London: The Hogarth Press.

Freud, S. (1923). The ego and the id. *The Standard Edition of the Complete Psychological Works of Sigmund Freud, 19*, 12-59. London: The Hogarth Press.

Freud, S. (1925). An autobiographical study. *The Standard Edition of the Complete Psychological Works of Sigmund Freud, 20*, 7-70. London: The Hogarth Press.

Freud, S. (1927). The future of an illusion. *The Standard Edition of the Complete Psychological Works of Sigmund Freud, 21*, 1-56. London: The Hogarth Press.

Freud, S. (1930). Civilization and its discontents. *The Standard Edition of the Complete Psychological Works of Sigmund Freud, 21*, 59-145. London: The Hogarth Press.

Freud, S. (1933). New introductory lectures on psycho-analysis. *The Standard Edition of the Complete Psychological Works of Sigmund Freud, 22*, 5-182. London: The Hogarth Press.

Freud, S. (1939). Moses and monotheism: Three essays. *The Standard Edition of the Complete Psychological Works of Sigmund Freud, 23*, 1-137. London: The Hogarth Press.

Friedman, R. (1986). The sayings of Rabbi Kahane. *New York Review Books, 3* (February 13), 19.

Galton, F. (1872). Statistical inquiries into the efficacy of prayer. *Fortnightly Review, 12*, 125-135.

Gardner, M. (1986). Niebuhr and supernaturalism. *New York Review of Books* (March 27), 52-53.

Gibbon, E. (1899). *Decline and Fall of the Roman Empire.* New York: Peter Fenelon Collier.

Grünbaum, A. (1984). *The Foundations of Psychoanalysis: A philosophical critique.* Berkeley and Los Angeles: University of California Press.

Grünbaum, A. (1987). Psychoanalysis and Theism. *The Monist, 70*, 152–192.

Grünbaum, A. (1990a). Meaning connections and causal connections in the human sciences: The poverty of hermeneutic philosophy. *Journal of the American Psychoanalytic Association, 38*, 559-577.

Grünbaum, A. (1990b). Pseudo-creation of the Big Bang. *Nature, 344*, 821-822.

Grünbaum, A. (1991). Creation as a pseudo-explanation in current physical cosmology. *Erkenntnis, 35*, 233-254.

Grünbaum, A. (1992). In defense of secular humanism. *Free Inquiry, 12*, 30-39.

Grünbaum, A. (1993). *Validation in the Clinical Theory of Psychoanalysis: A Study in the Philosophy of Psychoanalysis*. Madison, CT: International Universities Press.

Hook, S. (Ed.) (1959). *Psychoanalysis, Scientific Method, and Philosophy.* New York: New York University Press.

Küng, H. (1979). *Freud and the Problem of God.* New Haven: Yale University Press.

Küng, H. (1984). *Eternal Life? Life After Death as a Medical, Philosophical, and Theological Problem.* Garden City, NY: Doubleday.

Laplanche, J. and Pontalis, J. B. (1973). *The Language of Psychoanalysis.* New York: Norton.

McGrath, W.J. (1986). *Freud's Discovery of Psychoanalysis*. Ithaca, NY: Cornell University Press.

Meissner, W. W. (1978). *The Paranoid Process.* New York: Jason Aronson.

Meissner, W. W. (1984). *Psychoanalysis and Religious Experience.* New Haven: Yale University Press.

Meissner, W. W. (1990). Foundations of psychoanalysis reconsidered. *American Psychological Association, 38*, 523-557.

Meissner, W. W. (1992). The pathology of belief systems. *Psychoanalysis & Contemporary Thought, 15*, 99-128.

Ricoeur, P. (1966). Der atheismus der psychoanlyse Freuds. *Concilium, 2*, 430-435.

Rieff, P. (1959). *Freud: The Mind of the Moralist.* Chicago: University of Chicago Press.

Russell, B. (1954). *A History of Western Philosophy.* New York: Simon & Schuster.

Safire, W. (1986). Secs Appeal. *New York Times Magazine*, January 26, 68.

Shinn, R. L. (1986). Tillich as interpreter and disturber of contemporary civilization. *Bulletin of the American Academy of Arts & Sciences, 39*, 7-27.

Stepansky, P. E. (1986). Feuerbach and Jung as religious critics: With a note on Freud's psychology of religion. In P.E. Stepansky (Ed.), *Freud, Appraisals and Reappraisals*. Hillsdale, NJ: Analytic Press.

Sulloway, F. J. (1977). *Freud, Biologist of the Mind.* New York: Basic Books.

Wallace, E. R. (1983). *Freud and Anthropology. Psychological issues,* Monograph 55. New York: International University Press.

Yudofsky, S. C. and Hales, R. E. (Eds.) (1992). *Textbook of Neuropsychiatry.* Washington, DC: American Psychiatric Press.

Zilboorg, G. (1962). *Psychoanalysis and Religion.* New York: Farrar, Straus & Cudahy.

Chapter 2
A Problem for Freud's Disjunctive Argument

David Livingstone Smith

O! who can . . . cloy the hungry edge of appetite
By bare imagination of a feast?
Or wallow naked in December snow
By thinking on fantastic summer's heat?
—William Shakespeare (*Richard II*, Act I scene 3)

The anti-theistic argument presented by Freud in *The Future of an Illusion*, and elucidated by Adolf Grünbaum in "Psychoanalysis and theism" is in many respects an appealing one. The idea that religious beliefs are motivated by wishes is intuitively attractive, but it is precisely the seductiveness of Freud's rhetoric—its power, subtlety and incisiveness—that may lead the unwary reader to overlook difficulties in his arguments. In the present paper, I will focus on Freud's assumption that beliefs are motivated either by evidence or by wishes. I will argue that this unwarranted assumption plays havoc with his analysis of the psychological wellsprings of religious belief and undermines the anti-theistic argument that flows from it. Finally, I will show how Freud's arguments can be reformulated in a manner that makes them more plausible while, at the same time, preserving both their spirit and much of their substance.

Freud's Epistemology

One of the most impressive aspects of *The Future of an Illusion* is the insight that it gives us into Freud's epistemological views. His analysis of religion cannot be properly done without an understanding of these views. The key concept in Freud's psychology of religion is *illusion*. In the vernacular, illusions are false beliefs, but Freud uses "illusion" as a term of art denoting beliefs that are motivated by wishes. "Error" also has a technical sense in Freud's vocabulary, albeit one that is closer to ordinary usage. Errors are false beliefs. "Illusion" and "error" are therefore different types of concept. A belief is an illusion in virtue of its causal history, but it is an error in virtue of its failure to correspond to the facts. It follows from this that illusions can be either true or false: the fact that *S*'s wishing that *p* causes his believing that *p* has no bearing on whether or not *p* obtains. It is this feature of illusions that guarantees their irrationality. Rationality demands that one apportion the strength of a belief to the strength of one's evidence for it. A rational person withholds belief from propositions for which she has insufficient evidence. But in cases of illusion, the strength of belief is apportioned instead to the strength of one's desire. One believes in a proposition to the extent that one wishes it to be true. Now, contrast illusion with errors. Errors are always false, but they are not necessarily irrational. One might adhere to an erroneous belief because the evidence at one's disposal is misleading or incomplete, or because one's method for analyzing the evidence is inappropriate or insufficiently powerful. Newton's conception of gravitational force was erroneous in this respect, but it was certainly not irrational.

Freud believed that although veridical illusions exist, they are "difficult to find." It seems to me that he understated their prevalence. True illusions are relatively common in situations where strong emotional commitments are coupled with uncertain outcomes. In elections, supporters often believe that their preferred candidate will win for no better reason than their desiring that he win, and the same applies to the attitude of citizens towards victory in war, and of sports fans anticipating the outcome of an important match. But if Freud exaggerated the infrequency of veridical illusions, we can readily grant him the more modest claim that *most* illusions are errors. This proposition seems to be vouchsafed by an analysis of what it is for a belief to be wishfully motivated. When one wishes that *p*, one does so against the background of a prior belief that *p* does not obtain, where *p*'s not obtaining is undesirable. Given that this prior belief is not a wishful belief, it is more likely to be grounded in evidence than the wishful belief that negates it (even if the prior belief is wishfully motivated, it must have been preceded by a belief that is not wishfully motivated, as chains of wishful belief must ultimately terminate in a belief that is not wishfully motivated). Suppose I wish that today were a sunny day. The fact that I *wish* this indicates that I have reason to believe that today is not a sunny day (perhaps I looked out the window, or listened to the local weather forecast). Although the fact that a belief is justified is no guarantor of its truth, a justified belief is more probably true than an unjustified one, and, trivially, the negation of a justified belief is less likely to be true than the belief of which it is a negation. When illusions are true they just *happen* to be true—they conform to the facts by accident rather than design, and such meshings of belief with fact are merely fortuitous.

Unlike illusions, assertions of knowledge "demand belief in their contents, but not without producing grounds for their claim" (1927, p. 31). To count as knowledge, a belief must be true. Knowledge is factive—to know that *p* it must be the case that *p* obtains. Although this criterion raises some difficult questions about the possibility of true theoretical knowledge, it works perfectly well in ordinary cases. If I *know* that there is a porcupine in my garden, there must actually be one there, and I must have concluded that it is there on the basis of some sort of evidence (for example, visual evidence). Knowledge is a form of evidentially motivated belief. The factivity of knowledge demarcates it from error, and its evidential grounding distinguishes it from veridical illusion.

To understand Freud's analysis of the relationship between knowledge and veridical illusion, we need a more detailed account of his views on the roles played by wishes and evidence in their genesis. Although Freud defined illusions as beliefs that are caused by (and which fulfill) wishes, he did not claim that they are motivated *solely* by wishes, as is evident from his remark that "we call a belief an illusion when a wish-fulfillment is a prominent factor in its motivation" (1927: 31), which allows that a belief can be illusory even though *some* evidential considerations played a role in bringing it about. It is, for example, consistent with this criterion that one is initially attracted to a proposition because of the evidence in its favor, but comes to believe it because it fulfills a wish. Although it is not entirely clear what Freud had in mind when he referred to wishes playing a "prominent" role, all things considered I think that it is reasonable to interpret him as asserting that a belief is an illusion if a wish is causally *sufficient* for its acceptance. Consider a scenario in which *S* believes that *p*, p is true, and *S* both wishes that *p* and has evidence that *p* obtains. In these circumstances *S* might believe that *p* either because of *p*'s desirability or because of *p*'s warrant. In the former case, *S* would have believed that *p* even if it were unwarranted for *S* to do so, while in the latter, *S* would have believed that *p* even if doing so were unappealing.

Delusion is a kind of illusion. Like all illusions, they are generated by wishes, but in the case of delusions "we emphasize as essential their being in contradiction with reality" (1927, p. 31). I will henceforth use the term "ordinary illusions" to denote those illusions that are not delusions. Delusions are false illusions, but they are not *just* false illusions. Ordinary illusions fulfill conscious wishes, but delusions fulfill wishes of which the wisher is unaware. This causal difference accounts for a formal one. Ordinary illusions are semantically transparent—they wear their wishful content on their sleeve—whereas the wishful content of delusional beliefs is far from obvious. To set this out more precisely, I will need to make use of a concept drawn from the philosophy of mind. Philosophers describe mental states in terms of what are called *propositional attitudes*. As the name implies, propositional attitudes are attitudes towards propositions. The attitudes are denoted by psychological verbs like "knows", "believes" and "wishes", and their content is fixed by the propositions towards which they are directed. Applying this analysis to the cases at hand, we can say that Freudian illusions are structured in such a way that the proposition towards which an illusory belief is directed is identical to the proposition towards which its motivating wish is directed. Expressed schematically, one believes that *p* because one wishes that *p*. Because illusions share the content of their motivating wishes, it is child's play to infer the content of the wish from the content of the belief. But in delusion, sameness of content does not obtain. The wish that *p* is covertly fulfilled in the belief that *q*, and it is therefore impossible to infer the content of a delusion's motivating wish from the delusion's content, its so-called manifest content.

I will illustrate this distinction by means of two hypothetical examples. Suppose that Diane believes that someday soon she will win the Maine state lottery. She has recently had difficulty making ends meet, so she is excited about the impending win, and tells all her friends how it will change her life. All things considered, it is reasonable to think that Diane's belief is an illusion motivated by a wish to win the lottery. Three considerations support this inference.

1. Diane has no grounds for believing that she will win—in fact, the evidence at her disposal points in the opposite direction. So, her belief is the negation of a justified belief. This excludes the possibility that she either knows or rationally believes that she will win.

2. There is independent evidence that she desires to win the lottery. Diane is under financial pressure, she purchased a ticket, and she is happily anticipating getting all that money. Clearly, Diane has a wish with the right sort of content to bring the illusion about. But this does not, in itself, give us reason to think that this wish was the *cause* of her belief.

3. The content of her belief coheres with the content of her desire. Desiring that she will win the lottery and believing that she will win the lottery are different attitudes towards the same proposition. The conjunction of (2) and (3) supports the inference that Diane's belief is caused by her desire, and is therefore an illusion rather than a simple error.

Now, contrast this with a schizophrenic delusion—Elisabeth's terrifying belief that her head is full of rats. As in the previous case, the belief is unmotivated by evidence, but the similarity ends there. We need have no reason to think that Elisabeth harbors a wish of the sort that might produce an ordinary illusion that her head is full of rats. Such a wish would have to have the same propositional content as the belief—namely, that her head is full of rats. But Elisabeth does not *want* her head to be full of rats. So, we cannot infer, in any commonsensical way that her delusion is wishfully motivated. If her delusion is motivated by a wish, then it is not a wish that shares the content of the belief that it fulfills.

Given these facts, most people would insist that delusions are not wish fulfillments. However, Freud did not relinquish the wish-fulfillment hypothesis so readily. Instead, he proposed that the difference between delusions and ordinary illusions lies in the fact that the wishes motivating the former are of a different sort and follow a different causal trajectory from those that motivate the latter.

I will explain this with the help of Freud's theory of dreaming. Dreams are a class of perceptual belief—when one dreams that *p* one believes that *p*. In contrast to the views of many contemporary psychologists, Freud believed that dreams are motivated by wishes, and in his view, discovering the meaning of a dream—*interpreting* the dream—is just inferring the content of the wishes responsible for bringing the dream into being. Some dreams are transparently meaningful. Dreams of convenience are a highly plausible example. "It is easy to prove that dreams often reveal themselves without any disguise as fulfillments of wishes . . ., " Freud wrote, when introducing his readers to the wish-fulfillment hypothesis, "For instance, there is a dream that I can produce in myself as often as I like—experimentally, as it were."

> If I eat anchovies or olives or any other highly salted food in the evening, I develop thirst during the night which wakes me up. But my waking is preceded by a dream; and this always has the same content, namely, that I am drinking. I dream that I am swallowing down water in great gulps, and it has the delicious taste that nothing can equal but a cool drink when one is parched with thirst. Then I wake up and have a real drink.
>
> He then goes on to spell out the dynamics of his wish-fulfilling dream. This simple dream is occasioned by the thirst which I become aware of when I wake. The thirst gives rise to a wish to drink, and the dream shows me that wish fulfilled (Freud, 1900, p. 123).

Dreams of convenience are structurally similar to ordinary illusions in that the wishes that they fulfill share their propositional content: one dreams that *p* because one wishes that *p*. Of course, there are significant differences between dreams of convenience and ordinary illusions. Dreams have sensory and perceptual components—they are "hallucinatory"—whereas ordinary illusions do not, but Freud (1900) explained this as a consequence of the neurophysiology of sleeping state (he called it "topographical regression") while insisting dreams and illusions are of a piece with respect to their wish-fulfilling character.

Once we leave the realm of transparently meaningful dreams, the wish-fulfillment theory encounters a notorious difficulty. Overtly wish-fulfilling dreams are not the norm. In fact, most dreams are unpleasant or threatening, and some are extremely disturbing (Revonsuo, 2000). Freud conjectured that even these dreams are fulfillments of wishes—albeit *disguised* fulfillments of *unconscious* wishes. Unconscious wishes are actively excluded from consciousness by a mechanism that Freud called the "censorship". To circumvent the censorship, the content of unconscious wishes is disguised to prevent the dreamer from recognizing their authentic nature. Dream images are thus proxies for the wishes that instigate them. Freud called the process of dream creation the *dream work*.

Consider the following childhood dream, reported by Freud's patient Sergei Pankeyev.

> I dreamt that it was night and that I was lying in bed . . . Suddenly the window opened of its own accord, and I was terrified to see that some white were sitting on the big walnut tree in front of the window. There were six or seven of them. The wolves were quite white, and looked more like foxes or sheep-dogs, for they had big tails like foxes and they had their ears pricked like dogs when they pay attention to something. In great terror, evidently of being eaten up by the wolves, I screamed and woke up (Freud, 1918, p. 29).

Pankeyev did not wish for wolves to be outside his bedroom window. He was terrified of them. Nevertheless, Freud inferred that this eerie and menacing dream both concealed and fulfilled a disturbing unconscious wish—Pankeyev's wish to have sexual relations with his father. The whole visual apparatus of the dream—the window, the tree, and the six or seven white wolves—were, he proposed, creations of the dream work. This example illustrates another distinguishing feature of delusional beliefs. The wishes that bring them to life are unconscious because they would otherwise cause traumatic distress. No one having such a dream could, without using specifically Freudian inferential procedures, see through its façade to discern the latent wish at its core. Disguised dreams are thus structurally on a par with delusions. Pankeyev was in the same position with respect to the meaning of his dream of the wolves as Elisabeth was with respect to the meaning of her belief that her head is full of rats—or so Freud would have us believe.

Freud's Disjunctive Argument

Having described Freud's epistemological framework, we are in a position to examine his use of it to explain theistic beliefs. Although primarily concerned with the psychological sources of religious belief, Freud recognized that his psychological explanation of religious belief had some bearing on the question of God's existence. In this section, I will confine myself to an examination of certain aspects of Freud's psychological hypothesis about religious belief. Having done this, I will go on to evaluate this hypothesis, and to critically examine Freud's use of it to argue for atheism.

Freud pointed out in *The Future of an Illusion* that a psychological theory of religious belief must satisfy several desiderata. First, it must account for what he called the source of the "efficacy" of religious belief—the mental processes that give rise to religious conviction "independent as it is of recognition by reason" (p. 29). Second, a psychological explanation of religion ought to address the "inner force" of religious beliefs—their remarkable power to influence human behavior. Throughout history, the faithful have sacrificed their lives, committed terrible atrocities against unbelievers, subjected themselves to privations and austerities, and spent vast resources building religious monuments and performing religious rituals. It is difficult to think of any other form of belief, except, perhaps, quasi-religious political ideologies like National Socialism, with comparable impact on human behavior. A third desideratum for a psychological theory of religious belief is that it should explain the specific content of religious beliefs: it should provide an explanation of why God is so often portrayed as a divine Father who intervenes in human affairs, protecting believers from the hostile forces of nature and ensuring that the good are rewarded and the wicked are punished, either in this life or in the next.

Freud's theory addresses all three of these desiderata. Religious beliefs originate in "the oldest, strongest and most urgent wishes of mankind" (p. 30), and it is these wishes that dictate their doxastic content. The force of religious convictions is derived from the strength of the immensely powerful wishes that they fulfill. Reading between the lines, Freud seems to have used something like the following argument to ground his hypothesis that religious beliefs are illusions (I will refer to as "Freud's Disjunctive Argument," or "FDA" for short).

1. Forceful beliefs are either motivated by evidence or they are not.

2. If forceful beliefs are not motivated by evidence, then they are motivated by wishes.

3. Religious beliefs are forceful.

4. Religious beliefs are not motivated by evidence.

5. Therefore, religious beliefs are motivated by wishes.

6. Beliefs motivated by wishes are illusions.

7. Therefore, religious beliefs are illusions.

The argument is valid, so if all of its premises are true then its conclusion must also be true. The first premise is uncontroversially true. Any proposition of the form 'P or not-P' is true as a matter of logical necessity. Premise three is uncontroversially true. Let us grant the truth of premise four, even though in doing so we come close to begging the question against theism (I intend to show that FDA fails even if its fourth premise is true). Premise five is true just in case premises two, three, and four are true, and premise six is a straightforward definitional truth. As we have already granted the truth of premises three and four, this entails that premise five is true if premise two is true. *So, the conclusion of FDA is false only if premise two is false.*

It is indisputably true that *some* forceful beliefs are motivated by evidence and some are motivated by wishes. But premise two asserts something far stronger than this—namely, that *any* forceful belief that is not evidentially motivated is wishfully motivated. This is an empirical claim, and to justify it one must consider a range of alternative explanations for the acquisition of forceful irrational beliefs and demonstrate that none of these candidates have an explanatory advantage over the wish-fulfillment hypothesis. But Freud made no effort to do this. He seems to have simply assumed that, if a forceful belief has no evidential basis, it must be wishfully motivated. That Freud was well aware of the norms of inductive reasoning is clear from Grünbaum's (1984, 1993) insightful analysis of his struggle to exclude the possibility that suggestion is the agent of psychoanalytic cure. This is not to say that Freud always pursued this procedure responsibly. Indeed, it is consistent with the charge that he sometimes merely paid lip service to it. But paying lip service to a principle is a far cry from paying it no service at all.

It seems unlikely that Freud's failure to present evidence in favor of premise two of FDA can be put down to a highhanded disregard for scientific reasoning. It seems much more likely that had a reason for thinking that forceful irrational beliefs *must* be wishfully motivated. I think his reason was fairly obvious. Freud recognized that premise two is entailed by propositions that are so fundamental to psychoanalytic theory that questioning it would be tantamount to questioning psychoanalysis itself. In the terminology developed by Imré Lakatos, the principle that forceful irrational beliefs are wish-fulfilling was part of the inviolable "hard core" of the psychoanalytic research program. That is why Freud took its truth for granted.

Freud's use of the wish-fulfillment hypothesis is conterminous with psychoanalysis. It emerged as a critical component of the theory of the mental apparatus in the 1895 *Project for a Scientific Psychology*, and was central to the account of the dreaming mind introduced in *The Interpretation of Dreams.* It is no exaggeration to say that the concept of wish fulfillment probably plays a significant role in every one of Freud's psychoanalytic works.

Freud was a neuroscientist before he was a psychoanalyst, and he incorporated a number of neuroscientific ideas into psychoanalytic theory (Kitcher, 1992). The wish-fulfillment hypothesis was ultimately based on the nineteenth century neuroscientific idea that the nervous system tends toward the discharge of tension—a proposal that was advocated by Ernst Brücke, Theodor Meynert, John Hughlings Jackson and other distinguished scientists whose work influenced Freud's thinking (Macmillan, 1991). In creating psychoanalysis, Freud translated this neuroscientific conjecture into a psychological idiolect. In his view, every human being must manage tensions arising from endogenous somatic sources, which he called the *drives.* Unpleasure is the subjective perception of drive tension, while the diminution of drive tension is experienced subjectively as pleasure. Freud held that the configuration of the mental apparatus is such that we are disposed to seek relief from mounting drive tension by reanimating memories of prior satisfactions (wish-fulfillment).

Freud referred to the tendency to discharge drive tension by means of wish fulfillment as the *pleasure principle.* In his writings on the subject, he stressed both the ontogenic priority of the pleasure principle and its ongoing impact on adult mental life. With regard to ontogenesis, he argued, "the state of psychical rest was originally disturbed [during infancy] by the preemptory demands of internal needs."

When this happened, whatever was thought of (wished for) was simply presented in a hallucinatory manner, just as still happens today with our dream thoughts every night. It was only the non-occurrence of the expected satisfaction, the disappointment experienced, which led to the abandonment of this attempt at satisfaction by means of hallucination. Instead of it, the psychical apparatus had decided to form a conception of the real circumstances in the external world and to endeavour to make a real alteration in them. A new principle of mental functioning was thus introduced; what was presented in the mind was no longer what was agreeable but what was real, even if it happened to be disagreeable. This setting up of the *reality principle* proved to be a momentous step (Freud, 1911: 219).

With the establishment of the reality principle, the tendency to deal with unpleasure by means of wish-fulfillment is gradually supplanted by "an *impartial passing of judgment*, which had to decide whether a given idea is true or false—that is, whether it was in agreement with reality or not" (221). Although Freud's language sometimes suggests that the pleasure principle is wholly left behind during the course of development, this impression does not reflect his views. A disposition towards wish fulfillment persists to some extent in all of us alongside the mature capacity for objective judgment.

> A general tendency of our mental apparatus . . . seems to find expression in the tenacity with which we hold onto the sources of pleasure at our disposal, and in the difficulty with which we renounce them. With the introduction of the reality principle one species of thought-activity was split off; it was kept free from reality-testing and remained subordinated to the pleasure principle alone (222).

Freud's discussions of the pleasure and reality principles suggest that his epistemological commitments were deeply intertwined with psychoanalytic views about the configuration of the human mind. Illusions, both true and false, are a function of the pleasure principle, while the capacity for rational belief, a necessary condition for knowledge, is dependent on the operation of the reality principle. The tension between illusion and evidentially motivated belief, as exemplified by the conflict between religious and scientific modes of thought, reflects the inevitable antagonism between the pleasure and reality principles in the human mind.

Should We Accept the Second Premise of FDA?

If Freud's theory of the pleasure principle is correct, then the second premise of FDA succeeds, and its conclusion is assured. On the other hand, if the second premise fails, this does not establish the falsity of the argument's conclusion. The failure of the second premise would mean that Freud's argument fails to establish that theistic beliefs are illusions.

So, what conclusions should we draw? If there is evidence calling Freud's theory of the pleasure principle into question, this will be sufficient to undermine his disjunctive argument. We can look for such evidence from three sources: the neuroscientific ideas that Freud used to support his claims, facts about child development, and psychological research into motivated irrationality.

Let us begin with neuroscience. The principles of psychophysics that Freud invoked in support of his psychological theories have long since been abandoned. In her book on the role of interdisciplinarity in the development and demise of psychoanalytic theory, Patricia Kitcher gives a nuanced account of how progress in neuroscience undermined the neurophysiological rationale for Freud's confidence in the pleasure principle.

Although psychoanalysis was a complex theory with many detailed and intertwined claims, this hypothesis was a keystone. If it could not be maintained, then the rest of the structure would collapse. But neither Freud nor his followers ever found any direct evidence for this hypothesis, and advances in endocrinology and neurophysiology made both halves seem considerably less plausible (Kitcher, 1992, p. 156).

Freud's psychological explanations were not *dependent* on the truth of the neuroscientific explanations that he invoked. They played the more modest role of lending it support. It would therefore be an error to dismiss Freud's theory of the pleasure principle on the grounds that the neuroscientific claims that Freud invoked in support of it have been disconfirmed (in fact, this would be a version of the genetic fallacy). At best, we can say (echoing Kitcher), that progress in neuroscience makes this aspect of Freudian theory look less plausible.

We must therefore turn to other sources of evidence to arrive at a verdict. One of these is developmental psychology. Although developmental psychologists cannot pass judgment on Freud's assertions about the role of wish fulfillment in the adult mind, they are well positioned to confirm or disconfirm Freudian claims about the primacy of wish fulfillment during infancy. Not only have psychologists failed to confirm Freud's thesis that hallucinatory wish fulfillment is the characteristic form of infant cognition, they have discovered that infants' cognitive capacities are far more sophisticated than Freud and his contemporaries assumed (Gopnik, 2009). According to best scientific opinion, then, Freud's speculative account of the ontogenetic emergence of the reality principle out of the pleasure principle is more fantasy than fact.

What about the adult mind? It may be that although Freud's developmental conjectures were misconceived, his account of the role of wish fulfillment in the adult mind is correct. Recall that what is at stake here is the very strong claim that *all* forceful unjustified beliefs are wishfully motivated. This claim fails if there are any such beliefs that are not wishfully motivated. Recent research into self-deception demonstrates that we should not consider wish fulfillment as the only game in town for explaining motivated irrationality.

It is tempting to think of self-deception as the process of causing oneself to falsely believe that a desirable state of affairs obtains. This was Freud's view, as well as that of the philosophers David Pears (1984) and Donald Davidson (2004). According to this thesis, if *S* self-deceptively believes that *p* it must be that *S* wishes for *p* to be true. Certainly, many ostensible cases of self-deception seem to conform to this formula. However, the philosopher Alfred Mele calls attention to a form of self-deception that falls foul of it. He calls it "twisted self-deception."

In twisted cases, people are self-deceived about something that they want to be false (and do not also want to be true). For example, an insecure, jealous husband may believe that his wife is having an affair despite his possessing only relatively flimsy evidence for that proposition and despite his not wanting it to be the case that she is so engaged. If some self-deception is twisted in this sense, then at least one relatively common claim about self-deception is false—the claim that *S*'s being self-deceived that *p* requires *S*'s desiring that *p* (Mele, 2001, p. 4).

The obvious Freudian rejoinder is that the husband's self-deceptive belief concealed an unconscious wish with an entirely different content. However, Mele draws on research into lay hypothesis testing to propose a different sort of explanation. Investigations undertaken by James Friedrich, Yakov Trope, and Akiva Liberman suggest that for rival hypotheses *p* and not-*p*, if *S* assesses that it would be more costly to him to incorrectly assess *p* as true than it would be for him to incorrectly assess not-*p* as true, *S* will tend to be more exacting when gathering and assessing evidence in favor of *p* than when gathering and assessing evidence for not-*p,* and these cognitive biases may lead *S* to the self-induced false belief that not-*p* (Friedrich, 1993; Trope, Gervey & Liberman, 1997; Trope & Liberman, 1996). Perhaps the jealous husband desires to have a monogamous relationship with his wife, and this desire provides the motivational basis of his self-deception. If the proposition that she is *not* having an affair turns out to be false, this will be more costly to him than if the proposition that she *is* having an affair turns out to be false. Wrongly believing that she is faithful would place him in a more disadvantageous position that wrongly believing that she is faithful would, and this cost differential biases his cognitive processes to favor evidence that she is having an affair, which causes him to fall victim to twisted self-deception (Mele, 2001). If motivational biases can lead to false beliefs that are not wish fulfilling, than Freud's disjunctive premise should not be assumed to be true.

Assessing and Reformulating Freud's Anti-Theistic Argument

As mentioned earlier, Freud was mindful of the fact that his view that religious beliefs are illusions does not entail any conclusions about the existence of God. Illusions can be either true or false, and this applies to religious illusions just as much as to any other. However, Freud emphasized that the majority of illusions are probably false, and therefore that any given illusion is probably false. So, although the notion that theistic beliefs are illusions does not entail their falsity, it does have some bearing on the probability that they are false.

Clearly, Freud's failure to substantiate his claim that all forceful irrational beliefs are wish fulfilling, and therefore his failure to underwrite the claim that religious beliefs are illusions, has dire implications for his anti-theistic argument.

I would now like to assess those implications and determine whether Freud's argument can be salvaged.

The core of Freud's anti-theistic argument is condensed in the following passage from *The Future of an Illusion*:

> We know approximately at what periods and by what kind of men religious doctrines were created. If in addition we discover the motives which led to this, our attitude to the problem of religion will undergo a marked displacement. We shall tell ourselves that it would be very nice if there were a God who created the world and was a benevolent Providence, and if there were a moral order in the universe and an after-life; but it is a very striking fact that all this is exactly as we are bound to wish it to be. And it would be more remarkable still if our wretched, ignorant and downtrodden ancestors had succeeded in solving all these difficult riddles of the universe (Freud, 1927, p. 33).

Grünbaum interprets these remarks as expressing the following syllogism:

1. All archaic, evidentially ill-supported illusions are very probably false.

2. Anyone's belief in theism is an archaic, evidentially ill-supported illusion.

3. Therefore, anyone's belief in theism is very probably false.

The argument is valid, but it has a perplexing feature. It is not clear why Freud appears to give evidential weight to the archaic character of religious doctrines. Grünbaum tells us that his inclusion of the phrase "evidentially ill-supported" is semantically redundant, and included for emphasis only. Should we not treat the word "archaic" in the same way? If Freud was concerned with our ancestor's efforts to garner evidence in favor for God's existence, the reason for including it would be obvious. Our archaic ancestors did not have access to the sorts of evidence that would allow them to make good inferences about the existence of God. But Freud's discussion concerns illusions rather than evidentially motivated beliefs, and it is puzzling why he would consider ancient illusions to be any more disreputable than more recently minted ones. On the face of it, then, the syllogism appears to be logically equivalent to one that omits any mention of the primitive pedigree of religious doctrines, namely:

1. All illusions are very probably false.

2. Anyone's belief in theism is an illusion.

3. Therefore, anyone's belief in theism is very probably false.

I think that the archaic character of religious doctrines does play a significant role in Freud's argument. Consider the example of a twenty-first century theist who insists that only those religious doctrines that are consistent with the claims of modern cosmology or the theory of evolution are candidates for belief. Any religious belief that satisfies these criteria will be a member of subset of possible religious beliefs. Having set constraints on possible religious beliefs, this person might then adopt one or another of them because of its wish-fulfilling character. In other words—as I noted earlier in this paper—Freud's account of the role of wish-fulfillment in the formation of religious belief is consistent with the believer's making use of *some* evidential considerations (this seems to be what happens when believers decide to interpret embarrassing passages of scripture allegorically). Now, the "wretched, ignorant and downtrodden" originators of the world's religions had very little scientific evidence to constrain their doxastic options—which is why these religions are, in many respects, inconsistent with current scientific opinion. It is obvious that religious beliefs that are inconsistent with current scientific knowledge are more probably false than those that are consistent with current scientific knowledge (although, as we have seen, both are likely to be false simply in virtue of their being illusions), so the archaic pedigree of religious doctrines does have some relevance to judgments about their probable falsity.

Freud's anti-theistic argument is valid, but it does not succeed, due to its reliance on the claim that all theistic beliefs are illusions. Grünbaum is alert to the problem, pointing out that "there still remains the motivational question whether some of the faithful, when giving assent to theism, had not, in fact, been decisively moved by supposed proofs rather than by deep-seated wishes" (p. 19). Although these doubts are warranted, this remark suggests that Grünbaum underestimates the problem by implicitly accepting the supposition that beliefs are motivated either by wish fulfillments or the assessment of evidence—the offending premise of FDA. He concludes his discussion with the somewhat conciliatory remark that "we can *allow* that all cases of belief in God may perhaps be inspired by conscious favoritism for consoling beliefs over ominous ones, combined with any repressed wishes that do turn out to have such psychogenetic credentials" (p. 20).

Even this extremely weak rendition of Freud's position is vulnerable to refutation. For it to be true, all religious doctrines would have to be consoling. But, as cognitive anthropologist Pascal Boyer observes, "A religious world is often every bit as terrifying as a world without supernatural presence, and many religions create not so much reassurance as a thick pall of gloom" (Boyer, 2001, p. 20). And as far as promise of immortality goes, he adds that "we must . . . discard the parochial notion that religion everywhere promises salvation, for that is clearly not the case" (p. 21). The minimal Freudian proposal that *all* theistic doctrines are consoling may be based on too limited a sample of religious doctrines.

The failure of Freud's psychological explanation of religion, and the anti-theistic argument derived from it, can be attributed largely to its immoderate aspirations. Not content with accounting for the psychology of *some* (perhaps most) examples of theistic belief, Freud attempted—in typically Freudian style—to fashion a psychological explanation for *all* theistic belief, on the assumption that religious belief admits of a single, universal causal explanation. But there is no *prima facie* reason to think that all instances of religious belief can be captured by a single psychological explanation. Freud's psychological theory *might* suffice as an explanation for certain instances of religious belief, or even certain religious movements or doctrines, but, as Boyer implies, it is insufficiently general to capture the psychological basis of theism as such.

It is possible to modify Freud's arguments so that they no longer rely on the claim that beliefs are either evidentially justified or wish fulfilling, and in that modified form they are immune from the objections that I have leveled against them. In doing this, it is important to avoid discarding the Freudian baby with the bathwater. An acceptable reformulation of Freud's arguments should do justice to his intuition, which I regard as immensely plausible, that theistic beliefs are sometimes wishfully motivated. So, what needs to be done? For a version of Freud's psychological argument to pass muster we need only substitute the expression "non-rationally motivated" for the more theory-laden locution "motivated by wishes," and enlarge the notion of illusion to include all non-rationally motivated beliefs (or, equivalently, use a different term for the category of non-rationally motivated beliefs, and reserve the term "illusion" for the subset of these beliefs that are wish-fulfillments). The revised argument unfolds straightforwardly.

1. Forceful beliefs are either motivated by evidence or they are not.

2. If forceful beliefs are not motivated by evidence, then they are non-rationally motivated.

3. Religious beliefs are forceful.

4. Religious beliefs are not motivated by evidence.

5. Therefore, religious beliefs are non-rationally motivated.

6. Non-rationally motivated beliefs are illusions.

7. Therefore, religious beliefs are illusions.

Given that wishfully motivated beliefs are a subset of non-rationally motivated beliefs, this version of the argument allows that any instance of theistic belief may, in fact, be wishfully motivated, but it eliminates the overly strong claim that forceful irrational beliefs *must* be wish fulfillments. With these modifications in place, the conclusion that religious beliefs are illusions follows unproblematically, and can therefore be inserted in Freud anti-theistic argument as follows, to yield a satisfactory conclusion:

1. All archaic, non-rationally motivated beliefs are very probably false.

2. Anyone's belief in theism is an archaic, non-rationally motivated belief.

3. Therefore, anyone's belief in theism is very probably false.

Conclusion

If I am correct in imputing FDA to Freud, then his argument that theistic beliefs are illusions does not succeed because its premise that all forceful, evidentially unmotivated beliefs are fulfillments of wishes is unwarranted. If any such beliefs are produced by a psychological mechanism other than wish fulfillment, then the conclusion that all theistic beliefs are illusions fails to follow, and Freud fails to rule out this possibility, or even demonstrate that it is unlikely. Consequently, Freud's argument for atheism, the two premises of which rely on the conclusion of FDA, does not succeed. However, these difficulties can be rectified by judiciously weakening the second premise of FDA to allow that irrational beliefs may be produced by psychological mechanisms including, but not restricted to, wish fulfillment.

References

Boyer, P. (2001). *Religion Explained: The Evolutionary Origins of Religious Thought.* New York: Basic Books.

Davidson, D. (2004). Deception and division. In *Problems of Rationality (*199-212). Oxford: Oxford University Press.

Freud, S. (1900). The interpretation of dreams. *The Standard Edition of the Complete Psychological Works of Sigmund Freud,* 4-5, 1-338, 339-627. London: Hogarth Press.

Freud, S. (1911). Formulations on the two principles of mental functioning. *The Standard Edition of the Complete Psychological Works of Sigmund Freud*, 12, 218-226. London: Hogarth Press.

Freud, S. (1918). From the history of an infantile neurosis. *The Standard Edition of the Complete Psychological Works of Sigmund Freud*, 17, 7-122. London: Hogarth Press.

Freud, Sigmund (1927). The future of an illusion. *The Standard Edition of the Complete Psychological Works of Sigmund Freud, 21*, 3-56. London: Hogarth Press.

Friedrich, J. (1993). Primary error detection and minimization (PEDMIN) strategies in social cognition: A reinterpretation of confirmation bias phenomena. *Psychological Review, 100,* 298-319.

Gopnik, A. (2009). *The Philosophical Baby: What Children's Minds Tell Us about Truth, Love, and the Meaning of Life.* New York: Farrar, Straus & Giroux.

Grünbaum, A. (1984). *The Foundations of Psychoanalysis: A Philosophical Critique.* Berkeley: University of California Press.

Grünbaum, A. (1993). *Validation in the Clinical Theory of Psychoanalysis: A Study in the Philosophy of Psychoanalysis.* Madison, CT: International Universities Press.

Kitcher, P. (1992). *Freud's Dream: A Complete Interdisciplinary Science of Mind.* Cambridge, MA: Bradford/MIT.

Lakatos, I. (1978). *The Methodology of Scientific Research Programmes: Philosophical Papers Volume 1.* Cambridge: Cambridge University Press.

Macmillan, M. (1991). *Freud Evaluated: The Completed Arc.* Amsterdam: Elsevier.

Mele, A. R. (2001). *Self-Deception Unmasked.* Princeton: Princeton University Press.

Pears, D. (1984). *Motivated Irrationality.* Oxford: Oxford University Press.

Revonsuo, A. (2000). Reinterpretation of dreams: an evolutionary hypothesis of the function of dreaming. *Behavioral and Brain Sciences* 23, 877-901

Trope, Y., Gervey, B. & Liberman, N. (1997). Wishful thinking from a pragmatic, hypothesis-testing perspective. In M. Myslobodsky (Ed.), *The Mythomanias: The Nature of Deception and Self-Deception* (105-131). Mahwah, NJ: Lawrence Erlbaum.

Trope, Y. & Liberman, A. (1996). Social hypothesis testing: Cognitive and motivational mechanisms. In E. Higgins & A. Kruglanski (eds.), *Social Psychology: Handbook of Basic Principles* (239-270). New York: Guilford Press.

Chapter 3
The Psychoanalysis of Religion and the Dissolution of Epistemic Certitude

Jerry S. Piven

Grünbaum (this volume) adumbrates Freud's psychological analysis of religion, probing the epistemic status of religious belief as delusion, and the notion that religious arguments are *post hoc* rationalizations that occlude and disguise deep wishes. Grünbaum also elegantly dismantles theistic arguments, illustrating how modern critics of Freud fail to undermine the psychoanalytic assessment of religion or to offer convincing arguments for the plausibility of God. He then concludes his chapter by providing numerous examples of untenable and senseless theological claims to illustrate how much they resemble paranoid projections and seem to reflect deep psychological conflicts, rendering such fantasies ripe for psychoanalytic exploration. Grünbaum somewhat reductively describes religion in terms of obvious wish fulfillments and projections and does not fully appreciate the immensely complicated aspects of religious fantasy, belief, and behavior. This chapter therefore elucidates the psychoanalytic dissection of religion, tracing its profound convolutions and complexities, and finally rejects Grünbaum's notion that psychoanalysis lacks the evidential support to bolster its analysis of religion. Not only is there copious support for major psychoanalytic concepts, but psychoanalysis is a radical epistemology that subverts the notion of a rational mind that can use "scientific" methods to ascertain facts without investigating the way our own irrationality distorts our perceptions.

Theological Arguments, Motives, and Fantasies

In *Dialogues on Natural Religion*, David Hume (1779) provides a host of absurdly droll arguments to demonstrate that theological claims are conceptually baseless and contradictory. In the absence of evidence, what exactly can one say about God, or anything else? Nothing qualifies as actual evidence of the existence of God because every cause and creation can be attributed, hypothetically, to virtually any figment of the imagination. The cosmological argument asserts that God exists because everything must have a cause, and the ultimate cause must be God. But why one god instead of many? Why not Vishnu or the Keebler elves or the Flying Spaghetti Monster? Why not a race of omniscient space aliens who always existed, just like God? There is no evidence that a divine being created everything, so in the complete and utter absence of knowledge, what claims can one make about that imaginary being? The argument "it must be God" can be countered with "it can also be" any of the aliens or other deities suggested above. Hume demonstrates that the argument by design is pathetically flawed as well. Scientists can now explain how certain organs of the body are designed rather poorly, but even in Hume's day it was clear that the universe was not designed like a watch. Hume suggested that its creator would resemble a senile dotard rather than an intelligent designer.

Theological arguments attempt to fill in the gaps of knowledge with fantasies. For all we know, there may be a God, but the logic of such arguments is faulty. One just cannot say "there is no evidence" and "it must be this specific being with these specific intentions who gave us these specific commands," and so on. That is purely a figment of the imagination. Nor can one claim that this being is infinite and beyond human understanding and then claim any knowledge whatsoever of his workings. No form of indoctrination or habit can provide knowledge of that which is beyond human understanding, even if one dons the accoutrements of piety and authority. A tall hat and gilded stave does not an expert on the infinite make. To claim such knowledge is, actually, not only argument by devotion or authority; it is an argument *ad verecundiam*, pretense at expertise in something one cannot possibly have.

That does not, however, prevent people from expressing absolute certainty of God's expectations and demands, or from excoriating or filleting those who do not accept such certainties on faith. To paraphrase Davis (2006), the intellectual exertions and mendacity summoned to inflict or excuse the pain, destruction, and injustice people suffer is a marvel of ingenuity in the service of arrant delirium. Distressed by the dissonance between the notion of a merciful God and the Nazi genocide of the Jews, Buber proposed that God went into temporary eclipse during the Holocaust. Grünbaum (this volume) claims this is "perhaps one of the lamest in the history of theodicy" (p. 24), but is it really so atypical in terms of the absurdity of its reasoning and the utter lack of evidence for its conjectures?

The theologian Jack Haught recently gave a talk called "God After Darwin" at Case Western Reserve University, where he proposed that all of history is just a wonderful part of God's divine plan, and that we are all approaching de Chardin's noosphere, an era of impending universal God-consciousness. The Holocaust and all other wars and genocides are part of this happy plan. Or take Leibniz' *Theodicy*, which struggles to explain how a good and benign God could allow such misery and evil. Leibniz decides that though there are more evil than good people on earth, the kindly angels flitting around the atmosphere balance the scales toward goodness. The same brilliant mind that independently conceived the calculus, could also write 500 pages of sheer fiction devoted strenuously to fantasizing his way out of the horrid thought that perhaps there were no God, or that he didn't care whether people suffered. A complete absence of knowledge did not prevent him from asserting things for which there was no proof whatsoever. Hence Grünbaum (this volume) could conclude, appropriately, that theological claims are so illogical and incoherent as to suggest profoundly psychological forces motivating such nonsensical beliefs: "Thus it becomes imperative to explain *psychologically* what stake such theists have in paradoxically demanding credulous assent to those utterances" (p. 31).

This is why contemporary thinkers such as Dawkins, Hitchens, and Harris could go back to Hume, Feuerbach, Nietzsche, and Freud to understand the formation of fantasies and delusions. For eloquent, ribald essays that demolish theological arguments, by all means read *Letter to a Christian Nation* or *The Gospel of the Flying Spaghetti Monster*. However, these don't really explain *why* people imagine or defend their beliefs. Harris (2005) does a fantastic job of obliterating theological arguments, but he tends to explain all the credulity and destruction of religion as proceeding purely from faith. If you have faith, he avers, you will believe or do just about anything.

Clearly people can be motivated by faith, but this never explains how they acquire faith, what draws them to religion, what motivates them to believe certain ideas in the first place, how they are suddenly buoyed and possessed by faith in things unseen, why they sometimes undergo radical moral and personal transformations, why they are so devoted to those beliefs, or cling tenaciously to them in the face of all evidence to the contrary. It doesn't explain why people would believe that a few drops of water, a special bath, or a wafer would be so terribly crucial for "salvation." It sheds no light on why people can be preoccupied and terrified by sin, obsessed and disgusted with sexuality, or convinced that God gets angry when they touch themselves at night. It never explains what such beliefs gratify or salve, why people can feel so threatened by doubt and disbelief, or consider people of other faiths contemptible emissaries of evil, and in some cases, engage in inquisitions, witch hunts, and crusades.

Why would someone be convinced that a person could walk on water or rise from the dead? Why would one believe that an evil devil exists beneath the earth's crust (or netherworld) waiting to punish the sinful? Why would one believe that some divine being made a covenant involving foreskins, that he would care if you had a solitary orgasm, won a boxing match, or dialed a phone on a particular day? Are those beliefs any more reasonable than the notion that giant subterranean beetles cause earthquakes, that there are seven score virgins waiting in a celestial paradise, or that one can be reincarnated as a poodle or intestinal parasite depending on one's behavior? Are canonical theological claims any more likely than the belief that a divine tangle of spaghetti lurks in the skies above, or that a syndicate of cookie-baking elves presides over the workings of the universe? At least we have some proof that the Keebler elves exist; more than proof that Jesus performed miracles or even lived.

Why can people possessing such immense cerebral cortices believe in what is no more plausible than Santa Claus, or for that matter lacerate parts of their own anatomy, believe in talking reptiles, and maintain with rapt certainty that someday there will be a cosmic battle where the dead shall rise from their graves and myriad monsters, including a seven-brained dragon, will join the bloody fray? If one is willing to believe in dragons, why believe in *Revelation* instead of *The Hobbit*? Why is Satan more plausible than Sauron? Just because one knows that certain works are fiction does not make another fantasy book chock full of monsters and wizards any more believable. So why believe?

The usual explanation is that people believe what their parents and community do, that they need to fit in, that they do not question what seems to be the reality around them. This doesn't explain, however, how religions *do* change, how some people *do* question their faiths, and how theologies *do* regularly modify what was previously apodictic truth. The Catholic catechism reformulates the structure of the universe, and even God's relation to Jesus and the Holy Spirit every few generations. One year Limbo is a fact, the next a fiction. Initially Jesus is the adopted son of God, later he is the same substance.

Religious beliefs change, and people draw *selectively* on their texts. They ignore (or rationalize) passages that don't gel with their creeds and zero in on (or distort) passages that do mesh with their faiths. There are numerous unequivocal passages in the canonical biblical texts that support slavery (e.g., Exodus 21:2-8, Leviticus 25:44-46, Ecclesiastes 33:25, Ephesians 6:5-6, Colossians 3:22, Titus 2:9-11, 1 Peter 2:18, Judges 11:30-36, Genesis 19:4-8). The Qur'an asserts that Allah does not love aggressors (2:190), but it also tells people to slaughter infidels lest the passive, disobedient Muslim be punished (9:29). Something distinguishes the peaceful, pious Muslim from the self-appointed *mujahid* (holy warrior) who decides that God wants him to immolate a crowd of civilians to enter paradise. Some *jihadis* may be indoctrinated, and some may be heroes of their communities, but others are drawn to theologies that differ from the indigenous Islam into which they were born. The "psycho-logic" of those deemed terrorists weaves communal theology and personal history into an individual quest for identity and desire for martyrdom (Post, 1990; Wirth, 2004a, b). It is a complicated and variegated process, and cannot be reduced to merely obeying the dictates of the religion they have been taught (Davis, 2006; Piven, 2004a, 2006, 2007; Stein, 2004).

The notion that once you have faith you will perform any action, no matter how unsavory, makes it seem as though piety can be equated with following commands like robots. Nietzsche often invoked the notion of the herd mentality to describe religious people, making believers moronic sheep. As tempting as it is to accept such a scenario, it is quite an insult to suggest that all people of faith are devoid of independent thought, and it ignores the countless people of conscience who would never harm another human being. Frenzied persecutions, lynchings, autos-da-fe, crusades, and martyrdom operations (suicide bombings), however, are not acts carried out by intellectual flatliners who merely obey. The very ecstasy, fervor, hate, malice, or even love for God that inspire such acts, demonstrate how passionate people are about their religions. Even the flocks of sheep Nietzsche envisioned were not mindless, but craven, resentful, envious, and malicious souls who would form a mob or priesthood and crucify anyone possessing independent will or intellect.

When people obey or commit violent acts out of piety, we must ask what gratification that subservient devotion affords, and what longing is so intense that a person will do anything for his God. We must ask why someone needs to submit oneself before a grandiose power, yearns to obey, and hungers for deliverance. In many cases we need to fathom why someone is filled with feelings of loathsomeness or sinfulness, or needs forgiveness. Why would a person believe that possessing an intellect and independent will were so perilous, arrogant, or disloyal as to risk God's wrath, and that the only way to attain his love was to prostrate oneself before him and surrender that will and independent judgment? For those who *do* abdicate their intellects are not just sheep, they are desperate for love and forgiveness, and live in dread of divine condemnation. To take it a step further, why would a person feel that flagellating oneself, or even slaughtering himself, would be the only conduits to redemption? That the only way to attain God's love was one's own extinction?

Similarly, we must ask what arouses such malice, or such rapture, in the act of punishing or killing heretics or infidels. Even more commonplace, banal acts of intolerance and judgment involve derisiveness toward those considered sinners and apostates. The person who scorns someone of another faith, calls someone sinful, or castigates a child, may be repeating the unquestioned fictions he or she has been told. But his alarm, fear, anger, contempt, and disgust transcend mere obedience.

Hence it is *not* the case that people of faith just believe or do whatever they are told, and it is just *not* the case that people live in insulated religious worlds where their beliefs are the only reality they know. They also distend and rend the reality they have inherited. They fabricate and defend their own sanctified reality, sometimes with immense hostility.

The simplistic argument that people just believe what they are told never explains why people believe such strange things, especially when other ideas (like evolution) can be rejected virulently, and when their intellectual faculties can otherwise function with immense scientific skepticism and acumen. One recalls Freud's (1907) caveat about "the ease with which our intellect is prepared to accept something absurd provided it satisfies powerful emotional impulses . . . under these psychological conditions people of even the most powerful intelligence react as though they were feeble-minded" (p. 71). Grünbaum (this volume) cites the example of "medical experts, who invent far-fetched diagnostic hypotheses to discount their own ominous symptoms of serious illness" (p. 27). He also puzzles over "the virgin birth, whose ubiquity in Christendom cries out for psychological explanation, especially among those to whom you could never sell the Brooklyn Bridge" (p. 29). Consider also the person who studies cell biology but still believes in life after death, or the scientist who joins an apocalyptic cult and believes that a blind masseur is God, Buddha, and Krishna rolled into one.

One must ask why such ideas resonate with people, what they get out of such beliefs and rituals, what pleasures and relief such dogmas and massacres afford. Do the beliefs soothe a person in the face of death? Do they make a person feel significant, loved, and protected? Do they quell the despair of those fearing infinities on all sides, or those who lament this quintessence of dust? What so fills one particular person with such a dread of being engulfed by infinity that he hurls himself into faith in divine power and subservience to figments of his imagination? Do such creeds necessarily make people of different beliefs, attitudes, and ethnicities into despicable sinners who will be punished for all eternity? Do they enable one to escape struggling over certain intellectual, existential, or sexual conflicts? Is it faith that compels the pious to believe that sex is dirty, or that women are the stain on the holy life, or that they are impure, inferior, or loathsome? Here again we are describing intense emotional states, not just ideas that are taught.

One does not feel contempt for women as filthy, contemptible things just because teachers have conveyed that mistaken notion and one doesn't know any better. One must delve into the catalysis of revulsion, the genesis of hate, the need for purity, and disparagement of things perceived as weak, vulnerable, messy, and feminine. Whence the rage? The accusation of others as sinful, vile, and evil? Why does a person get angry when someone holds different beliefs? (Anger isn't the only possible response; some people, religious or no, regard other ideas as intellectually nourishing.) Why are the beliefs so important that they cannot be questioned? To echo Nietzsche, how do merciful people devoted to pacifism come to say "unbeliever, you have no right to exist"? What transforms ordinary, peaceful, moral individuals, who maintain a faith purporting to cherish compassion and love, into a frenzied mob bent upon the conversion, punishment, or death of heretics and infidels? To blame *faith*, ignorance, or mere credulity for such beliefs, desires, feelings of revulsion, disgust, hatred, malice, and violence, explains *nothing*. We have to ask what abyss in the psyche spawns such beliefs and behaviors. Why is one willing to do anything to defend, enforce, or inflict that faith on others? What is so emotionally and existentially crucial, or volatile, or fragile, that such faith must be so desperately vouchsafed, even to the point of torture and slaughter?

All these examples and questions serve the purpose of illustrating how religious beliefs and actions are not derived from mere errors or prejudices. They aren't just historically and culturally conditioned worldviews based on the available facts. As Freud (1940) avers, errors can be understood as *hallucinations* (p. 162). People fantasize. They disregard evidence, deny it, and disavow realities they cannot tolerate, invent other worlds, and murder out of their own feelings of dread, terror, yearning, and rage. This is why a psychoanalytic inquiry into religion is so fertile. It delves into theology as fantasies of the imagination that reflect the intricate workings of a self-deceiving, delusion-projecting, profoundly irrational psyche. One does not rationally choose to despise women, loathe sinners, or live in abject fear that some being in the sky will cast one into a lake of fire, and one does not conclude that there are virgins in paradise or demons in the netherworld because of the available evidence at hand. Grünbaum's (this volume) argument is difficult to refute: a spectrum of theistic assertions too much resemble wish fulfillments, thought pathologies, paranoid projections, and delusions to explain in terms of reasonable belief (pp. 24-30).

The Roman Catholic exorcism, attribution of death in the world to Satanic machinations, and the asseveration that Lucifer or Satan is "a cosmic liar and murderer" whose suave badinage seduces people into disavowing his existence in the name of rationalism are all fantasies about sinister invisible forces that deliberately cause suffering, madness, evil, and death. Never does the believer subject the belief to rigorous scrutiny, confront the crucial epistemological question of how one could really know for sure whether unseen sentient beings exist, or peruse other disciplines that research the causes of seizures and death. The appeal is made to faith, or to the phenomena themselves as evidence of satanic activity. The argument is circular in appealing to the end result as proof of the existence of the cause of the end result, and it is sustained by nothing but a self-confirming theological system. Hence Grünbaum aptly observes how "John Paul II tries to render the purported satanic activity immune to evidential discreditation by precisely the sorts of reasoning featured in the arguments characteristically employed by paranoiacs in defense of their delusions" (p. 35).

Here again, one asks why the Pope, or anyone subscribing to the belief in demonic possession or satanic causation, would find such ideas so compelling in the first place. What convinces them of the existence and ubiquitous exertions of Satan? Why do they imagine demons hovering around them? There are innumerable believers who do not believe in demonology. Other pious individuals may actually interpret God as causing death, whether as punishment for breaking the covenant in the garden, as the benign order of the cycle of life, or some other mysterious but non-Luciferian godly purpose. So one cannot reasonably argue that it is just what one has been taught. Here we are speaking about a belief that may or may not be shared by one's community, that involves not blithe acceptance of inculcated ideas, but conviction that malicious sentient entities swarm around and wreak havoc on humanity, invade people's bodies, cause insanity or sexual perversion, and otherwise inflict all manner of pestilence and death. This is the realm not only of paranoid reasoning and the defense of an idea, but intense feelings of persecution and terror.

One critical nuance about delusions: while Freud emphasized how they were characterized by being "in contradiction to reality" (1927, p. 31) or as a wish-fulfillment that turns away from reality (1940), this does *not* actually mean that delusions are false, but that they contradict what is "known." Hypothetically, elves, balrogs, and gods *could* exist. That would not, however, legitimate belief in such entities. Belief in things that may really exist can still be delusional in the absence of anything that can be described as reliable evidence, when such beliefs deny the evidence that is available, and when such beliefs are so precious that they are defended and coveted against any alteration.

The actual falseness is not even the issue in some cases. What is crucial is that delusions are compromise formations, and beliefs in which fantasy subjugates the ego's *perceptions* of the world (Freud, 1907). Paranoid, grandiose, messianic, and apocalyptic delusions are projections of internal conflicts and catastrophes (Freud, 1911). Delusion is thus determined not only against the scientific facts, but against what the person sees but distorts with sundry defenses and fantasies. One can turn one's back on reality (as if one really perceived reality objectively), or, one can turn one's back on what one has already observed *subjectively*. Indeed delusions are mutilations not of reality per se, but of the world that is painful, distressing, disappointing, terrifying, and horrifying (Freud, 1911, 1930). This is a rejection of experiential, not actual reality. One need not know what "really" happens after death to be so horrified by putrefaction, or even by fictions about torture in hell, that one withdraws into a paradisiacal fantasy that contradicts what one *believes*. Consider the irony: theistic delusions may evolve when people cannot tolerate the religious fictions that distress them. As intimated previously, that is the mendacious struggle of theodicy. It is so anguished by a disappointing delusion that it creates a more soothing, rationalizing delusion to modify its own fiction. Thus the measure of a delusion is not whether it contradicts reality, but how much of a distortion it is of what the person actually perceives.

Further, a person may even be aware of the evidence for something, but be so passionately, obsessively focused that the belief—even when supported—becomes pathological, a symptom and index of his psychological architecture. When examining religion (or any other belief or practice), one may seek to discern whether the person's belief accords with the available facts about the world, *or*, focus instead upon the person's fantasies and emotional convolutions, the currents of pain, dread, rage, yearning, humiliation, guilt, sadness, woundedness, despair, desire, affection, ecstasy, euphoria, and lust that saturate his beliefs, what his beliefs, acts, and supplications are supposed to accomplish, what will be transformed, conquered, or transcended.

Theology, Paranoia, and Delusion

How then does psychoanalysis explain religion? A host of philosophers before Freud suggested that religion derived from the fear of death, reflected the terrors of the soul, and created God in humanity's image. Marx is infamous for having described religion as "the opium of the people." In his essay "A Criticism of the Hegelian Philosophy of Right" Marx (1844) writes of "the Vale of Tears whose aureole is religion" and deems it the task of philosophy "to unmask human self-alienation in its unholy shape, now that it has been unmasked in its holy shape" (p. 13). Feuerbach saw religion as a dream of the human mind, the entrancing splendor of imagination and caprice. Nietzsche wrote incessantly about religious delusions, how we can only tolerate a world we have made, how truth kills, how reality is a mobile army of metaphors, metonymies, and anthropomorphisms. As Grünbaum (this volume) aptly observes, Freud acknowledged how much he had been influenced by his predecessors. His humility notwithstanding, it would be an egregious error to accept Freud's word here. With all due respect to his mentors, the psychoanalytic understanding of religion is a quantum departure.

According to Freud, religion is a wish-fantasy. It may seem commonsensical to imagine how suffering people dream of a more satisfying reality where a divine paternal being watches over us, delivers us from evil, and provides a blissful life after death. The reality of fantasy is more complicated, however, for Freud is describing not just conscious desire but compromise formation and transference that reflect developmental wounds, fixations, and struggles projected onto the world (cf. Meng & Freud, 1963, letter to Oskar Pfister, November 25, 1928). Religious beliefs and behaviors are manifest content; they distort and symbolize archaic wishes. The conscious belief or ritual action is not simply the expression of what one consciously wishes at all, but enacts unconscious desires in disguised form. The fantasy is a strategy that recapitulates and compulsively strives to resolve those archaic desires and conflicts. The psyche employs myriad defenses that repress or dissociate painful perceptions, that magically occlude, alter, isolate, or undo the world. If other brilliant minds fathomed religion as dream and desire, they had no sense of the course of child development, the phases and struggles children traverse, the profusion of defenses employed to reorder perception and sensation, the obscure pathways and transformations of desire, the modes of rendering desires and perceptions unconscious while making waking belief symbolic of those inner processes.

Thus, for Freud religion supplies not only illusions of loving divine parents and eternal joy beyond death. It involves a delusional remolding of perceived reality, a desperate self-infantilization, regression, and abdication of the will and intellect to that delusion, as well as a projection into the cosmos of inner torment and discord such that those internal struggles are perceived as evils in the outer world.

Sin, sexual depravity, and demonic machinations are psychic states confused with innate evil in the world. The misogynist who sees women as loathsome, polluted, or disgusting is projecting his own terror of female sexuality and death onto them as inherently despicable. As Grünbaum (this volume) observes, the need to render Jesus' birth asexual and free his conception from taint or pleasure "bespeak a strong desire to *dissociate* motherhood from sexuality . . . it is the *purity* of Mary's motherhood—rather than *just* its miraculousness—that is being steadily celebrated in the adulatory references to her as the Virgin" (p. 28). Grünbaum attributes this dissociative impetus to the oedipal craving for mother, so that her virginity diminishes the father as rival because he did not possess her sexually. I might also suggest that the transformation of Mary into an ethereal, nonsexual, noncorporeal being reflects sexual discord, and the need to split off the dangerous, erotic, sultry, putrid, carnal aspects of mother (Davis, 2006; Piven, 2004a). The desire may be pre-oedipal—a defensive, delusional flight from female sexuality. Myriad religions have lamented their dread of the evil feminine, sometimes taming female sexuality like the Jicarilla Apache hero Slayer of Enemies, who domesticated the vagina dentata. Numerous Buddhist discourses disparage women as corpses, disease, and sewage. Ancient Judaism ritualized the circumcision to wash away the contamination of having been born of woman with purer, male blood (Eilberg-Schwartz, 1990; Lederer, 1968; Piven, 2004b). Sexuality, femininity, good, evil, and sin, are the stuff of delirium and dread, imagined as ineluctable perils of the world to be controlled, condemned, punished, purified, evacuated, or exorcised.

Hence Freud could describe religion not only as illusions, but as mass delusions, deeply pathological processes projected onto the world and confused with reality. Were they mere happy illusions, God would always be kind, there would be no devil perpetually causing suffering and temptation, and women would be seen as pristine mothers and wives. Not just the bizarre reasoning, as Grünbaum mentions, but the imagination and accusation of predatory evil deriving from unseen demonic forces (even from women who are seen but who are hardly succubae) is what resembles paranoid ideation.

Paranoid ideation symbolizes and projects inner strife. The devil, or other persecutor, is a disguised external representative of an internalized other, someone who victimized or terrorized one with abuse, invective, or malice. The identity of the original persecutor must be disguised so that the victimized child can retain the conscious fantasy that the persecutor is actually a protective, loving person. The victim also avoids the terrifying consequence of being aware of his own anger toward the hostile person, who could retaliate. Belief in an external evil occludes awareness of who the evil persecutor really is, and it disgorges the evil from the self so it may be escaped, avoided, and warded off.

Freud's (1911) analysis of the memoirs of Schreber also illuminates the way in which delusions of persecution can become delusions of grandeur. Schreber initially lives in terror because he imagines that God is transforming him into a woman, but he later comes to see himself as an avatar of God. The victim moves from feeling persecuted to conviction of his divine ordination. Emasculation by a sinister and merciless God becomes remasculation and apotheosis, a fantasy that might be interpreted as a psychological means of allying himself with the persecutor to partake of the strength and love of the symbolic father effigy instead of remaining his victim. Freud's daughter Anna (1936) would later coin the phrase "identification with the aggressor" to describe the way subjugated individuals become sycophantic toward tyrants or abusers to evade suffering while adopting the same aggressive behaviors. This again avoids retaliation for hostile feelings toward the persecutor, transforms ignominy into triumph and power, provides feelings of self-regard and control, and preserves the persecutor against being understood as a vile, hateful person, a thought that could lead to immense fear of loss and profound betrayal.

Such processes occur not only in individual cases of overt paranoia, but suffuse myriad other forms of religious ideation. Freud (1930) describes how the Jews reconciled their suffering with belief in a benign God by blaming themselves. The God of the Old Testament is spiteful, vindictive, and capable of obliterating humanity in his mercurial wrath, while his chosen people suffer a plethora of persecutions, conquests, humiliations, and injustices. One might be tempted to believe that God was really evil, and that he treated his people like flies he could torture. Anger and the accusation of malignance were displaced away from God. This maneuver maintained the dream that there was a loving God in the universe who watched over them, avoided confrontation with the possibility that God was really an evil persecutor, and granted them the exalted status of a people of entitlement and destiny.

This is the rationalizing process of all theodicy, the ingenious legerdemain and mendacity that desperately seeks to preserve notions of God's existence and goodness in the wake of excruciating suffering; feelings of anger, betrayal, abandonment, loss of faith, and the dread of feeling alone, unloved, and unprotected in a universe where one will eventually die and rot in the ground.

Theodicy aside, hallucinating a divine protector, displacing evil away from him to some real or fantasized external agent, and sanctimoniously proclaiming a divine mission, implicate the profound narcissistic dimension of theology. Schreber may have believed he was God's avatar, and the Jews may have believed they were the chosen people, but all manner of religious groups and individuals for millennia have maintained the grandiose belief that God speaks to them, that they alone are privy to God's love, wisdom, and true message, and that they have the right to inflict it on others.

Whether one is an inquisitor who flays people alive, makes pronouncements about God's will, judges others in the name of celestial authority, or murders civilians under the auspices of divine mandate, one is using God to express one's own will. To invoke Grünbaum (this volume), "How do ecclesiastics acquire greater expertise than others" about God (p. 30)? The pretense of knowing God's will and having the authority to judge, coerce, or kill in his name is megalomaniacal, even when masked by performances of humility, subservience, and piety. Such sanctimony still makes God into one's own personal sock puppet no matter how much one feigns obedience to holy powers. God becomes a prosthetic self, a bloated pseudopod of the ego. If we are speaking of revelation, the only thing such theological utterances reveal is the speaker's own delusions of reference, that he imagines he knows God's will, that he has the right to enforce it, pronounce judgments on others, and in some cases, torture or kill them. That implicates the believer's own malice, sadism, and narcissistic grandiosity.

What Freud illuminates here is the fusion of the dread of victimization with compensatory ego inflation, the manner in which feelings of debasement, humiliation, and persecution can metastasize into delusions of grandeur as a way of transcending abjection, escaping persecutory wrath, transforming the ugliness of parental violence into a blissful idealization of a God who adores his prodigy, and displacing all the wickedness of the real fathers onto others now hallucinated as evil. Even further, the rage one has toward the real source of his misery and abjection can also be displaced onto others, who now become despicably loathsome and can be excoriated with impunity. It is infantile anger and hatred, one's own desire to punish and kill that are now turned away from the real parent and God onto others, who are deliriously imagined to be persecutory enemies.

The devil, or any satanic enemy terrestrial or infernal, is thus an amalgam of displaced parental malevolence and one's own retaliatory desires. The enemy becomes the container of all the iniquities one wishes to cleanse from the parent, and also from the dystonic aspects of the self; all the malice, sexually distasteful, and vile traits one refuses to acknowledge, all disgorged and projected outward on demons, devils, heretics, or infidels. One punishes or murders both the despised parent and the despised self in the other, delusionally conflated with ontic evil.

The psychoanalytic epistemology of evil becomes even more complex when we delve into group psychology. If illicit desires and despicable aspects of the self and parents may be displaced onto real or fictive others, who become embodiments of evil, so too may the community participate in a ritualized displacement of their own disavowed emotions onto those mythologized enemies. As Freud (1930) writes, "It is always possible to bind together a considerable number of people in love, so long as there are other people left over to receive the manifestations of their aggression" (p. 114).

Rituals that ward off, sequester, or vanquish evil may be magical solutions to genuine dangers, but their logic often resembles the kind of paranoid reasoning Grünbaum mentioned earlier. Fear of typhoons and floods may be realistic, but imagining them as punishment, for as the consequence of transgression is not. The medieval Japanese fear that clipping one's nails, washing one's hair, or taking a single step in the wrong direction might cause tidal waves or devastating fires is not realistic. Nor are the magical solutions for preventing such disasters, or the procedures for displacing dread and malice onto scapegoated enemies. Whether ritualized as the expulsion of evil in such rites as the Pharmakon, Buphonia, or Hadaka, or as the eradication of evil in witch hunts, lynch mobs, or pogroms, the communal dissipation of fear and rage engenders a rapturous bond with one's tribe in the feeling of having conquered imminent danger and catastrophe.

The sinister implication here, if it is not obvious, is that patriotism, nationalism, and all manner of group loyalties may be delirious trance states that realize loving bonds by displacing hostility and illicit emotions outward; that while actual enemies may exist, we also *need* and hallucinate them to exist as targets for those disgorged emotions; and that a similar hallucinatory process may well be suffusing their imagination of us.

The implications of this manner of understanding theistic belief, as well as its gradations of paranoia, sanctimony, or violence, are germane to the way we understand contemporary religious conflict. If we can move from interpreting ideas as basically rational given what people know about the world, and begin to fathom the ways in which imagination pervades and disrupts waking perception, we may be able to discern how these processes of displacement and projection saturate the claims people make about God, evil, and enemies.

Political and historical analyses of "terrorism" cite the injustices that motivate violence. While these should not be disregarded, the specific claims about the justification for violence, what is categorically evil, and what actions must be taken on behalf of God are susceptible to psychoanalytic dissection. Political events do not explain why someone believes that God will love him if he obliterates a bus filled with children. Nor can they explain why someone finds the intermingling of the sexes and female emancipation repugnant (even across an ocean in another culture), as did the radical Muslim Sayid Qutb in his influential treatise *Milestones*. Nor indeed could political explanations reveal much about why someone would be so preoccupied with contamination by women that they must be barred from proximity to his charred corpse, as 9/11 hijacker Muhammad Atta declared in his final will.

One may actually agree that the American government has engaged in imperialistic, violent acts, or that the Israeli government has inflicted unfathomable suffering, trauma, and misery, for instance, without assuming that terrorism is a rational response, or that martyrdom operations are rational acts devoid of psychological fantasies. Rather one can acknowledge the political injustice that motivates the rage, while also recognizing the complexity of an ideology, how a discourse may still be pervaded by paranoid ideation, delusions of reference, distortions of who the enemies are and what they have done, and so on. Real events may be imagined in terms of fantastical causes, such as Zionist conspiracies, final apocalypses, and signs from God. A political event can be imagined as a holy war and an opposing leader as Satan. Very real secular occurrences can be experienced as dire threats to the veracity of one's religion or salvation. Political or military actions can catalyze messianic visions, appeals to divine destiny, and theistic justification for bloodshed. Just because a real injustice occurs in no way guarantees that the perception of that event, or the response, will in any sense be rational.

The suicide bomber putatively believes that his death is a beloved thing, that God wills it, that it is not suicide at all but vengeance against infidels, that he will be rewarded in paradise, and that the act will be his apotheosis. Political and military strategies against oppressors are one thing; the belief that a celestial power desires one's own death in the act of murdering children is another. This suggests a fantasy of transforming the overwhelming pain of victimization, unfairness, helplessness, and shame into cosmic power over evil, where one displays stalwart courage in the face of one's own death, wrests control of one's fate from the hands of wicked others, obliterates iniquity, and ascends triumphantly to a hedonic afterlife where he is surrounded by pristine virgins unsullied by age, ugliness, and all manner of sexual messiness, while basking in the love of his divine father.

Beyond political purposes and military tactics, this fantasy not only seeks parental love, but engages in an act of self-destruction in order to attain that love and redemption. It implicates the deep feeling of already being sinful and in need of forgiveness so extreme that one is willing to die for it, or believes only self-slaughter is necessary. It suggests that an idealized, pure, divine father is the antidote to unrequited love on earth, that one fantasizes a perfect father in response to the all too human one who may have suffered his own frailties, failed to protect his son from anguish and injustice, or even persecuted him. Martyrdom is the conduit to paradise, immolation of physical and emotional boundaries in fusion with the idealized imaginary father, and magical transformation from helpless victim into invulnerable hero who bludgeons his enemies and conquers the dread of death.

This dread is psychologically complex as well. Philosophers from Plato to Lucretius to Cicero to Bacon to Montaigne have pondered the dread of death that inspires visions of protective gods and serene paradises that salve all the anguish of life on earth. Kant believed that the issues that preoccupy philosophy are God, freedom, and immortality. Heidegger was consumed by the project of living authentically in the face of death. But death is a fantasy. The cessation of life is one thing; the imagination of what one has not experienced is another. Human beings not only imagine what happens after death, they associate death with all manner of cultural and individual referents. Death becomes a floating signifier, whose image and meaning varies profoundly. Death may be imagined as sleep, serenity, light, heaven, fusion with God, rebirth through the divine body of mother, physical resurrection, reincarnation as a cow, or an eternal orgy. Death may be imagined as void, aloneness, darkness, hell, reincarnation as a hungry ghost, eternal suffering, suffocation, murder, monstrous predation, disease, decay, and decomposition, as wormfood, as so many have imagined from *The Epic of Gilgamesh* to *Hamlet*, the putrescing leak into green bile and black treacle, as Joyce limned in *Ulysses*. When we conceive the human reaction to death as the conscious realization of a specific thing, we ignore the vast spectrum of experiences that have filled a void with infinite meanings, anxieties, terrors, and fantasies. There is no abstract contemplation of death that is not generated by these associations and experiences, which is why the psychoanalytic deconstruction of death is so crucial.

Freud was inconsistent about death, and so complicated that an entire book could be written about the diverse implications of his thinking on the subject (Piven, 2004a). Freud (1900, 1927) asserted that the fear of dying and rotting in the icy ground motivated mythologies, and beliefs in the afterlife. But he also argued that what appears to be the fear of death may conceal other problems, like guilt or the dread of castration (Freud, 1912, 1915, 1923, 1926). The conscious fear is manifest content disguising and obscuring the myriad conflicts and crises below.

Guilt and fear of castration are themselves the end product of psychic processes, emerging from the internalization of the parental presence. One dreads losing the protection and love of the parent and internalizes him as a kind of intrapsychic presence, the super-ego. That parental presence still threatens the child with punishment, abandonment, and loss of love, so the ego acquiesces to that presence, remains a dependent child in order to placate and preserve that relationship (1923).

The fear of death can emerge from external violence or trauma, but it can also emerge from the fear of separation, abandonment, parental retaliation, rage, and violence. Guilt is (among other things) the fear of parental judgment and malice, as well as the fear of being killed for one's own anger. One can go through life feeling morally guilty, consumed with sin, enraged by the iniquity of those around him, dreading God's wrathful judgment, ever vigilant about infernal assaults, and fearing death in the outer world, when he may truly (unconsciously) be afraid of losing the love of his mother or father, being castigated by his parent, or killed for one's own vengeful, filicidal desires.

Ultimately what this means is that what one fears as external danger may be entirely internal danger, and both entirely imaginary. Thus again the fear of death is a floating signifier, an empty idea devoid of content unless one recognizes the latent fantasies that have gestated the architecture of those fears and the disguises those fears take as the psyche tries to mask and resolve those anxieties into manageable forms. The philosopher who believes the dread of death is the issue never realizes that the conscious, existential problem may conceal vastly different forms of anguish. His angst over suffocation, meaninglessness, purposelessness, or alienation may well obscure a far more humiliating inner wound, threat, or loss, despite his perceiving his torment as the inevitable consequence of awareness or the human condition. Indeed that fantasy may inflate his ego so that he feels that his pain is the consequence of intelligence and enlightened awareness, to hide from himself (and others) that his suffering is rather his own shameful weakness. His existentialism could be a confession and projection, rationalized as the universal conundrum of humankind, to avoid understanding and revealing himself.

If Freud (1927) claimed that the fear of death inspired the fantasy of a divine protector, like so many of his predecessors, he also wrote that death was a blow to human narcissism. Human frailty, limitation, weakness, and helplessness in the face of his own decay and demise, wound his self-regard. Narcissistic inflation is the compensatory response to the humiliating dread of our own vulnerability and demise. Human aspiration, our ambitions to become famous, to be remembered, to be somebody, to be powerful, invulnerable, logical, more intelligent than others, in control of our bodies and intellects, are desperate defenses against that dread of nothingness, of feeling as defenseless as whimpering children who need parents to suckle and soothe us.

The preceding précis of Freud's psychoanalysis of religion should give some sense of the intricacy of the psyche. What Freud brings to the study of religion is *not* merely a set of theories clumsily mapped on to explain everything, but a way of discerning the complexity of motives and the varied processes by which perceptions, desires, and terrors interweave, transform, and mutate, are disavowed, buried, and disguised. Those who believe that Freud sought to reduce religion to a simplistic oedipal wish for father, have no inkling of the spectrum of transformations those wishes go through, not the slightest grasp of how the very wishes gestate and evolve through the developmental process, how the disposition of the desire, the ways of coping with pain and dread, and the convolutions of those theistic fantasies emerge from the psychic encounter with the experience of life.

So while others have asserted that man makes God in his image, none before Freud has charted a psyche whose development, defenses, and modes of transforming and disguising ideas and awareness render God such a complicated fantasy. From this perspective God is not just an Oedipal projection of a protective father. God is a Frankensteinian mongrel, a confluence of past perceptions and past wishes, disavowed or magnified by desire and fear, at once the idealized divinized presence of love and succor, as well as the antidote to cruelty, frailty, and violence. The same mercurial aspects of real fathers metastasize into the personality of God, who thus becomes menacing and judgmental, even when we wish him to be placid and purely loving.

As we have seen, a surfeit of ingenuity plays into the way people rationalize and disavow the very brutality that infects God. We also project our own narcissism into God, and he thus manifests our own unconscious anger and cruelty, the need to punish and coerce others, our vengeance against our own vulnerability and anguish. This is why God's personality changes over time. It is also why theological systems similarly alter as fears, desires, and fantasies change. The renascent theology emerges as new visions of the cosmos and its inhabiting beings, new projections that reflect shifting psychic constellations, varying conflicts, wounds, terrors, traumas, and catastrophes, and seek resolutions to evolving existential crises.

Incidentally, it should be said that the psychoanalysis of religion has evolved considerably since Freud, so readers need not be troubled if the interpretations of religion above are imperfect. Some of Freud's ideas have been discarded and others supplemented. Developments in object relations and self psychology have advanced psychoanalytic thinking about religion, and a number of authors have argued that the impact of the mother and the dread of death are crucial (Becker, 1973; Beit-Hallahmi & Argyle, 1997; Lederer, 1968; Piven, 2004a,b, 2006; Pruyser, 1968; Rheingold, 1967; Rizzuto, 1979).

Grünbaum (this volume) is certainly correct that a phylogeny of theism that relies on the Lamarckian inheritance of repressed racial memories is dubious (p. 16), although some scholars (Paul, 1992) have suggested that the inheritance is symbolically, *not* biologically transmitted. What should be entirely clear, however, is that the psychoanalytic approach to religion is a drastic departure it is from the philosophies of Freud's predecessors, and elucidates the vicissitudes of fantasy and praxis with unparalleled intricacy.

Conclusion: Method, Madness, and Evidence

This chapter has tried to demonstrate how the psychoanalysis of religious phenomena provides a multifaceted and nuanced approach that addresses questions that other disciplines fail to answer with any cogency. Grünbaum would maintain, however, that the psychoanalytic approach to religion is only as reliable as the theories that undergird it. We must always ask the basic and indispensable epistemological question: how do I really *know* this?

Psychoanalysis does not entail Luciferic initiations or demand that members wear colanders on their heads to receive the divine thoughts of their master, but psychoanalytic claims often seem unjustifiable. Consider this passage from a recent psychoanalytic work on terrorism:

> Ultimately, a perverse coalition takes place between an anguished infant who . . . underwent a "primitive catastrophe" . . . became an outcast and orphan, on one hand, and a terrorist on the other, made a pact with the devil in order to survive (died a little in order to survive), the cost of which was to forfeit his/her

> future development, and then entered into a coalition with the devil's family, the psychic retreat, which consists of the retaliatory ghosts of the father's penis, the unborn children, and the blessed feces within a now traduced, corrupted, and mutilated mother's body (Grotstein, 2009).

It is quotes like this that open psychoanalysis to such scrutiny and skepticism. How indeed would someone know or prove such an assertion? What indeed would be sufficient clinical evidence to warrant the belief that driving an airplane into a building was unconsciously related to the ghost of the father's penis and blessed feces? It will always remain something of a problem if psychoanalysis cannot corroborate or disconfirm its findings. Critics like Grünbaum, and even those within the analytic community such as Rapaport (1944, 1948), Eagle (1984), and Edelson (1984), just to name a few, regard case evidence as anecdotal, unverifiable, or untestable. Thus Grünbaum (1993) could ask about the evidential support for psychoanalytic theories.

Grünbaum's assessment of the poverty of the evidential support is beguiling. There are literally *thousands* of studies that *do* support cardinal psychoanalytic ideas. Though Grünbaum (1993) cites Kline's admission that many Freudian claims concerning the neuroses have not been tested objectively (p. 45), Kline has marshaled, conducted, and analyzed *over 700* studies (1972, 1981, 1984). Kline's humility in the wake of the limitations of testing cannot be cited fairly without also incorporating the recurring unambiguous message of both his works: that there is copious evidence that *does* support numerous cardinal psychoanalytic propositions. Some of the most meticulous accumulation and analysis of evidence derived from the testing of psychoanalytic theories has been conducted by Fisher and Greenberg, who have marshaled some 2,500 studies pertaining to the testing of psychoanalytic propositions.

Though he is dismissive of Kline, Fisher, and Greenberg (at least the work published prior to Grünbaum's book on clinical validation), there seems to be a *surfeit* of evidence warrants the support of Freudian theories of primary process thinking, unconscious dynamics and conflicts, and the operations of defense mechanisms. The sheer number of studies testing Freudian theory should convince critics that a great many psychoanalytic propositions can and have been tested. Further, strong support has been accumulated for both the psychoanalytic framework of a dynamic unconscious, and for a number of the theories concerning character structure, neurotic syndromes, and oedipal phenomena. Space does not permit me to review each study individually, since again, they numbered in the *thousands*. Nor could I index every aspect of Freudian theory that has been tested.

Arlow (1959) and Hartmann (1959, 1964) have demonstrated that psychoanalytic theories have been measured against those in direct clinical investigation of children. The etiological factors so repudiated by Grünbaum have received strong empirical support by the "baby watchers," though certain hypotheses have *of course* been abandoned or modified since this began. The pioneering works of Spitz (1965) and Bowlby (1969), for examples, have done much both to solidify certain psychoanalytic concepts and to revise them. In recent years Schore's (1999, 2002a,b) pioneering studies on affect regulation and dysregulation have generated a truly massive body of evidence regarding unconscious regulatory mechanisms and the impact of trauma on attachment, the developing psyche, psychopathology, and violence. While his work modifies certain psychoanalytic concepts, Schore also states that "neuropsychoanalytic work clearly substantiates many of the basic assumptions of Freud's model" (email communication, June 24, 2009).

The impact of the fear of death on *unconscious* mental processing, self-esteem, ideology, and violence has been demonstrated and replicated over hundreds of studies worldwide by those involved in Terror Management Theory. Initially setting out to test Ernest Becker (1973) thesis that human beings invest in various religious beliefs and immortality projects to deny the dread of death, TMT research has repeatedly confirmed Freud's (1900, 1927, 1930) assertions that human beings unconsciously suffer from death anxiety, that it impinges on their narcissism (or self-esteem), that dread motivates terror-reducing ideology, that worldviews absorb the fear of death, and that subliminal triggers of death anxiety stimulate aggressive worldview defense (http://www.tmt.missouri.edu/publications.html). Thus there *is* substantial evidence supporting a variety of principal psychoanalytic concepts. And these discoveries provide a comprehensive and nuanced means of understanding our beliefs, fantasies, projections, and deliria, such as religion.

Nevertheless, I would shift the argument to examine the disposition of psychoanalytic epistemology. Psychoanalysis does not merely find what conforms to its preconceived notions. Psychoanalysis is neither naïve hermeneutics, nor shamanism, nor a fairy tale. Its value is not merely heuristic, but based on observation, hypothesis, and either confirmation from a massive amount of data, inquiry, observation, and further testing, or disconfirmation, from which the analyst attempts to learn his mistakes and make new hypotheses. The sheer wealth of clinical data should not be underestimated, nor the caution, patience and tentativeness, the skepticism of the analyst against his own speculations, feelings and reactions to the patient which might distort his *own* perceptions, and finally the constant testing of hypotheses against all of these factors.

For all its defects, psychoanalysis is a progressivist methodology that is the best available means of obtaining information on the dynamic workings of the human mind. Which is more precise, and more useful: the factoral results of a ten-minute questionnaire or experiment which enables one to determine what proportion of children are ambivalent toward their fathers, or ten years of repeated clinical inquiry into the deepest, most intense, complicated, and perplexing emotions and fantasies? To quote Laudan (1977), "far too much scientific research today is devoted to problems which are as cognitively trivial as they are socially irrelevant" (p. 225). As Irvin Yalom (1980) notes, "the precision of the result is directly proportional to the triviality of the variables studied" (p. 24). This is echoed by Kline (1988): "the demand for precision has led empirical psychologists to choose variables *because they can be so measured* and not for reasons of theoretical psychology. This has led to research into trivial issues . . . precision has overruled psychological significance" (p. 22).

The value of psychoanalysis resides not only in its vast capabilities in explaining the depths of the human psyche in wide ranges of behavior and imagination, but in its capacity to call into question the epistemic assumptions and rationales which define the modes of thought of individuals, societies, and even the sciences.

Psychoanalysis explores the nature of *knowing*. As Barratt (1984) writes, "by setting normal discourse against itself, psychoanalysis pursues a changeful inquiry upon the interiority of psychic reality. It is both scientific and emancipatory" (p. 173). Psychoanalysis therefore undermines the projection and solidification of any certainty, even scientific soundness. Unlike other forms of psychology, it is perpetually engaged in an epistemological enterprise that disallows its own speculations from becoming the apodictic measure of all phenomena, and continually reflects on itself in order to avoid seduction into pretensions of redefining the world according to its own ineluctable truths.

Psychoanalysis is grossly misunderstood when conceived as "yet another system of interpretation, a set of constructions to be imposed, ideologically, on the subtleties and vicissitudes of life's events" (1993, p. 15). As Barratt explains so eloquently, psychoanalytic method is a work of interrogation that seeks to expose the foundations and horizons of understanding as the fundamental devices of our own imprisonments (p. 20). What is unsealed are the psychodynamics of epistemic closure, whereby consciousness believes its own falsifications, self-deceptions, illusions projected upon reality as truth and causality (pp. 167-169). Psychoanalysis traces and exposes such projections in their polysemous complexity, calling the nature of knowledge itself into question.

Psychoanalysis resists facile closure, scientistic reductivism, and jejune simplicity. It is an epistemological enterprise that seeks to trace the elusive, irrational, entangled, confusing fantasies that form a psyche too complex to be reduced to simple, clean, single, conscious motives. For all its frailties psychoanalysis has yielded an immense array of material on the psyche, and has elucidated ways in which unconscious interfusing fears, wounds, and wishes distort and dream the world. Psychoanalysis discloses a psychic realm teeming with irrationality, madness, and hallucinosis. Here psychoanalysis begins to illumine the vast and opulent depths of religious fantasy, where these abysses remain opaque to other modes of inquiry. Whatever divine forces might hypothetically exist, beliefs about the divine are fabrications and fantasies of the psyche. And hence psychoanalysis moves us toward comprehending the efflorescence of religion, in its dreams and deliria.

The psychoanalytic study of religion suggests how easily people may delude themselves, derange their own perceptions, disavow and deny what they experience so that the world may conform to their fantasies. If one has the capacity to give up the defensive pretension of being absolutely rational and in control, one may then realize how this all too human propensity to fall into delusions applies to ourselves, not just others. It means that laborious self-deconstruction is the sine qua non of any interpretation of the world. For without this we have no way of knowing whether our most convincing certainties, even scientific ones, may be distorted according to our own wishes, terrors, and fantasies. The protest that one merely *knows* one's rationality is futile.

References

Arlow, J. (1959). Psychoanalysis as a scientific method. In S. Hook (Ed.), *Psychoanalysis, scientific method and philosophy* (pp. 201-211). New York: New York University Press.

Barratt, B. (1984). *Psychic Reality and Psychic Knowing.* Hillsdale, NJ: Analytic Press.

Barratt, B. (1993), *Psychoanalysis and the Postmodern Impulse: Knowing and Being Since Freud's Psychology.* Baltimore, MD: Johns Hopkins Press.

Becker, E. (1973). *The Denial of Death.* New York: Free Press.

Beit-Hallahmi, B. & Argyle, M. (1997). *The Psychology of Religious Behaviour, Belief and Experience.* London: Routledge.

Bowlby, J. (1969). *Attachment.* New York: Basic.

Davis, W. (2006). *Death's Dream Kingdom: The American Psyche Since 9-11.* Ann Arbor, MI: Pluto.

Eagle, M. (1984). *Recent Developments in Psychoanalysis.* Cambridge, MA: Harvard University Press.

Edelson, M. (1984). *Hypothesis and Evidence in Psychoanalysis.* Chicago: University of Chicago Press.

Eilberg-Schwartz, H. (1990). *The Savage in Judaism: An Anthropology of Israelite Religion and Ancient Judaism.* Bloomington: Indiana University Press.

Fenichel, O. (1945). *The Psychoanalytic Theory of Neurosis.* New York: W. W. Norton.

Fisher, S. & Greenberg, R. (1977). *The Scientific Credibility of Freud's Theory and Therapy.* New York: Basic.

Fisher, S. & Greenberg, R. (1996). *Freud Scientifically Reappraised.* New York: Wiley.

Freud, A. (1936). *The Ego and the Mechanisms of Defense.* New York: International Universities Press.

Freud, S. (1900). The Interpretation of Dreams. *The Standard Edition of the Complete Psychological Works of Sigmund Freud,* 4-5, 1-338, 339-627. London: Hogarth Press.

Freud, S. (1907). Delusions and dreams in Jensen's Gradiva. *The Standard Edition of the Complete Psychological Works of Sigmund Freud, 9*, 7-96. London: The Hogarth Press.

Freud, S. (1911). Psycho-analytic notes on an autobiographical account of a case of paranoia (*dementia paranoides*). *The Standard Edition of the Complete Psychological Works of Sigmund Freud, 12*, 9-79. London: The Hogarth Press.

Freud, S. (1915). Thoughts for the times on war and death. *The Standard Edition of the Complete Psychological Works of Sigmund Freud, 14*, 271-302. London: The Hogarth Press.

Freud, S. (1915). Our attitude toward death. *The Standard Edition of the Complete Psychological Works of Sigmund Freud, 14*, 289-302. London: The Hogarth Press.

Freud, S. (1923). The ego and the id. *The Standard Edition of the Complete Psychological Works of Sigmund Freud, 19*, 12-59. London: The Hogarth Press.

Freud, S. (1926). Inhibitions, symptoms, and anxiety. *The Standard Edition of the Complete Psychological Works of Sigmund Freud,* 20, 77-172. London: The Hogarth Press.

Freud, S. (1927). The future of an illusion. *The Standard Edition of the Complete Psychological Works of Sigmund Freud, 21*, 1-56. London: The Hogarth Press.
Freud, S. (1930). Civilization and its discontents. *The Standard Edition of the Complete Psychological Works of Sigmund Freud, 21*, 59-145. London: The Hogarth Press.
Freud, S. (1940/1938). An outline of psychoanalysis. *The Standard Edition of the Complete Psychological Works of Sigmund Freud, 23,* 14-207. London: The Hogarth Press.
Grotstein, J. (2009, in press). Waging holy war in the sacred body of the godhead. In *In God's Name: Psychoanalytic Perspectives on Terrorism.*
Grünbaum, A. (1984). *The Foundations of Psychoanalysis: A philosophical critique.* Berkeley: University of California Press.
Grünbaum, A. (1993). *Validation in the Clinical Theory of Psychoanalysis: A Study in the Philosophy of Psychoanalysis.* Madison, CT: International Universities Press.
Harris, S. (2005). *The End of Faith: Religion, Terror, and the Future of Reason.* New York: Norton.
Harris, S. (2006). *Letter to a Christian Nation.* New York: Knopf.
Hartmann, H. (1959). Psychoanalysis as a scientific theory. In S. Hook (Ed.), *Psychoanalysis, Scientific Method and Philosophy* (pp. 3-37). New York: New York University Press.
Hartmann, H. (1964). *Essays on Ego Psychology: Selected Problems in Psychoanalytic Theory.* New York: International Universities Press.
Henderson, B. (2006). *The Gospel of the Flying Spaghetti Monster.* New York: Villard.
Hume, D. (1779/2007). *Dialogues Concerning Natural Religion.* New York: Cambridge University Press.
Kline, P. (1981). *Fact and Fantasy in Freudian Theory.* London: Methuen.
Kline, P. (1984). *Psychology and Freudian theory: An Introduction.* London: Methuen.
Kline, P. (1988). *Psychology Exposed, or, the Emperor's New Clothes.* New York: Routledge.
Laudan, L. (1977). *Progress and its Problems.* Berkeley: University of California Press
Lederer, W. (1968). *The Fear of Women.* New York: Harcourt.
Marx, K. (1844). A critique of the Hegelian concept of right. In *Selected essays* (pp. 11-39). Retrieved from: http://www.gutenberg.org/files/21565/21565-h/21565-h.htm.
Meng, H. & Freud, E. (1963). *Psychoanalysis and Faith: Dialogues with the Reverend Oskar Pfister.* New York: Basic.
Paul, R. (1992). Freud's anthropology: A reading of the "cultural books. In E. Garcia (Ed.), *Understanding Freud: The Man and his Ideas* (pp. 10-30). New York: New York University Press.
Pickthall, M. M., Trans. (C. 632/1999). *The Glorious Qur'an.* Elmhurst, NY: Tahrike Tarsile Qur'an, Inc.
Piven, J.S. (2004a). *Death and Delusion: A Freudian Analysis of Mortal Terror.* Greenwich, CT: Information Age Publishing.
Piven, J.S. (2004b). Buddhism, death, and the feminine. In J.S. Piven (Ed.), *The Psychology of Death in Fantasy and History* (pp. 37-70). Westport, CT: Praeger.
Piven, J.S. (2006). Narcissism, sexuality, and psyche in terrorist theology. *Psychoanalytic Review, 93,* 231-265.
Piven, J. S., with Y. Katsuta (2007). *Nihon no kyoki (madness in Japan).* Tokyo: Nihon Hyoronsha.
Post, J. (1990). Terrorist psycho-logic: Terrorist behavior as a product of psychological forces. In W. Reich (Ed.), *Origins of terrorism: Psychologies, Ideologies, Theologies, States of mind* (pp. 25-40). Baltimore: Johns Hopkins University Press.
Pruyser, P. (1968). *A Dynamic Psychology of Religion.* New York: Harper & Row.

Rapaport, D. (1944). The scientific methodology of psychoanalysis. In (1967), *The Collected Papers of David Rapaport* (pp. 165-220). New York: Basic.
Rapaport, D. (1948). Discussion in "the psychologist in the clinic setting" round table. In (1967), *The Collected Papers of David Rapaport* (pp. 299-303). New York: Basic.
Rheingold, J. (1967). *The Mother, Anxiety, and Death.* Boston: Little, Brown and Company.
Rizzuto, A-M. (1979). *The Birth of the Living God: A Psychoanalytic Study*. Chicago: University of Chicago Press.
Schore, A. (1994). *Affect Relation and the Origin of the Self.* Hillsdale, NJ: Lawrence Erlbaum.
Schore, A. (2003a). *Affect Regulation and the Repair of the Self.* New York: Norton.
Schore, A. (2003b). *Affect Dysregulation and Disorders of the Self.* New York: Norton.
Spitz, R.A. (1965). *The First Year of Life*. New York: International Universities Press.
Stein, R. (2004). Evil as love and as liberation: The mind of a suicidal religious terrorist. In J.S. Piven, C. Boyd, & H.W. Lawton (Eds.), *Terrorism, Jihad, and Sacred Vengeance* (pp. 38-61). Giessen: Psychosozial-Verlag.
Wirth, H.-J. (2004a). Thoughts for the times on terrorism, war and death. In J.S. Piven, C. Boyd, & H.W. Lawton (Eds.), *Terrorism, Jihad, and Sacred Vengeance* (137-165). Giessen: Psychosozial-Verlag.
Wirth, H.-J. (2004b). Xenophobia and violence as a family and psychosocial disease. In J.S. Piven, C. Boyd, & H.W. Lawton (Eds.), *Terrorism, Jihad, and Sacred Vengeance* (pp. 237-264). Giessen: Psychosozial-Verlag.
Yalom, I.D. (1980). *Existential Psychotherapy.* New York: Basic.

Chapter 4
Psychoanalytic Theories of Religion and the "Catholic Problem"

Michael P. Carroll

Adolf Grünbaum stated his own goals clearly at the beginning of his chapter: first, to assess the relevance of Freud's theory of religion to the truth or falsity of theism and second, to assess Freud's personal attitude toward a belief in God—and in pursuit of his goals Grünbaum skillfully disentangles and explicates the different (but mutually reinforcing) arguments that Freud developed to explain religion. How well Grünbaum succeeded in regard to these two stated goals, however, is something that I leave to others (and in particular, to the other contributors to this volume). For myself, I want to consider Grünbaum's chapter through a lens fashioned from what has always been one of psychoanalysis's greatest methodological insights, namely, that there is often much to be gained by paying attention to things that might at first sight seem incidental or marginal. Freud himself, of course, as the readers of this volume well know, used this insight early on by studying dreams, jokes and parapraxes. In the case of Grünbaum's chapter, I want to focus on the fact that when Grünbaum reaches for a concrete example of a religious belief or ritual in order to illustrate a theoretical point, he typically reaches for an example that is distinctively *Catholic* (not just Christian, but specifically Catholic).

What I will be arguing is that there are reasons for Grünbaum's easy turn to Catholic examples and that uncovering these reasons provides us with a theoretical basis for thinking about something that is rarely discussed in psychoanalytic discussions of religion, namely, that some religious traditions may well be more amenable to psychoanalytic investigation than others.

Grünbaum's Catholic Examples

Grünbaum turns explicitly to the Catholic tradition at four points in his recapitulation of Freud's theories of religion. The first Catholic example appears in his discussion (p. 5) of Freud's contention that the feelings of helplessness we experience as adults awakens in us a desire for that sort of "protection through love" we enjoyed as infants as the result of protection by our parents, especially the father. Although Grünbaum spends much time here identifying earlier theorists (Feuerbach and Marx in particular) who made a similar argument, he in the end gives only one example of a concrete religious practice that illustrates this process: the fact that in the Catholic tradition priests are called "Father"; the Pope is called "the Holy Father"; and the Church is called "Holy Mother Church."

Grünbaum reaches for a second Catholic example when challenging Wallace's view that the repetitiveness of religious ritual is always ego-syntonic (something, Wallace claimed, Freud had ignored). Thus, Grünbaum (p. 11) points out, that many Catholics may find the penitential repetition of Holy Marys and Our Fathers less than congenial. Grünbaum's comments on Wallace aside, the important point is that here again Grünbaum is using a Catholic example to illustrate a theoretical point drawn from Freud's theory of religion, in this case, a point about the repetitiveness of religious ritual.

Grünbaum (p. 23) uses a third distinctively Catholic example when discussing Meissner's contention that paranoid delusions and religious belief are often similar in being immune to disproof. Thus, says Grünbaum, Catholic belief in the Real Presence, that is, the view that through transubstantiation the consecrated bread and wine becomes the literal Body and Blood of Christ, is safeguarded by Aristotelian distinctions between "essential" and "accidental" attributes. At the end of this same discussion, however, Grünbaum uses this same example to illustrate Freud's phylogenic theory of religion. Thus, Grünbaum points out (p. 24), Freud saw Christian communion as reminiscent of the cannibalism of the Brothers after they had killed the Primal Father, and so as a practice that on the one hand perpetuates the guilt over that deed while simultaneously expiating that guilt by bowing to religious authority.

Grünbaum's fourth explicitly Catholic example appears (p. 31) where he suggests that the mystery surrounding an "incomprehensible" belief like the Assumption (i.e., the belief that Mary's physical body was taken up into Heaven) facilitates acceptance of beliefs that are more clearly wish-fulfilling (like the belief in Mary's virginal motherhood).

Apart from these four overtly Catholic examples, Grünbaum uses a fifth Catholic example as well, though without ever quite recognizing it as such. This occurs in the context of his extended discussion of the Virgin Birth (pp. 27-29).

True, as Grünbaum notes, the belief that Jesus was born of a virgin is common to all variants of Christianity (and so not just Catholicism). Grünbaum, however, uses this example to illustrate Freud's ontogenic theory of religion, and in particular, Freud's contention that religious belief is often appealing because it gratifies the remnants of Oedipal desire. In the end, Grünbaum's argument is that Mary's complete disassociation from sexuality gratifies the Oedipal cravings of sons and daughters. In his own words, "the son has the satisfaction that the rival father did not possess the mother sexually; and the daughter gets her wish that the rival mother did not get her sexual tentacles on the father" (p. 29). But this line of reasoning works, or at least works well, only for the Catholic tradition. Thus, while all variants of Christianity do indeed embrace the Virgin Birth of Christ, Catholics have also embraced the view that Mary was both an "in partu" virgin (meaning her hymen remained intact despite giving birth to Christ) and a perpetual virgin (meaning she never had sexual relations even after the birth of Christ). Protestants, by contrast, taking literally the references to Christ's brothers in the New Testament, have never insisted that Mary was a perpetual virgin. In other words, the complete disassociation of Mary from sexuality that is key to the Oedipal interpretation that Grünbaum develops here (but see also Carroll, 1986 for a similar argument) works well only if the Catholic tradition is assumed.

A total of four, possibly five, examples may not seem like much, but this must be balanced against the fact that they are the only examples of religious belief and ritual discussed at any length in the chapter. Thus, although Grünbaum does make occasional reference to the work of theologians like Paul Tillich and Martin Buber, he does not have much to say about the popular practice in the Jewish or Protestant traditions beyond pointing to their common emphasis on theism. I now want to argue that there is a theoretical basis for this easy recourse to Catholic examples.

The Catholic Imagination

Grünbaum notes (p. 17) that, by definition, theistic religions commonly posit "the existence of an omnipotent, omniscient and omnibenevolent paternal creator, at once immanent and transcendent, who is accessible to personal communion with us." At one level, such a descriptive statement probably does capture the God posited by Christianity, Islam, and Judaism (the traditions that seem mainly to be the focus of Grünbaum's analysis). Some time ago, however, the Catholic theologian David Tracy (1981) noted that at least as regards two of the attributes mentioned here by Grünbaum, namely, immanence and transcendence, there is a dramatic, and conceptually important, difference between the Catholic and the Protestant traditions. Simply put, Catholics place far more emphasis on immanence, that is, on the presence of God (or more generally, the sacred) in the material world while Protestants place far more emphasis on transcendence, that is, on the distance between God and the world. Tracey went on to argue that this initial difference, in turn, has given rise to other differences. Because Catholics see the created world as pervaded by the sacred, they are, he suggested, predisposed toward analogical thinking, i.e. toward the use of relationships drawn from everyday experience both as a way of thinking about God and his relationship with human beings, *and* as a way of drawing closer to God. By contrast, the Protestant emphasis on transcendence, and the resulting sense that there is an "infinite qualitative difference" between God and the created world, predisposes Protestants toward a form of dialectical thinking that emphasizes God's Word, that is, God's revealed message to humanity, and the need for human beings to accept that message (Tracy, 1981). Subsequent commentators—notably Andrew Greeley and Mark Massa—have expanded upon Tracy's initial argument.

Greeley, in particular, has argued that the "Catholic Imagination" (his preferred term, equivalent to Tracy's "Analogical Imagination"), by virtue of its predilection to see God in the world and to use metaphors drawn from daily experience as a way of drawing closer to God, has resulted in a range of other differences between Catholics and Protestants, only some of which would be seen as having anything to do with religion. To take one example: contrary to popular expectations, survey data (Greeley, 2000) indicate that American Catholics are more likely (than American Protestants) to embrace the fine arts (to visit an art gallery or museum; to attend a live performance of classical music, etc). For Greeley this derives from the fact that the Catholic Imagination predisposes Catholics to find God "in the world" and in particular, in those everyday human experiences that are uplifting. The fact that this effect is *strongest* for Catholics who attend church on a regular basis, he suggests, lends even more support to this interpretation.

Mark Massa has extended Tracy's analysis in another direction. Simply put, Massa's argument is that because Protestants tend to see God as absent from the world, they are predisposed to see social relationships as "unnatural and oppressive" (2001, p. 567). Given the predominance of Protestant culture in the United States, Massa continues, this predisposition has given rise to that distrust of government that has long been a hallmark of American political culture. Catholics, by contrast, because they see God as immanent in the created world, are more likely to see human social relationships as natural and good and so are more trusting of government.

One of the central insights about the study of religion that falls out of the work by Greeley and Massa (and Tracy), as Dillon (2001, p. 265) notes, is that "inter-religious differences are not fundamentally doctrinal or ethical" but rather "outcomes of distinct imaginations or narratives that preconsciously inscribe different views of the world" on individuals.

It is important to note that Greeley et al. are not saying that the Catholic Imagination is a personality trait that will inevitably be found in all Catholics. Quite the contrary, Greeley (1995) in particular, has argued that Catholicism is characterized by what he calls a "popular tradition" and "high tradition." The popular tradition is the tradition that derives from the experience and actions of ordinary Catholics and it is here—he argues—that the Catholic Imagination, with its emphasis on metaphor, flourishes. The high tradition derives from the experience of "religious adepts, leaders, thinkers, teachers, philosophers, and theologians" and is more likely to be "systematic, rationalized, elaborate, detailed, reflective, precise, prosaic, and formal" (p. 49). So: what does all this have to do with the psychoanalytic study of religion?

Psychoanalysis and the Catholic Imagination

What can get overlooked in psychoanalytic discussions of religion, if only because it is so obvious (at least to psychoanalytic investigators), is that in *all* psychoanalytic formulations religious belief is seen to be the *disguised* reflection of unconscious impulses and desire. The totem and the monotheistic god, after all, may be father-surrogates, but they are surrogates, that is, disguised reflections of the father, only. My first contention, then, is that because the Catholic Imagination predisposes Catholics to draw metaphors from daily life when thinking about God (or more generally, the sacred), the imagery used by Catholics will be familiar to psychoanalytic investigators, and so the process of disguise will be easier to uncover than might otherwise be the case. After all, the analysis of images drawn from daily life, with a goal of linking that imagery to the unconscious, has been a central element in psychoanalytic thinking from *The Interpretation of Dreams* on forward.

For example: because Catholics conceptualize their relationship to the sacred *both* in terms of the mother-son relationship (and this, incidentally, is Greeley's argument about the Mary cult) *and* in terms of the father-son relationship, they are likely to use fairly obvious paternal and maternal imagery when thinking both about God and about the Church that brings them closer to God. As Grünbaum notes, this is precisely what Catholics *do* in using terms like "father" (for priests), "Holy Father" and "Holy Mother Church." But it is precisely because this Catholic recourse to paternal and maternal imagery when thinking about God and the sacred is so blatant that it is so easy for commentators like Grünbaum to come up with Catholic examples when discussing the link between religious practice and "the wish for parental protection."

Let me be clear: I am not arguing that religious belief is more shaped by unconscious desire in the Catholic case than in the Protestant (or Jewish or Hindu, etc.) case. Rather, my point is that the Catholic recourse to concrete and familiar metaphors drawn from daily life when thinking about the sacred results in the use of imagery that makes it easier for psychoanalytic investigators to *see* the link between that imagery and the unconscious

Quite apart from the "obviousness" of the imagery that falls out of the Catholic Imagination, there is something else that makes Catholic imagery so accessible to psychoanalytic interpretation: a common emphasis upon the body. Thus, Robert Orsi (2005) has argued that the immanental worldview that defines the Catholic Imagination predisposes Catholics toward what he calls the "corporalization of the sacred." In his own words

> The materialization of the religious world includes a process that might be called the corporalization of the sacred. I mean by this the practice of rendering

> the invisible world visible by constituting it as an experience in a body—in one's own body or in someone else's body—so that the experiencing body itself becomes the bearer of [a sacred] presence for oneself and others (p. 74).

That Catholics do invest bodies with religious significance, in a way not true of, say, the Protestant and Jewish traditions, seems clear. This different is perhaps best encapsulated in the distinction between the "crucifix" (a cross to which is attached the nearly naked body of the crucified Christ) so important in the Catholic tradition and the stark (body-less) "cross" that epitomizes Protestant iconography. At the level of abstract theology, this same Catholic emphasis on the body is seen not only in the central position given to doctrines relating to the Incarnation and the Eucharist but also in beliefs about the Immaculate Conception (that Mary was free from original sin from the moment of her physical conception) and about the Assumption (that Mary's physical body was taken up into heaven). This Catholic fascination with bodies is also seen in the historical importance of relic cults in the Catholic tradition; in saintly hagiographies that describe in minute detail the ways in which the flesh of early martyrs was torn and mangled; and in the great variety of behaviors historically associated with the bodies of Catholic mystics (e.g., living without eating; the stigmata; bilocation; etc.) that were long ago discussed (critically) by the Catholic historian (and Jesuit) Herbert Thurston (1952). Heartney (2003) suggests that this same tendency to see the body as a "medium through which we make contact with God" helps to explain why Catholic artists (in the sense of artists who were raised Catholics) in the United States have been especially likely to create works of art that challenge conservative (implicitly Protestant) artistic norms—and here she points to the work of Andy Warhol, Martin Scorcese, Robert Mapplethorpe, Andres Serrano, etc.

But this tendency to use the body to "think about" the sacred, like the recourse to metaphors drawn from daily experience, again results in the use of imagery familiar to psychoanalytic investigators. After all, a focus on the imagery associated with a particular body (or bodies) is central to many of Freud's most well-known analyses (his studies of Michelangelo's *Moses* and da Vinci's *The Virgin, St Anne and the Christ Child* come easily to mind), and the suggestion that the process of disguise often makes use of "displacement upwards" to associate repressed sexual impulses with areas of the body (the head, teeth, etc.) that have no overt sexual connotations is one that Freud made recurrently in *The Interpretation of Dreams* and other works.

Finally, there is still another affinity between psychoanalysis and the Catholic Imagination, though at first it is an affinity that might not come easily to mind to observers unfamiliar with the lived experience of Catholicism: a common emphasis on *sexualized* imagery. Greeley (2000), in particular, has argued that ordinary Catholics are predisposed to take sexual union as a metaphor for union with God. In his words:

> The Catholic imagination in all its many manifestations tends to emphasize the metaphorical nature of creation. The objects, events and persons of ordinary existence hint at the nature of God and indeed make God in some fashion present

> to us . . . The love of God for us, in perhaps the boldest of all metaphors (and one with which the Church has been perennially uneasy), is like the passionate love between man and woman (pp. 6-7).

And although Greeley uses "passionate love" in this particular passage, he's talking mainly about sex. Later in the same book, for example, he says "Erotic metaphors are part of the Catholic religious sensibility, though Catholic teachers and leaders rarely address them" (p. 75)—and points to Bernini's St. Teresa in ecstasy; Leo Steinberg's work on renaissance depictions of Christ's genitalia; the writings of St. John of the Cross, etc. as examples of works that have been influential among Catholics precisely because of their use of sexual arousal as a metaphor for spiritual arousal. Heartney (2004), building on Greeley's argument, suggests that the ease with which the Catholic Imagination makes use of erotic metaphors is another reason why artists raised Catholic are so often at the center of public controversy in the United States.

For Freud, the repressed impulses and desires that give rise to religious belief are disguised, often by shifting their affect to objects and images that are decidedly non-sexual, because a failure to do so would be disturbing to the conscious mind. But if sexual images are relatively less disturbing to the Catholic Imagination when thinking about God and the sacred (which in the end is what Greeley et al. are arguing), then here again we should expect *less* disguise—thereby making it that much easier for psychoanalytic investigators to detect that the unconscious impulses and desires that make particular beliefs appealing. Heartney (2004) provides a useful example here when describing her own experiences growing up Catholic.

Heartney talks first of the statue of St. Joseph in her local church, who seemed "gentle but slightly remote in the way that *ideal fathers* were supposed to be" (emphasis added), and then, in the very next sentence, about her fascination with the statue of Jesus above the altar. In her own words, "but of course the central focus was Jesus, positioned directly above the altar so that he could be seen from all corners of the cruciform church; Jesus was naked but for a slightly fluttering loin cloth [and] even to a nine-year-old the physicality of his perfect male body was unmistakable" (2004, pp. vii-viii). Even granting that any interpretation of Heartney's conscious recollections here must be entirely provisional, it seems difficult not to start with the possibility that the cluster of associations found in this stated memory (a gentle but remote ideal father contrasted with the "perfect male body" of a figure of Jesus set in a central and commanding location within the church) has been shaped by a daughter's Oedipal desire. Such an interpretive possibility, however, only comes easily to mind because Heartney is at ease in describing her pre-pubescent experience of Catholicism as being intimately bound up with the physicality of the "perfect male body" she saw on the crucifix that commanded her attention in her parish church.

And yet, if I am correct, and Catholic belief and Catholic practice are especially well-suited to psychoanalytic interpretation, there is an obvious difficulty that must now be confronted: the fact that Freud himself—quite unlike

Grünbaum—showed little inclination to draw upon the Catholic tradition when discussing religion.

Freud and Catholicism

Anyone familiar with Freud's work knows that he was quite clear about his antipathy toward the institutional Roman Catholic Church throughout the entirety of his career. Thus in the *Interpretation of Dreams*, he (1900) explained his early identification with Hannibal by first pointing to his own experience of anti-Semitism and then to the fact that "to my youthful mind Hannibal and Rome symbolized the conflict between the tenacity of Jewry and the organization of the Catholic church" (p. 196), thereby implicitly holding the Church responsible for anti-Semitism. And of course in his final years, Freud expressed disgust over the fact that the Catholic Church in Austria had proven to be a "broken reed" in the face of the Nazi invasion and the resulting threat both to the psychoanalytic movement and Austria's Jewish population (Freud, 1939).

Vitz (1988) has developed a psychoanalytically informed account of Freud's atheism generally and his special antipathy toward Catholicism specifically. Like other commentators, Vitz argues that Freud's atheism derived mainly from a rejection of his father, Jakob Freud, and so a rejection of God as a father substitute. But Vitz also argues that the Catholic nanny who cared for Freud until he was 2-3 years old (and who took Freud to Catholic Church services) functioned as a "good mother" whose loss engendered in Freud a lifelong ambivalence toward Catholicism. Thus, on the one hand, his intense anger over the loss of his nanny led to a strong rejection of Catholicism since a devaluation of his nanny's Catholicism was a way of coping with this loss. But (Vitz argues) the other part of this ambivalence was that there was a strong "Christian unconscious" in much of what Freud did and said.

Nevertheless, in giving examples of this supposed "Christian unconscious" in Freud, the best that Vitz can do is point to things like Freud's fascination with the city of Rome (and Italy generally) and his theoretical emphasis on the mother (Catholicism having a strongly maternal emphasis as a result of the Mary cult). The fact remains, Vitz's argument notwithstanding, that Freud did not use Catholic examples when discussing religion. On the contrary, as Vitz himself notes (p. 213), most of the concrete examples that Freud uses when discussing religion come from the Old Testament via the Philippson Bible he knew when growing up and from New Testament references found in literary works.

Ingham (1992), building on Vitz, also argues that Freud was strongly influenced by Catholicism as a result of his early relationship with his nanny. But again, like Vitz, by "influence" Ingham means "intellectual influence"—as when he suggests that Freud's emphasis on reproductive imagery, on Oedipal themes, on suffering as redemptive, etc. may have been derived from Catholicism. In the end, Ingham acknowledges that Freud paid little attention to the specifics of Catholic belief and ritual when discussing religion.

Reasonably, of course, the absence of images and ideas drawn from the Catholic tradition in Freud's work might be attributed to the fact that his patients did not confront him with such images and ideas. As Gay (1987, p. 128) points out, although we typically have to rely on conjecture and inference in deciding on the background of Freud's patients, it does seem likely that most of his early patients were Jewish. And when Freud did begin seeing an increasing number of gentile patients in the 1920s and 1930s most of these (see Gay, p. 128, for a list) seem to have been Protestant, with Princess Marie Bonaparte, who was Catholic, being the obvious exception. But the more important point, I think, is that there is no evidence (in the analytic material that Freud reports) that any of his patients, whether Jewish or Christian (with at best one or two exceptions), were especially religious. Freud's inattention to Catholicism, in other worlds, might reasonably be due to the fact that he treated few (if any) devout Catholics. But this seems incomplete. After all, some of Freud's most well-known analyses were based not on material supplied by his patients but on material derived from various literary or artistic traditions. Freud, for example, was quite at ease for example in providing interpretation of religious imagery created by Catholic artists, again, as in his well-known analyses of Michelangelo's *Moses* and of da Vinci's *The Virgin, St Anne and the Christ Child.*

So, despite the fact that Freud was living in a Catholic society (Austria), regularly vacationed in another Catholic society (Italy) and was clearly drawn to artistic works embodying religious themes by Catholic artists—he, unlike Grünbaum, shows no inclination to use Catholic examples when discussing religion. This apparent disinclination to confront Catholic practice seems most apparent in Freud's encounter with Italy. Thus, though he regularly visited Italian churches, these visits seem mainly to have been in pursuit of particular works of art. For the most part, as is evident in Simmons's (2006) discussion of Freud's Italian vacations, Freud was concerned mainly with Italy's Greek and Roman past or with using details of his experience in Italy to illustrate processes having little to do with religion.

Freud's failure to use Catholic examples in discussing religion is all the more puzzling given that here and there, at the fringes of a discussion typically concerned with something *other* than religion, Freud provides evidence that he was aware of popular Catholic practices that would otherwise seem well suited to psychoanalytic investigation. For example, in a well-known example from *The Psychopathology of Everyday Life*, he explains why he forgot the name of the artist (Signorelli) responsible for a fresco he had seen the year before in the cathedral at Orvieto. In the end, through a process of free association, Freud related this parapraxis to the repressed memory of a patient who had committed suicide. But to ordinary Catholics, Orvieto is especially well known on account of a Eucharistic miracle that supposedly occurred in 1263, when a German-speaking priest from Prague, in the midst of a pilgrimage to Rome, had doubts about the Real Presence while celebrating Mass in Bolsena. Suddenly, in apparent response to such doubt, the consecrated host started bleeding on the corporal that the priest held. The Priest took the bloodied corporal to Orvieto, where the Pope was then in residence, and after the matter had been investigated, the stained corporal was enshrined in the Cathedral.

And yet despite the juxtaposition of elements similar to those that Freud routinely considered (bleeding—doubt—approbation by a father surrogate); despite the fact that Freud visited both Orvieto and Bolsena several times, making it highly likely that he would have been familiar with the story of this Eucharistic miracle—and despite the similarities to himself (after all, wasn't he also a German-speaking pilgrim from central Europe on his way to Rome, given that on two of his trips he visited both Bolzano and Orvieto before visiting Rome; cf. Simmons, 2006), Freud says nothing specific about the Bolsena/Orvieto miracle in any of his works on religion.

Similarly, in describing why a traveling companion in Italy forgot the word "aliquis" in a famous quote from the Aeneid, Freud tells us that the man's free associations led to (among other things) the miracle of St. Januarius's blood relic at Naples (and he described the ritual in some detail) and to the memory of a year when the relic did not liquefy. Freud, focusing on the "failure of blood to liquefy" element, traces the slip to the man's anxiety over the fact that a woman with whom the man had had sexual relations had missed her period. And yet despite the fact that Freud was obviously familiar with the St. Januarius cult, and despite the fact that he visited Naples on three different occasions (Simmons, 2006), he nowhere—in his writings on religion—discusses the juxtapositions of elements in the case of this cult that might otherwise seem well-suited to psychoanalytic investigation (i.e., the fact that the blood relic was supposedly obtained when St. Januarius was decapitated; that a failure to liquefy was taken as premonition of disaster; that a hereditary group of women, the *Zie* [aunts] *di San Gennaro*, attended the ritual and shouted obscenities at the blood relic in order to encourage liquefaction. For more on this particular cult, see Carroll, 1989.)

Freud also said very little about the Mary cult, even though that cult has long been central to Catholicism (all the more so during Freud's lifetime given the upsurge in Marian devotion that occurred in the nineteenth century). Vitz (1988) attributes this lack of attention to Mary to the fact that "Freud's nanny (who for Vitz, remember, is Freud's link to Catholicism), being rather old, would not have made a good psychological symbol for the Virgin Mary" (p. 191). Ingham, making a slightly different argument, suggests that for Freud "suppressing" (Ingham's term) Mary's importance was a way to denying the importance of his early identification with his Catholic nanny.

Yet here too, at the fringes of what Freud does say about Mary, it seems clear that he had some awareness of phenomena that would have been well suited to psychoanalytic investigation. Towards the end of his brief "Great is Diana of the Ephesians" (the main point of which is that veneration of Mary at Ephesus is the historical reemergence of Diana worship) he makes a brief allusion to Katherine Emmerich, whose visions in the nineteenth century supposedly led to the rediscovery of Mary's home at Ephesus. As Vitz (p. 192) points out, Emmerich's story was especially well-known in the Austro-German Catholic community and so Freud's reference to this Catholic mystic is not really surprising. What is surprising, all the more so given the likelihood that Freud would have had easy access to Emmerich's story, is he never thought to discuss her visions in the way that he discussed, say, the hallucinations of the painter Christophe Heisman (Freud, 1923) nor did he discuss the other phenomena that Emmerich is described as experiencing (the stigmata, living without eating) even though such phenomena seems similar to the phenomena that Freud encountered in female hysterics.

This failure to "think about" a connection between hysteria and Catholicism seems most puzzling in the case of "Anna O," whose real name was Bertha Pappenheim. Although it was Breuer who wrote up the Pappenheim case for *Studies in Hysteria*, the fact that this was the case that introduced the "talking cure" insured that it would always be seen—by Freud and others—as central to the development of psychoanalysis. Although born into a Jewish family, Pappenheim had as a young girl attended a Catholic school in Vienna (Kaplan, 2004) and so certainly would have acquired some familiarity with famous Catholic mystics. Then too the fact that in 1879 Sigmund Pappenheim (Bertha's father) had been appointed guardian for Martha Bernays, Freud's future wife (Kaplan, 2004), makes it likely that Freud would have had some familiarity with Bertha's background. And yet, although the similarity between Bertha's hysterical symptoms and those of famous nineteenth century Catholic mystics like the Belgian stigmatic Louise Lateau (1850-1883) has been noted by later investigators like Peter Swales (Kaplan, 2004), it was something that Freud himself never investigated.

Finally, one of the most important sites (in all senses of that word) of Marian devotion during Freud's lifetime was the shrine at Lourdes. Just after the turn of the century, for example, when Freud was developing his theory(ies) of religion, about one million pilgrims a year were arriving at the railway station at Lourdes (Bertrin, 1913). And certainly the founding events at Lourdes, notably the series of apparitions (eighteen in total) of Mary to young Bernadette Soubirous were well-described in the Catholic devotional literature of the period. It is again no surprise, then, that Freud was aware of Lourdes's popularity and of the miracles that were the basis of its popularity. Thus, in discussing the usefulness of psychoanalytic therapy, he noted (Freud, 1964) candidly "that I do not think our cures can compete with those of Lourdes" and then quickly provides an explanation "There are so many more people who believe in the miracles of the Blessed Virgin than in the existence of the unconscious." Yet here again, he never thought to take the apparitions at Lourdes, nor the belief in the miracles that supposedly occurred here, all of which he knew about, as an object of study

So, why did Freud (apparently) turn away from the specifics of Catholic practice when talking about religion, despite the likelihood (as I have argued earlier in this chapter) that the Catholic Imagination makes popular Catholic practice ideally suited to psychoanalytic investigation) and despite the fact that he was almost certainly familiar with examples of Catholic belief and practice that that could have been used to illustrate his theoretical argument(s) about religion? As mentioned, Ingham, and presumably Vitz, trace this to Freud's experience with his nanny and a resulting ambivalence toward Catholicism. Possibly. But I think that there's something else at play as well and it is has to do with something that has been ignored by previous commentators: as a religion, Catholicism is not easily compatible with the social evolutionary paradigm that provides the theoretical foundation for Freud's general theory of religion. Phrased differently, Freud was reluctant to confront the particulars of Catholic belief and practice because Catholicism is a religion that does not really "fit" with the evolutionary (what Grünbaum call the phylogenic) sequence that Freud posited for religion in *Totem and Taboo* and *Moses and Monotheism.*

Freud's Social Evolutionary Emphasis

As any number of commentators have pointed out, the latter nineteenth century saw the rise of a social evolutionary paradigm that dominated European thinking about society and social life. Although the theories developed by the central figures in this tradition—including here scholars like Auguste Comte, Herbert Spencer, John Ferguson McLennan, James Frazer, William Robertson Smith—were different in many ways (especially as regards the process seen as fueling social evolution), what they had in common—as regards religion—was a teleological emphasis on a common end point: the emergence of monotheism among "civilized" (read: modern European) societies. But a second common element, especially after the publication of McLennan's influential *The Worship of Animals and Plants* in 1869, was the view that totemism had been an early stage in the social evolutionary sequence that led to monotheism. Moreover, as Jones (2005) has demonstrated in his review of theories of totemism, Freud's theory of religion was very much a part of this social evolutionary tradition. After all, in Freud's account, totemism had come into existence shortly after the primal parricide as a way of relieving the guilt that that crime had occasioned. The totem was a disguised father-substitute, and over time the repressed image of the father came more and more to consciousness in religious thinking, resulting in a paternalistic monotheism

Freud's evolutionary argument, however, encountered a problem when confronted with the facts of European history. After all, in many ways Judaism represented the logical endpoint of the "return of the Father" process that he posited, given that Judaism was not simply monotheistic but also intensely focused on a strongly paternalistic God. But of course Judaism had remained a minority religion in the Mediterranean basin and had increasingly lost ground to Christianity, a religion that was clearly *less* Father-centered religion than Judaism. So, in both the first and third chapter that made up *Moses and Monotheism*, Freud brought his posited evolutionary sequence a step beyond Judaism. After first talking about the guilt that pervaded Jewish culture just before the Christian era, he argued that one particular Jewish thinker, Saul of Taurus (St. Paul), implicitly traced this guilt to the fact that "God the Father" had been murdered. This element was never explicit, of course, but it was implicit (Freud argued) in the Pauline suggestion that there must have been an "Original Sin" against God the Father that required the sacrifice of the Son of God. Freud linked this to his evolutionary argument by arguing that in becoming a Son-centered religion, Christianity was popular because it gratified the desire to replace the Father that had given rise to the original parricide in the first instance.

Freud's theoretical argument to this point, then, could (possibly) have been reconciled with the facts of European history if Christianity had indeed triumphed as the sort of Son-centered religion described by Freud. But of course, as Freud knew full well, Christianity very quickly became *more* than just a Son-centered religion and in fact moved away from monotheism. In his words,

> In some respects the new religion meant a cultural regression as compared with the older, Jewish one, as regularly happens when a new mass of people, of a lower level, break their way in or are given admission. The Christian religion did not maintain the high level of things of the mind to which Judaism had soared. It was no longer strictly monotheistic, it took over numerous symbolic rituals from surrounding peoples, it re-established the great mother-goddess, and found room to introduce many of the divine figures of polytheism only lightly veiled, though in subordinate positions. Above all, it did not, like the Aten religion and the Mosaic one which followed it, exclude the entry of superstitious, magical and mystical elements . . . (1939, p. 88).

And again:

> After the Christian doctrine had burst the framework of Judaism, it took up components from many other sources, renounced a number of characteristics of pure monotheism and adapted itself in many details to the rituals of other Mediterranean peoples. It was as though Egypt was taking vengeance once more on the heirs of Akhenaton (1939, p. 136).

What these passages are referring to, of course, are precisely those religious elements that would later come to distinguish Catholicism from Protestantism, namely, an emphasis (in Catholicism) on the Mary cult ("the mother-goddess of earlier religions reestablished") and on cults organized around a variety of powerful saints ("divine figures of polytheism only lightly veiled").

Freud's account of early Christianity, and how it came to be transformed into Catholicism, is entirely consistent with a Protestant meta-narrative that had, and has, long structured European thinking on religion. Thus, in the Protestant worldview, Christianity had originally been a pristine religion focused on the figure of Jesus and on an interiorized concern with otherworldly salvation. What had happened over the centuries, however, was that magical and superstitious elements had been allowed (by corrupt Church leaders) to seep into Christian practice. The end result of this supposed process of religious degradation was Roman Catholicism, and it had been left to the Reformation to return Christian practice to the purity of the early Church. This Protestant "degradation narrative" not only structured the views of Protestant historians on Christianity but their views on other religions as well. Almond (1988), for example, has shown how this narrative shaped Victorian perceptions of Buddhism (by casting Buddha as a Luther-like figure who sought to reform a sacramentalized Brahmanist religion) and Smith (1990) has shown how his same narrative shaped historical scholarship on Roman mystery cults by treating them as surrogates for Roman Catholicism in confrontation with an implicitly Protestant "early Christianity." (The Protestant degradation narrative, and its influence on European thinking about religion, is discussed in more detail in Carroll, 2007.) In any event, Freud's account of what happened to Christianity after Paul is quite obviously a variant of this entrenched degradation narrative.

In the end, however, and notwithstanding the fact that Freud could reach outside the confines of his "return of the Father" theorizing in order to cobble together an argument that would explain Catholicism away, the fact remains that the distinctive features of Catholicism would have been a constant reminder to Freud that the progressive sequence otherwise posited by his phylogenic theory of religion, i.e., a smooth sequence that starts with totemism and ends with a Father (or Son) centered monotheism, does not really fit with the historical record unless you ignore the last 1500 years of European history. Within the logic of Freud's theory, in other words, Catholicism was a step backward, a throwback to an earlier stage of social evolution that should have ended once repressed memories of the primal parricide had to return to near-consciousness. And indeed, in saying that "It was as though Egypt was taking vengeance once more on the heirs of Akhenaton" (1939, p. 136). Freud seems implicitly to be saying just that, i.e., that Catholicism had much in common with the polytheistic religion that had prevailed in Egypt prior to the rise of the Aten religion and (the first) Moses and his religion.

(Suggesting that Freud saw the pre-Aten religion of ancient Egypt as a surrogate for Catholicism provides us with a new perspective on Freud's well-known fascination with the Egyptian artifacts that he displayed on his desk, i.e., it becomes possible to see those artifacts as a way for Freud to associate himself with Catholicism on a daily basis in a disguised manner, but that is a subject for a different essay!)

The main point, again, is this: the fact that Catholicism was still flourishing in many areas some two thousand years after the emergence of Paul's Son-centered religion was a theoretical embarrassment for Freud and helps to explain why he turned away from investigating the details of Catholic belief and practice.

Conclusion: Freud's Misguided Legacy and the Continued Neglect of Catholicism

This chapter started with a seemingly peripheral element in Grünbaum's article: his tendency to use examples drawn from the Catholic tradition when explicating Freud's argument about religion. But in pursuit of an explanation for this fact we have arrived at conclusions that tell us something about the psychoanalytic study of religion generally, namely, that because of the influence of what Greeley and others have called the Catholic Imagination, Catholicism is a tradition that is especially well suited to psychoanalytic investigation.

On the other hand, as noted, Grünbaum's use of Catholic examples is an anomaly. Most psychoanalytic authors writing on religion—starting with Freud himself—do not draw heavily (or at all) from the Catholic tradition. For example, in his annotated bibliography of psychoanalytic studies of religion published (in English) between 1920 and 1993, Beit-Hallahmi (1996) identifies forty-nine studies that take "Judaism" as their primary focus; the corresponding figures for

"Christianity" and "Asian Religion" (mainly Buddhism and Hinduism) are twenty-seven and ten studies, respectively. But of the twenty-seven studies that take Christian belief or ritual as their primary focus, only three focus specifically on Catholicism (and two of those are mine).

In the case of Freud I have argued that he turned away from the analysis of specifically Catholic beliefs and rituals (even when he was at least vaguely aware of those beliefs and rituals) because the continuing triumph of Catholicism in many parts of the world was a theoretical embarrassment given his social evolutionary perspective on religion. But now—and in conclusion—what of psychoanalytic authors more generally? Why have they continued to pay so little attention to Catholicism? Partly, I suspect, it's because many psychoanalytic investigators have little familiarity with the rituals and beliefs that have comprised popular Catholicism over the centuries. Partly too, I think that Freud's inattention to Catholicism has meant that investigators who take Freud as their starting point (as many do) never think to look to the Catholic tradition for examples. But most importantly, the continuing inattention to Catholicism among psychoanalytic investigators likely derives from a theoretical legacy that modern investigators, including some Catholic commentators, continue to share with Freud: a predilection for theoretical arguments that implicitly allow for the invidious ranking of different religious traditions.

For Freud himself, as mentioned, it was the use of a social evolutionary paradigm that allowed certain religions to be seen as more advanced than others. Social evolutionary theorizing, however, fell from fashion following the First World War (which did much to bring the notion of "progress" into disrepute). But what is popular (and has been for several decades) are theoretical arguments that link different types of religions and different types of religious experience to different points along a (psychological) developmental sequence. A good example here involves an author heavily cited by Grünbaum: William Meissner.

In his seminal work on psychoanalysis and religion, Meissner (1984)—a Jesuit priest—first discusses Freud's theory and then goes on to offer an "expanded" version of that theory. Simply put, Meissner's argument is that the human personality goes through a developmental course characterized by different "attainments, resolution of crises, deviations, distortions and developmental defects" and that differing religious experiences are linked to what happens at each point in that process and to residues of that process in the mature adult. In the end, the developmental sequence posited by Meissner is one that will be familiar, at least in its broad outlines, to readers of this book. Thus, the first stage of religious experience, for Meissner (1984), is dominated by primary narcissism, by the absence of self and object differentiation, by a merger of self-representation and God representation, etc. Subsequent stages are characterized by:

> . . . the metamorphosis of infantile narcissism, the changing quality and integration of object relations, the progressive and modification of instinctual derivatives, the transition from absolute dependence toward increasing autonomy in function and structure, the progressive internal organization that provides stability and coherence to the psyche, and the gradual emergence, definition and

> stabilization of the self as a coherent and integral part of the subjective world (p. 158).

Freud's error, according to Meissner, lay in restricting his analysis to one particular segment of this developmental sequence whereas he (Meissner) takes the entire sequence into account.

Although Meissner's theory posits a developmental (not a social evolutionary) sequence, the net result is still a schema that allows for the invidious ranking of different types of religious experience. This is evident in one of the passages from Meissner's book that Grünbaum reproduces:

> A caricature of [ideal] religion, which Freud employed as an analogy to obsessional states, is not infrequently found among religious people in whom blind adherence to ritual and scrupulous conscientiousness, as well as conscience, dominate religious life. In fact, we can safely say that the great mass of believers led credence to Freud's formulations.
>
> More mature and integrated forms of religious experience are modestly distributed among the people of God. Those who reach the highest level to religious experience and achieve the maximum expression of religious ideals are very rare indeed (p. 12).

Meissner here is contrasting a type of religious experience associated with a relatively early point in the development sequence he has described with a type of religious experience associated with the endpoint of that sequence. And at one level, the contrast that Meissner draws here mimics the contrast between "intrinsic" religiosity (where a person has internalized thoughts and beliefs that bring him or her closer to God) and "extrinsic" religiosity (which consists of behavioral conformity only), that routinely appears in the psychology of religion literature. Further, although Meissner himself (p. 159) warns against using his formulation to establish an "evaluative scale," this seems disingenuous. On the contrary, given the semantic loading of terms like "a caricature of religion," "blind adherence," and "more mature and integrated," as well as the contrast he sets up between "the masses" who embrace extrinsic religion and the more "modest" number who embrace intrinsic religion, Meissner's discussion clearly, if only implicitly, privileges intrinsic religion just as older social evolutionary theories (including Freud's) privileged the religions of "civilized" societies over totemic religion.

Although Meissner is a Catholic priest, his argument, characterized as it is by abstract theorizing and an emphasis on universal developmental sequences, falls more into Greeley's "high tradition" than anything else. Certainly there is no evidence in Meissner of the Catholic imagination and its emphasis on metaphors drawn from daily life. So where does popular Catholicism "fit" within the (invidious) developmental sequence that Meissner posits? It is hard to tell, mainly because Meissner rarely discusses specific religious experiences. Still, on those few occasions when he does, the evaluative biases of his formulation become apparent.

Thus, in a paragraph commenting on the religious significance of Paleolithic cave art, he suggests (p. 174) that such art created "a world of illusion in which all distinction between symbol and object was lost and omnipotent magical wishes had their play." Putting aside the fact that we have absolutely no way of knowing what cave art "meant" to those who created and/or viewed that art, Meissner here is associating prehistoric religion with the early stages of the developmental schema he has posited (with its emphasis on the absence of a distinction between self and object; on omnipotent thought, etc.). By implication, then, prehistoric religion is "primitive" both in a chronological and developmental sense.

A few pages later, in one of Meissner's very few references to Catholic practice, he first posits that religious objects and experience are often transitional, in Winnicott's well-known sense of that term, and then goes on to argue

> Just as the transitional object of the child can degenerate into a fetish object, transitional religious experience can be distorted in *less authentic,* relatively fetishistic directions that tend to *contaminate* and distort the *more profoundly meaningful* aspects of religious experience (p. 181-182; emphases added).

Here again, the semantic loading of the italicized terms leave no doubt as to the low valuation that Meissner puts on religious practice centered on what he calls fetish objects. He only gives one example of such an object however and it is a Catholic example:

> At least in some degree, the Catholic devotion to the rosary has been vulnerable to this distortion. In this sense, religious objects are reduced to talismans, religious rites become obsessional rituals, and religious faith is corrupted into ideology (p. 182).

What we are catching sight of in this passage, brief though it is, is—I suggest—disdain for a range of popular Catholic practices that Meissner associates with the earlier modalities in his developmental schema and that he sees as the preserve of the "masses" and not the smaller number who embrace what he would call mature religiosity. In short, for Meissner as for Freud, popular Catholicism may not be quite as primitive as totemic (or Paleolithic religion) but it is still less advanced than other forms of religion.

Although I have focused on Meissner's analysis, his implicit categorization of popular Catholicism as a "less advanced" form of religiosity is one that would likely fall out of *all* psychoanalytic formulations that link religious experience to a psychoanalytically-informed developmental schema given that the Catholic emphasis on immanence produces a type of "blurring" at least superficially similar to the sort of blurring associated with early infantile development. In the end, then, the absence of Catholic examples from most psychoanalytic discussions very likely derives from a continuing disdain (never stated explicitly, of course, but present nonetheless) for "less advanced" religions that shape psychoanalytic thinking on religion now as it did in Freud's time.

References

Almond, P. C. (1988). *The British Discovery of Buddhism*. Cambridge: Cambridge University Press.

Beit-Hallahmi, B. (1996). *Psychoanalytic Studies of Religion: A Critical Assessment and Bibliography*. Westport, CT: Greenwood Press.

Bertrin, G. (1913). Lourdes. In C. G. Herberman et al. (Ed.), *The Catholic Encyclopedia* (Vol. 9, pp. 389-391). New York: The Encyclopedia Press.

Carroll, M. P. (1989). *Catholic Cults and Devotions*. Montreal: McGill-Queens University Press.

Dillon, M. (2001). Review of "The Catholic Imagination." *Contemporary Sociology, 30*, 265-266.

Freud, S. (1900). The Interpretation of Dreams. *The Standard Edition of the Complete Psychological Works of Sigmund Freud,* 4-5, 1-338, 339-627. London: Hogarth Press.

Freud, S. (1923). A neurosis of demoniacal possession in the seventeenth century. *The Standard Edition of the Complete Psychological Works of Sigmund Freud, Standard Edition,* 19, 67-105. London: Hogarth Press.

Freud, S. (1964). New Introductory Lectures on Psychoanalysis. *The Standard Edition of the Complete Psychological Works of Sigmund Freud,* 22, 1-182. London: Hogarth Press.

Freud, S. (1939). Moses and Monotheism. *The Standard Edition of the Complete Psychological Works of Sigmund Freud,* 23, 1-137. London: Hogarth Press.

Gay, P. (1987). *A Godless Jew: Freud, Atheism and the Making of Psychoanalysis*. New Haven: Yale University Press.

Greeley, A. (2000). *The Catholic Imagination*. Berkeley: University of California Press.

Greeley, A. M. (1995). *Religion as Poetry*. New Brunswick, NJ: Transaction Publishers.

Heartney, E. (2003). Thinking through the body: women artists and the Catholic Imagination. *Hypatia, 18*, 3-22.

Heartney, E. (2004). *Postmodern Heretics: The Catholic Imagination in Contemporary Art*. New York: Midmarch Arts Press.

Ingham, J. M. (1992). Freud in a forest of symbols: the religious background of psychoanalytic anthropology. In D. Spain (Ed.), *Psychoanalytic Anthropology after Freud* (pp. 139-161). New York: Psyche Press.

Jones, R. A. (2005). *The Secret of the Totem: Religion and Society from McLennan to Freud*. New York: Columbia University Press.

Kaplan, R. (2004). O Anna: being Bertha Pappenheim—historiography and biography. *Australasian Psychiatry*, 12, 62-68.

Massa, M. S. (2001). The new and old anti-Catholicism and the analogical imagination. *Theological Studies*, *62*, 549-570.

Meissner, W. W. (1984). *Psychoanalysis and Religious Experience*. New Haven: Yale University Press.

Orsi, R. A. (2005). *Between Heaven and Earth: The Religious Worlds People Make and the Scholars Who Study Them*. Princeton: Princeton University Press.

Simmons, L. (2006). *Freud's Italian Journey*. Amsterdam: Rodopi.

Smith, J. Z. (1990). *Drudgery Divine: On the Comparison of Early Christianities and the Religions of Late Antiquity*. Chicago: University of Chicago Press.

Thurston, H. (1952). *The Physical Phenomena of Mysticism*. London: Burns Oates.

Tracy, D. (1981). *The Analogical Imagination: Christian Theology and the Culture of Pluralism*. New York: Crossroads.

Vitz, P. C. (1988). *Sigmund Freud's Christian Unconscious*. New York: The Guilford Press.

Chapter 5
Freud, Jewish Universalism, and the Critique of Religion

Carlo Strenger

It has been fashionable to say for some time that Freud's attitude towards religion has been overly reductive; that he didn't really understand religious experience; that he took religion to be bad science instead of understanding that it is a form of life, and that it is important to see religion in a very different context, as a spiritual and communal form of life. Critiquing religion, in the context of the more relaxed multicultural point of view that evolved since the 1960s seemed politically incorrect, and hence Freud was, in this respect, *passé*.

But over the past decade, atheist critiques of religion (Harris 2004, Dennett 2005, Dawkins, 2006) have generated much attention and heated discussion and have become an important topic again. In this context Adolf Grünbaum's chapter on Freud's theory of religion is timely. Grünbaum, in his customary precision and thoroughness, analyzes a number of Freud's arguments about religion in depth and great detail.

I would like to address a somewhat different aspect of Freud's critique of religion. I will be less concerned with the epistemic credibility of Freud's specific arguments and instead ask what was Freud's guiding motivation in his critique of religion? What ethos is reflected in his uncompromisingly negative stance towards religion?

My argument will be that Freud's views on religion were guided by an ethos that was adopted by a large number of Jewish thinkers in the second half of the nineteenth and the onset of the twentieth century. What connects Freud with figures like Albert Einstein, Franz Boas, one of the founders of American Anthropology, with Yehuda Magnes, the first president of the Hebrew University of Jerusalem, philosopher of culture and science Ernst Cassirer and many other Jewish scientists, intellectuals, writers and artists was a profound gratitude to the values of the European Enlightenment.

Jews, for many centuries, had been condemned to live an existence between pariahs and parvenus, in Hanna Arendt's (1951, 2006) felicitous phrase. At best they had the status of *Ausnahme-Juden,* of Jews tolerated because of the financial or commercial services they rendered to kings and countries, or, in many cases, they had no legal and political rights worth speaking of. Only with the advent of the political and epistemic values of the enlightenment, Jews could, in ever growing numbers, lead lives as equal citizens in a number of countries.

The phenomenally quick and successful influx of Jews into academia and the sciences has been explained in Yuri Slezkine's (2004) groundbreaking *The Jewish Century*. For most of their European history, Jews were denied access to land-ownership and a variety of occupations, and had hence developed a tradition of what Slezkine calls 'mercurian' professions. Hence, once they had access to the modern university as it evolved according to the Humboldt's model in Prussia in the early nineteenth century, they flooded the professions.

Slezkine's explanation is certainly valid, but it misses out on an important aspect of this influx of Jews into academia. The Jewish tradition of learning has been essential to the Jewish forms of life throughout the Diaspora, and the value of thought and logical thinking had been nurtured in its community for many centuries.

In the nineteenth century, when the opportunity to gain access to higher education arose, the combination of the value of learning with the gratitude towards the ethos of the Enlightenment created a unique synergy. Jews owed universalism their dignity as citizens. The idea of knowledge that could be corroborated by universally applicable standards was uniquely appealing to a group that had suffered for so many centuries from religious persecution, prejudice and often quite simply irrational fear and bigotry.

I will try to show that Freud's critique of religion was part and parcel of his wider project of ridding the scientific investigation of the human psyche from racial conceptions and irrational prejudice. In particular, I will argue that there is a strong subterranean connection between two of Freud's projects that *prima facie* seem unrelated: his attempt to rid the psychiatry of his times from racial prejudice and his analysis of religion. Finally, I will argue that even if Freud's arguments and theories have not stood the test of time, the Jewish universalist ethos is far from having lost its historical function.

The Resurgence of Atheist Critiques of Religion

The belief in tolerant coexistence between religion and secularism has been badly shaken since the onset of the twenty-first century for a number of reasons. In the United States, during the two G.W. Bush terms, there was a massive attack of Christian Fundamentalism on science in general and the theory of evolution in particular. The so-called Theory of Intelligent Design was pushed as an alternative to evolution by a number of political groups, and it seemed that religious intolerance of naturalism, atheism and even agnosticism was making a comeback (Brockman, 2006).

In parallel, a series of events indicated the frightening possibility that secular liberalism was coming under attack from political Islam. In retrospect, the writing had been on the wall at least since 1989, when Ayatollah Ruholla Khomeini issued a fatwa condemning novelist Salman Rushdie to death for his *Satanic Verses* that, presumably, blasphemously depicted the prophet Mohamed. The West, as has been documented (Hitchens, 2000), reacted rather timidly. Instead of making it very clear that liberal secularism would defend itself and its values, both governments, and, surprisingly, some writers took a conciliatory stance. Some accused Rushdie of insensitivity; others said that it was important to keep a calm modus vivendi vis-à-vis the Islamic world. As a result, Rushdie had to live undercover for a number of years, and a number of translators and editors of the book were killed or wounded in terror attacks.

The quietists who hoped the problem would go away were to have a rude awakening. 9/11, the event that truly opened the twenty-first century and changed our world completely was only the most gruesome and spectacular of a number of events that showed that liberalism needed to rethink its foundations and to find ways to defend its core values against the forces of bigotry and religious fanaticism. The killing of Dutch Filmmaker Theo van Gogh, the threats on Somali-born activist and writer Ayaan Ali Hirsi, the outbreak of violence after the publication of the Danish Cartoons depicting Muhammad, as well as the terror attacks in London and Madrid made clear to all that were willing to open their eyes, that tolerance and secularism were values that needed defending.

If Freud's radical critique of religion had been deemed *passé* for years, and psychoanalysis was attempting rapprochements with religion (Beit-Hallahmi, 2008), such critiques returned to the forefront with a vengeance. The opening salvo was Sam Harris (2004) The *End of Faith,* a sharp, if not very carefully argued, critique of the role of religion in human affairs. Philosopher Daniel Dennett (2005) followed suit with his polemical, but more carefully argued, *Breaking the Spell.* But the man who put the atheist counterattack into the headlines and generated a whole new discourse was the dean of contemporary Darwinian thought, Richard Dawkins (2006) with his uncompromising *The God Delusion*, which has sold more than 1.5 million copies to date and has been translated into dozens of languages. Journalist Christopher Hitchens (2007) joined the fray with a delightfully enraged, even though not very systematic *God is not Great: Why Religion Poisons Everything.*

These four authors, humorously called the 'four apocalyptic riders,' expressed a growing sentiment that atheism had to strike back; that the timid, politically correct respect for religious belief had been counterproductive. It was no longer tenable that atheists could be attacked for spiritual shallowness, immorality and lack of human depth without being able to counterattack, and thus radical critique of religion became an important aspect of contemporary discourse.

Freud's Program of De-Racializing Psychiatry

What was the context of Freud's critique of religion? Freud has been one of the most influential, admired but also feared and reviled critics of religion. It is of interest to view his critique in the larger background of the burning questions of his time.

The nineteenth century had seen spectacular developments in all domains of knowledge. Newtonian physics was supplemented by Maxwell's electrodynamics, and it looked as if natural science was on the way to decipher the basic structure of nature. Darwin had provided the missing link needed to bridge the gap between the physical and the biological sciences. In parallel, the development of historical and philological methods sprouted a veritable explosion of knowledge in the domain of the humanities.

Yet, the romantic idealization of *Volkstum* found its way into the science, in particular medicine and psychiatry (Gilman 1994). The emerging power of nationalist ideas led many intellectuals to reject the idea of universal reason which had been at the foundation of the enlightenment project. The German *Volksgeist,* the French civilization, the Russian soul, these thinkers argued, were a much more concrete embodiment of the actual psyche than the bloodless construct of universal reason (Noll, 1994).

Julian Benda (1926), in his classic *The Treason of the Intellectuals* has documented this tendency in detail. Suddenly, the aim was no longer to produce knowledge or contribute to science *tout court.* It mattered to contribute to the German Spirit, to French knowledge.

But how could these nationalist ideas be incorporated into the emerging edifice of modern natural science? The answer was the notion of race; a notion that seemed to have scientific respectability gradually became the vehicle through which nationalist ideas were transformed into seemingly scientific, biological language. German *Volkstum*, French greatness, Russian spirituality were now supposedly based on racial foundations. One of the most important notions that emerged during the second half of the nineteenth century was the notion of an Aryan race, supposedly superior to all others in its achievement, nobility and character.

In hindsight it is, of course, impossible to disregard the catastrophic consequences of race-based thinking. Hence it is easy to underestimate how respectable the notion of race was in mainstream science in the second half of the nineteenth century, as Sander Gilman (1994) demonstrated in detail in his groundbreaking work on the role of the notion of race in the nineteenth century medicine.

Once again, in hindsight, it is easy to see how ideologically colored, how scientifically inexact and unfounded was all this talk of race in general, and the superiority and inferiority of races in particular. Jared Diamond (1997) has magisterially shown how all the claims that the West's technological and scientific superiority was due to Europeans' biologically ingrained superior intelligence fly into the facts of what is actually known.

Even at the time, there were some who realized how catastrophic the implications of racial discourse could become. Ernest Renan was among the first to recognize that the combination of the newly emerging passion for nationalism and the mythical constructs of races that went back into the Gaelic, Germanic or Slavic past could be lethal, and set out to counteract this thesis in his classic and justly famous attack on the myths of nationalism.

Sigmund Freud grew into a profession, psychiatry, which was gaining enormous power in the fabric of the modern state, as Michel Foucault (2006) has shown in a variety of investigations. Psychiatry was about to become the discipline that would 'objectively' describe human nature, 'objectively' describe normality and pathology, and 'objectively' determine the biological foundations of the differences between individuals and groups.

I put 'objectively' in quotation marks, because many of the claims of nineteenth century psychiatry, ranging from the female propensity to hysteria, the Jewish propensity for hyper-sexuality to the connection between soil and race that was to play such an important role in C.G. Jung's thinking, have turned out to be thinly disguised attempts to give nationalism in its new racial form scientific respectability.

The story of these notions have been recounted in details primarily in Sander Gilman's work, but also in Noll's (1994) investigation of the intellectual foundations of C.G. Jung's work in the German romantic tradition of *voelkisch* thought. Gilman (1994) has also shown convincingly how many of Freud's ideas were designed to counteract the tendency to connect forms of mental illness and psychological dysfunction to racial types, and I will only briefly mention some of Gilman's findings.

Freud was particularly concerned with the tendency of racial stereotyping of Jews, which was ubiquitous in the anthropology and medicine of the second half of the nineteenth century. Jews were supposed to be somewhat effeminate, overly intellectual on the one hand, and overly sexual on the other hand. They were supposed to have less of a moral sense and hence tended to be both sexually and morally perverse and of weak character (Gilman 1994).

All these stereotypes were taken very seriously, and, paradoxically, accepted by many Jews (Gilman 1988). The most spectacular instance of such Jewish internalization of racial stereotypes and the resulting self-hatred was Otto Weininger's *Sex and Character,* published in 1903. Weininger turned all these stereotypes into an integrative system based on male and female characterizations. The male principle was intellectual, moral, active, productive and stable; the female principle was emotional, amoral, passive, reproductive and instable.

Races were characterized by the predominance of the male or the female principles. Unsurprisingly, Weininger claimed that the Aryan race was predominantly male and the Jewish race predominantly female.

Weininger was a young, very gifted man of vaulting ambition, who only saw value in his life if he could contribute something grand to human knowledge. He also happened to be Jewish. Applying his own theory to himself quite consistently, he came to the conclusion that he would not produce anything of lasting value. Hence he rented the room in which Beethoven had died, and told the landlady not to disturb him until the morning. He shot himself and died in the morning. Weininger's suicide was also precipitated by his disappointment at the reception of *Sex and Character.* Paradoxically, his suicide may have contributed to the phenomenal success that this book would have, going through more than twenty editions and selling hundreds of thousands of copies.

Freud was actually quite impressed by Weininger's work; he had played with the idea of universal bisexuality for a few years, and the development of his biological ideas has been documented in detail by Frank Sulloway (1979) in his classic *Freud, Biologist of the Mind.* Freud took both the notion of inborn bisexuality and his notion of polymorphous perversity of human sexuality a different direction from Weininger and others who connected them to racial stereotyping. He was to argue that bisexuality was a universal trait of the human unconscious, derived from the phylogenesis of the human mind.

Freud's emphasis was precisely on the universality of these traits, and the importance of this claim needs to be understood within the context of the pervasive tendency of medicine and psychiatry to attribute racial characteristics to different ethnicities. By claiming that the human psyche *per se* was polymorphous perverse, Freud wanted to counteract the tendency to re-cast nationalism in general, and anti-Semitism, the racially formulated, new embodiment of hatred of Jews.

It was to turn out that the fight against nationalist conceptions of psychiatry would not be won easily. Freud's erstwhile disciple and crown-prince C.G. Jung was to turn into a radical representative of this perspective. Notoriously, he was to write in 1928 in a footnote to the *Two Essays in Analytic Psychology* that "It is a quite unpardonable mistake to accept the conclusions of a Jewish psychology as generally valid," and was to make his view of the racial unconscious even clearer in 1934 when he wrote:

> Freud did not understand the Germanic psyche any more than did his Germanic followers. Has the formidable phenomenon of National Socialism, on which the whole world gazes with astonishment, taught them better? Where was that unparalleled tension and energy while as yet no National Socialism existed? Deep in the Germanic psyche, in a pit that is anything but a garbage-bin of unrealizable infantile wishes and unresolved family resentments (Jung, 1934, in Samuels, 2009).

Andrew Samuels, one of today's leading Jung interpreters, gives a few other examples for the way Jung incorporated race into his conception of human nature in general, and Germans and Jews in particular.

In the same paper, which clarifies the somewhat cryptic language above, Jung asserted (about Jews): "The 'Aryan' unconscious has a higher potential than the Jewish." "The Jew who is something of a nomad has never yet created a cultural form of his own and as far as we can see never will, since all his instincts and talents require a more or less civilized nation to act as host for their development." "The Jews have this peculiarity with women; being physically weaker, they have to aim at the chinks in the armour of their adversary." Jung also warned against "applying Jewish categories indiscriminately to Germanic and Slavic Christendom" (Samuels, 2009).

In the present context, neither Jung's nor Freud's personal histories, complexes nor the deriving motivations are in focus: we are really dealing with the underlying ethos and the conflict between universalism and particularism that was carried out under the guise of a scientific dispute about the nature of the unconscious. And on this level, Freud had one overriding goal: the human psyche needed to be studied objectively; and its phylogenetic structure needed to be deciphered, and this phylogenesis was to be shown as a *universal trait of humankind.* This was Freud's great evolutionary project which was largely dropped by psychoanalysis, because Freud's version of it was irreparably doomed by his Lamarckism (Strenger, 2006). Yet Freud can be seen as one of the great precursors of contemporary evolutionary psychology, and most of all a proponent of a study of human nature fuelled by enlightenment universalism.

Psychoanalysis of Religious Epistemology

Grünbaum's thorough analysis of the logical structure of Freud's critique of religion stands by itself. I would now like to complement it by analyzing the Enlightenment ethos that guided it and its connection to Freud's attempt to invalidate the notion of race in psychiatry. Reading *The Future of an Illusion* is an interesting experience, because it is far more a philosophico-political tract than a pure exercise in psychoanalytic thinking. Freud's psychoanalytic elucidation of the psychogenesis of religion is driven by the credo he enunciates towards the end of the book: 'The Voice of Reason is a soft one. But it does not rest until it gets a hearing' (Freud 1927, p. 53).

Freud starts *The Future of an Illusion* by analyzing the functions of civilization. One crucial function of civilization is the protection of the social order and the reigning in of human drives, many of which can be destructive. Obviously religion largely fulfills some of these functions, and throughout the entire book Freud points out the major difference between religion and the 'laborious acquisition of knowledge.' Religion fulfills certain psychological needs that science cannot possibly fulfill for the simple reason that it cannot provide more protection from the powers of nature than is technologically possible, whereas religion's content is, as Freud says, driven and shaped by our wishes rather than by the function of reality testing.

Freud's argument is complex and intricate, and I will focus on an aspect particularly pertinent to his universalist ethos. In section five Freud succinctly summarizes what could be called the epistemology of religious belief. He says that in most religions the main argument for maintaining religious beliefs is that they have been passed down through the ages; that they were believed by our ancestors, and that hence it is forbidden to question them.

The next move Freud makes is to connect religious epistemology to its ontogenetic origin. He hypothesizes that the attachment to ancestry is a fixation on the reassuring authority and protection of parental figures in childhood. As such it is a wish-fulfillment rather than a belief based on a realistic strategy of gaining control over nature. As our experience of parental protection was more soothing than the essentially conjectural basis of all science and the realistic limitations of technological control, it is more attuned to our desire for total safety than the enterprise of science.

The aspect of religion that is most likely to lead to strife and irresolvable conflict is obviously this epistemology of blind loyalty to ancestry. Different groups, tribes, nations and religions are loyal to different ancestries; as a result they are attached to beliefs that are bound to clash with each other without there being, in principle, a way to resolve these clashes.

Various enlightenment movements throughout history have one aspect in common: whether in India in the middle of the first millennium BCE, in Greece in the fifth and fourth centuries BCE, in Islam during the ninth and tenth centuries, or in the European Enlightenment beginning in the seventeenth century, there was one central common theme. Beliefs and values were no longer valued just because they had been held by ancestors, and critical thinking was valued above tradition.

It is this valuation of critical thinking and the combined effort of humans to generate knowledge about the world that differentiates all enlightenment movements from the epistemology of religion as Freud describes it. Most of all, an enlightenment does not recognize any prohibition on critical thinking and inquiry, because enlightenment assumes that such prohibition is likely to inhibit progress in human knowledge.

The central move here was described by Nietzsche (cf. Foucault, 1971) when he criticizes the idealization of *Ursprung*: all religious thought was based on the idea that an idea's *origin* determined its value. A God, a prophet, or a priest had revealed a truth that derived its dignity from this origin.

As opposed to that, the enlightenment model assumes consistently that it is the way ideas are generated and tested rather than their origin that matters. There is no idea or statement whose truth is guaranteed by its origin; only its constant critical scrutiny in the cooperative venture of human inquiry can provide the hope that this venture called *episteme* in ancient Greece and science in modernity will gradually converge towards truth by eliminating error to the extent possible.

Here we come to what I take to be the most important contribution of Freud's *The Future of Illusion.* Obviously, Freud was not the first to point out the basic, structural opposition between religious and enlightenment epistemologies. It had been a basic theme of all great epistemological theories starting with classical Indian and Greek philosophies, and it had, of course, been central to modern enlightenment critiques of religion from Voltaire and Hume to Schopenhauer, Feuerbach, and Nietzsche.

Freud was also not the first to try to explain the psychological foundation of religion. Such explanations had been given many times before, and Schopenhauer and Nietzsche had applied psychodynamic explanatory structures quite similar to Freud's. Freud's most important contribution was to provide a psychodynamic explanation of *religious epistemologies,* by showing that they were structurally analogous to early infantile attachments.

In doing so, he also showed that there was a basic, irreducible conflict between religious and enlightenment epistemologies; a conflict which, as we saw at the beginning of this paper, has once again come to the forefront of international relations and of the culture wars inside the United States.

For Freud there was no compromise and no mediation between the enlightenment credo to 'liberate man from self-imposed tutelage' and the demands of religion for unquestioned loyalty to ancestry. Demanding respect for beliefs because of their origin was diametrically opposed to the demand to examine them critically.

This leads us to the strangest and most criticized of Freud's writings: *Moses and Monotheism* (1938). I will not go into the details of Freud's explanatory structure and its weaknesses, since Grünbaum's essay shows both in detail. Speculations about Freud's personal motivations for writing this strange essay have abounded, and some of the analyses are interesting and instructive (Robert, 1974; Yerushalmi, 1991).

I would like, once again, to connect the *Moses* book, unconvincing as it is, to the ethos that had guided Freud's lifework. Freud himself suffered from many qualms about publishing the *Moses* at a time when the persecution of Jews had reached new heights—and would lead to a degree of inhumanity that Freud was not to know because of his death in 1939.

Edward Said (2003) has made a convincing case for interpreting Freud's *Moses* as an attempt to dismantle notions of race and ethnicity. Beyond all the speculations and argumentative contortions of Freud's argument a very simple thesis stands out: Moses, the man who, according to Judaic myth, led the Israelites from slavery to freedom, from polytheism to monotheism, was an Egyptian. In other words: he was not part of the Jewish tribes. He was part of an African dynasty.

While this was certainly a thesis that could hurt the sensibilities of Jews, it was most of all a thesis that frontally attacked the whole idea that there was such a thing as the Jewish race that, for its defenders, embodied the 'Jewish genius,' and for its detractors, Jewish depravity and neuroticism. The most defining idea of the Jewish tradition, monotheism, was not connected to Jewish ancestry, but was transmitted by an Egyptian nobleman who tried through the Jewish tribe to revive the failed experiment to introduce monotheism in Egypt itself.

Hence monotheism neither belongs to the Jews nor to the Semites. In Biblical terms Africans were the descendents of Ham, the Semites, as their name implies, the descendants of Shem, and the Greeks, the founders of counter-culture to the Jews, those of Japheth.

Freud now mixes this up completely: the origin of the Jewish creed was in a descendant of Ham; and he, Freud the Jew (i.e. 'Semite'), was analyzing the racial stereotypes with the tools developed by the descendants of Japheth: Western science, which, according to popular lore, began its history in ancient Greece (Said, 2003). It would have suited Freud's agenda very well had he known how intricate the interaction between Greek philosophy and science and ancient India had been. It would have given him a further reason to deconstruct the ancestral myths connecting between ideas and races.

Behind the historical and scientific inaccuracy of Freud's reasoning, we see a deep drive. Freud in his old age tries everything to convince his readers that classifying humans according to their biological provenance is wrong. What matters about ideas are not who formulated them, but only their validity and their ethical implications.

Here two of Freud's great projects connect: the project of excluding race from psychiatric discourse and the critique of religion. The common theme of these two projects is to deconstruct the notion that origins provide honor, dignity and value. Freud opposed the importance of origins both with respect to human beings, and with respect to theories, beliefs and ideas. In the same way as Aryan, Jewish, aristocratic or other descent could not be the reason why we should respect human groups or individuals more than others, the origin of a belief or command could not provide the grounds for its authority.

Freud was intransigent in this respect. While his undermining of the notion of race in psychiatry was primarily directed against his Germanic surrounding and its anti-Semitic undertones, his undermining of the specialness of Jews as a race, group, or religion was a logical implication of the very same project. For him there was no way he could protect Jews against the attack of racial inferiority without, with the very same argument, denying them any special status because of their provenance or beliefs.

Freud's Jewish Universalist Identity

Freud's deconstruction of myths of origin and his critique of religion are intrinsic to his own Jewish identity, which he addressed in two famous texts. As we have seen, he neither believed that Jews were a race, nor that they were special in having invented monotheism. And in any case, Freud was as critical toward Judaism as he was toward any other religion. In what sense, then, did he feel Jewish? The latter of the two texts is the preface to the first of his works to be translated into Hebrew, *Totem and Taboo.*

> No reader of [the Hebrew version of] this book will find it easy to put himself in the emotional position of an author who is ignorant of the language of holy writ, who is completely estranged from the religion of his fathers—as well as from every other religion—and who cannot take a share in nationalist ideals,

> but who has yet never repudiated his people, who feels that he is in his essential nature a Jew and who has no desire to alter that nature. If the question were put to him: 'Since you have abandoned all these common characteristics of your countrymen, what is there left to you that is Jewish?' he would reply: 'A very great deal, and probably its very essence.' He could not now express that essence clearly in words; but some day, no doubt, it will become accessible to the scientific mind.
>
> Thus it is an experience of a quite special kind for such an author when a book of his is translated into the Hebrew language and put into the hands of readers for whom that historic idiom is a living tongue: a book, moreover, which deals with the origin of religion and morality, though it adopts no Jewish standpoint and makes no exceptions in favour of Jewry. The author hopes, however, that he will be at one with his readers in the conviction that unprejudiced science cannot remain a stranger to the spirit of the new Jewry. Vienna, December 1930 (Freud, 1930).

Freud describes the complex emotions he felt about this Hebrew translation. He does not apologize for his ethos. He makes it clear that he is critical of religion and repudiates nationalism, and that his critique of religion is not about to spare Judaism, the religion of his ancestors. He says very clearly that *Totem and Taboo* doesn't adopt a 'Jewish standpoint.' What, then, could Freud possibly mean when he said 'a great deal of him' had remained Jewish? It is easy to disqualify this as nothing but a sentimental utterance, possibly meant to please the readers of the Hebrew edition who, obviously, had to be consciously Jewish, as no one else at the time would know Hebrew.

I think that Freud did not just play up to his audience. All his major biographers from the classic three volume work by Ernest Jones to Peter Gay's magisterial *Freud: a Life for our Time* agree that his Jewishness was essential to his identity.

There were, of course, Jews who were on the way to complete assimilation, and who were confronted with their Jewishness primarily through the experience of anti-Semitism: most famously, of course, Theodor Herzl; to a large extent Albert Einstein; and also one of the most incisive inquirers into the nature of modern Jewish identity, Hannah Arendt.

This was not Freud's case; he never tried to avoid or suppress his Jewishness. Part of this could have been due to the very lively group of Jewish intellectuals, writers and scientists concentrated in the ninth *Bezirk* in Vienna. There was no dearth of secular Jews for Freud to connect to, and they were connected to each other through the precariousness of their situation: on the one hand they had achieved an ever growing influence in Viennese cultural life, and on the other hand they knew that anti-Semitic sentiments were part of reality, as the election of the openly anti-Semitic Karl Lueger as mayor of Vienna showed beyond any doubt (Schorske, 1981).

Freud therefore certainly felt a community of fate with his Jewish brethren in Vienna. Mahler—one of his most famous short term cases—converted to Catholicism to gain access to the most coveted post in the world of music, the directorship of the Viennese opera. Freud himself often complained that his ideas were initially rejected because he was Jewish—a claim that has not been substantiated by historical research. Nevertheless, unlike Mahler, he never considered conversion for the sake of acceptance or advancement.

The question is whether the 'Jewish essence' he speaks of consisted in nothing but this adversity in advancing in Viennese society. The key to a positive content of Freud's Jewish identity may be found in the other major text that addresses this question explicitly: the letter he sent to the opening of the Hebrew University in Jerusalem.

> Historians have told us that our small nation withstood the destruction of its independence as a State only because it began to transfer in its estimation of values the highest rank to its spiritual possessions, to its religion and its literature.
>
> We are now living in a time when this people has a prospect of again winning the land of its fathers with the help of a Power that dominates the world, and it celebrates the occasion by the foundation of a University in its ancient capital city.
>
> A University is a place in which knowledge is taught above all differences of religions and of nations, where investigation is carried on, which is to show mankind how far they understand the world around them and how far they can control it.
>
> Such an undertaking is a noble witness to the development to which our people has forced its way in two thousand years of unhappy fortune.
>
> I find it painful that my ill-health prevents me from being present at the opening festivities of the Jewish University in Jerusalem. (Freud, 1925)

In this brief text Freud makes a connection between what he takes to be the essence of Jewish identity throughout most of its history: the 'transfer in its estimation of values the highest rank to its spiritual possessions, to its religion and its literature.' He then moves on to define the essence of the university as 'a place in which knowledge is taught above all differences of religions and of nations,' and finally speaks of the foundation of the 'Jewish University' as 'noble development to which our people has forced its way in two thousand year of unhappy fortune.'

I think that Freud does not just speak of the possibility of a Jewish homeland when he speaks of this 'noble development.' I think he speaks of another 'transfer in [the Jewish] estimation of values.' While Jews previously valued their religion and literature, the Jews that he was surrounded by had now moved to put the highest value on the 'objective investigation . . . [of] the world,' i.e. science, which Freud, throughout his life, had seen as humanity's highest achievement.

For Freud, this was not a falsification of Jewishness, as he understood it, but a creative transformation of its essence. To take the 'possession of spiritual values' from religion to science was the step that all of humanity had to make if it was ever to mature fully and to move from the pleasure principle to the reality principle.

Of course the following question is to be expected: 'But this is in no way unique to Jews! Freud thought that all of humanity needed to make this step. So how did this differentiate between Jews and Gentiles?'

This is the point at which we have to admit that the question of the particularity of Jewishness was not first and foremost on Freud's mind. The greatest value he saw for humanity was the ability to transcend 'all differences of religions and of nations'. Attachment to one's kin certainly is an ineradicable trait of human nature. Freud knew this and made it a cornerstone of his view of human nature: character was the reflection of our early love attachments, and these could not be erased from the psyche.

The question for Freud always was, to what extent, as individuals and as a species, humans would be able to transcend these early attachments when it came to formulating their worldview and their ethics. As we saw, Freud insists throughout *Future of an Illusion* that overcoming those early attachments and the move from religion to science is humankind's only chance to mature fully.

He doesn't make any exemption for Jews. In the preface to the Hebrew translation of *Totem and Taboo*, he expresses the hope that the ethos of 'unprejudiced science' will find its place in the 'new Jewry.' I think that, underlying this hope is his profound belief that Jews, like humankind as a whole, must move towards universalism.

This is why, despite his own misgivings about its timing, and his awareness that the argument was rather weak, he felt compelled to write the *Moses* book in his last years. For him it was crucial to formulate the decisive argument that Jews needed to overcome the myth of racial origins that he had fought all his life, and that was to achieve its most terrible expression, after Freud's death, in the Holocaust.

The Relevance of Freud's Universalism Today

We live in a time in which universalism is severely threatened again. In the United States, white supremacists seek to show that Obama is not really American born, a thinly disguised attempt to delegitimize the first black president of the United States. The issue, obviously, is not Obama's place of birth, but his ancestry: the fact that he is half black and a quarter Muslim.

The Middle East is in the throes of a series of conflicts that have been interpreted as a clash of civilizations by leading thinkers of the stature of Bernard Lewis and Samuel Huntington. Even if we do not accept this interpretation in full, it is no doubt that the unconscious of the Middle East (if the metaphor be forgiven) is structured by the family drama of the three Abrahamic religions.

Jews and Moslems are fighting for possession of the Temple Mount, or Haram al'Sharif. According to legend, this is the place where Abraham followed God's command to sacrifice his son, to be stopped only at the very last moment. This Biblical story is the epitome of the exaltation of blind obedience. Abraham is about to commit one of the most horrible acts as proof to his complete submission to God's will.

The paradox and the horrible reality of the myth of origin come to fullest expression in this conflict. Muslims claim that it was really Ishmael, the mythical forefather of Arabs who was almost sacrificed on the temple mount rather than Isaac, the no less mythical forefather of the Jewish people (Posmanik, 2009). The irony is that, in a sense, Jews and Moslems fight for the dubious honor to have been the victim of a trauma that both groups are willing to perpetuate forever. Both religions are willing to send their sons into death for the possession of a piece of land that, more than anything, expresses what Freud saw as immature attachment to the authorities of childhood.

Had Freud lived to see this he might have sighed, reiterating that the voice of reason indeed has great difficulty in making itself be heard. And yet he would have insisted that the hope must never be given up. He would have pointed out that in the Middle East people kill each other for nothing more than the claim of truth of their respective myths, and he would have seen this as another pernicious consequence of the refusal to mature into universally acceptable standards of truth and the fixation to religious belief. And he would have been happy to see psychoanalysis applied to the critical understanding of the Middle Eastern conflict (Bunzl and Beit-Hallahmi, 2002)

Freud's universalism accepted only one natural kind for humans: the species of *homo sapiens.* He did not think that there were biologically based sub-species within humanity. The unconscious was his metaphor for the biological nature of humans, and its structure was supposed to be universal. All humans had to live with the built-in conflict between the pleasure principle embodied in the Id and the reality principle, laboriously acquired in the process of maturation and embodied in the ego.

His critique of religion was universalist as well. All humans yearn for a sense of protection and the belief that they have a special, privileged place in the cosmos, and all humans suffer from the insight that we are but a transient species that has evolved by chance on a small planet in one of billions of solar systems. The desire to regain the sense of ontological specialness that has characterized our infancy is understandable. But we must by no means give in to this desire: the consequences are too dangerous.

History is filled with wars, persecutions and genocides built on the idea that one group is more special, more deserving than others. It is written in the blood of those killed in the name of religions and other belief-systems that tried to restore a pure faith, a pure race or a pure ideology.

For Freud there was but one way to counteract the regressive pull towards groupism, particularism, and claims to specialness: the disinterested study of the nature of humankind and the deciphering of the biologically ingrained forces that push us toward irrationality and inhumanity.

Freud's specific theories have, to a large extent, not survived the increase in knowledge. Biology has moved far away from the models in which Freud was educated and in which he formulated his ideas. As a result the models of contemporary cognitive evolutionary neurosciences look radically different from Freud's psychoanalytic theory (Buss, 2004).

But Freud's ethos, the research program that he believed in, flourishes. His idea that the evolutionary strata of the mind need to be deciphered has become the core of a research paradigm spanning the civilized world, evolutionary psychology, which is nowadays incorporating psychodynamic thought (Greenberg,

Koole, & Pyszczynski, 2004). Even his idea that the evolutionary roots of religion must be understood has turned into a flourishing domain (Atran, 2002). Current models of the evolutionary psychology of religion have achieved considerable complexity and they are based on an impressive array of interrelated disciplines ranging from physical anthropology through comparative religion to cognitive psychology and evolutionary theory.

None of the researchers working on the evolutionary roots of religion (or the evolutionary roots of the mind in general) believe that there are Black, Asian, Aryan, Jewish, or Moslem psychologies. There is human psychology which, depending on circumstance, leads to a wide variety of cultures, belief-systems, and religions. But the conflicts, yearnings and pitfalls of human nature are the same everywhere. In this respect, Freud has remained more than relevant.

References

Arendt, H. (1951). *The Origins of Totalitarianism.* New York: Meridian.

Arendt, H. (2006). *The Jewish Writings.* New York: Schocken.

Atran, S. (2002). *In Gods we Trust: The Evolutionary Landscape of Religion.* Oxford: Oxford University Press.

Beit-Hallahmi, B. (2008) Review of D.M. Black (ed.), *Psychoanalysis and Religion in the 21st Century: Competitors or Collaborators?*, 2006. *Mental Health, Religion & Culture*, 2008, 11, 355-358.

Benda, J. (1926). *The Treason of the Intellectuals.* New York: Morrow.

Brockman, J., (ed.) (2006). *Intelligent Thought: Science Versus the Intelligent Design Movement.* New York: Vintage.

Bunzl, J and Beit-Hallahmi B. (eds.) (2002). *Psychoanalysis, Identity and Ideology: Critical Essays on the Israel/Palestine Case.* New York: Springer.

Buss, D. (2004). *Evolutionary Psychology.* New York: Allyn & Bacon.

Dawkins, R. (2006). *The God Delusion.* New York: Houghton Mifflin.

Dennett, D.C. (2005). *Breaking the Spell: Religion as a Natural Phenomenon.* New York: Viking.

Diamond, J. (1997). *Guns, Germs and Steel: the Fates of Human Societies.* New York: Norton.

Foucault, M. (1971). Nietzsche, genealogy, history. In Rabinov, P. (ed.). (1984). *The Foucault Reader.* New York: Random.

Foucault, M. (2006). *Psychiatric Power: Lectures at the College de France 1973-1974.* New York: Palgrave.

Freud, S. (1925). On the Occasion of the Opening of the Hebrew University. *The Standard Edition of the Complete Psychological Works of Sigmund Freud, 19*, 252. London: Hogarth Press.

Freud, S. (1927). The future of an illusion. *The Standard Edition of the Complete Psychological Works of Sigmund Freud, 21*, 1-56. London: Hogarth Press.

Freud, S. (1930). Preface to the Hebrew Translation of Totem and Taboo. *The Standard Edition of the Complete Psychological Works of Sigmund Freud, 13,* xv. London: Hogarth Press.

Freud, S. (1939). Moses and monotheism: Three essays. *The Standard Edition of the Complete Psychological Works of Sigmund Freud, 23*, 1-137. London: Hogarth Press.

Gilman, S. (1988). *Jewish Self-Hatred: Anti-Semitism and the Hidden Language of the Jews.* Baltimore: Johns Hopkins University Press.

Gilman, S. (1994). *Freud, Race and Gender.* Princeton: Princeton University Press.

Greenberg, J., Koole, S. L., & Pyszczynski, T. (Eds.) (2004). *Handbook of Experimental Existential Psychology.* New York: Guilford Press.

Harris, S. (2004). *The End of Faith: Religion, Terror and the Future of Reason.* New York: Norton.

Hitchens, C. (2000). *Unacknowledged Legistlators.* London: Verso.

Hitchens, C. (2007). *God is NOT Great: How Religion Poisons absolutely everything.* New York: Twelve Books, Hachette Publishing Group.

Noll, R. (1994). *The Jung Cult: Origins of a Charismatic Movement.* New York: Free Press.

Posmanik, S. (2009). *The Theme of Akedat Yitzhak in Hebrew Literature.* Unpublished Doctoral Dissertation, Tel Aviv University

Robert, M. (1974). *D'0edipe a Moise. Freud et la conscience juive.* Paris: Calman Levy.

Said, E.W. (2003). *Freud and the Non-European.* London: Verso.

Samuels, A. (2009). Jung and Anti-Semitism. *Institute of Historical Research.* Retrieved August 18, 2009, at http://www.history.ac.uk/resources/e-seminars/samuels-paper.

Schorske, C. (1981). *Fin de Siècle Vienna: Politics and Culture.* New York: Vintage.

Slezkine, Y. (2004). *The Jewish Century.* Princeton: Princeton University Press.

Strenger, C. (2006). Freud's Forgotten Evolutionary Program. *Psychoanalytic Psychology, 23*, 420-429.

Sulloway, F. (1979). *Freud, Biologist of the Mind.* New York: Vintage.

Weininger, O. (1903/2005). *Sex and Character.* Bloomington, IN: Indiana University Press.

Yerushalmi, Y.H. (1991). *Freud's Moses: Judaism Terminable and Interminable.* New Haven: Yale University Press.

Part II: Interpretation and Meaning

Chapter 6
Interpreting Three Religious Constructs

Harriet Lutzky

In his chapter on "Psychoanalysis and Theism," Adolf Grünbaum carefully described and analyzed Freud's claim that belief in God is a wish-fulfilling illusion, and further, that this illusion may be qualified as a delusion, ergo false, because of its complex structure with an unconscious component, and its archaic nature Although Grünbaum says that Freud's claim that religion is delusion may not be entirely supported, it is of interest that another major theorist of religion, the French sociologist Emile Durkheim, has also called religion a delusion. This information has, however, been unavailable to readers of English because of the choices made in the two English translations of Durkheim's (1912) classic, *Les formes élémentaires de la vie religieuse*.

In that work, Durkheim states: "*En dehors de l'individu humain et du monde physique, il doit donc y avoir quelque autre réalité par rapport à laquelle cette espèce de délire qu'est bien, en un sens, toute religion, prend une signification et une valeur objective*" (p. 124). The important word is *délire*. But the two English translations of the work mask the stark meaning of this phrase by rendering *délire* as 'delirium.' Swain's translation is: "Aside from the human individual and the physical world, there should be some other reality, in relation to which this variety of delirium which all religion is in a sense has significance and an objective value" (Durkheim, 1915, p. 88). Field's translation is similar, maintaining 'delirium' for *délire*: "Beyond the human individual and the natural world, then, there must be some other reality in relation to which this species of delirium that every religion is, in some sense, takes on meaning and objective significance" (Durkheim, 1995, p. 85).

The translation of *délire* by delirium obscures an important statement of Durkheim's on religion, and conveys no intelligible meaning. The professional translator I consulted stated that translating French *délire* by English delirium is incorrect. The French *délire* has a more general application and connotations than the English 'delirium,' and refers to a departure from reality or reason, while the English 'delirium' usually refers to a disturbance or confusion of thought or consciousness due to a physical alteration, as from alcohol or fever. Thus it was agreed that the correct English rendition of *délire* in this context would be 'delusion,' which means that Durkheim here described religion as a departure from reality and/or reason.

The hypothesis that *délire* in this case should be translated 'delusion' (Lutzky, 1997, 1999) elicited several comments (Durkheimian Studies/Etudes Durkheimiennes, 1997, 1998, and 1999), mostly agreeing that 'delirium' was obviously incorrect, and claiming that 'delusion' was not necessarily the best replacement, but that 'hallucination' or 'illusion' were also possible. The last word was had by William Pickering (1999). He cited an article on the English translation of psychiatric terms used by Durkheim, which claimed that untold confusion had been caused by nineteenth century translations of *délire* by 'delirium.' It stated that although 'delirium' is one of the meanings of *délire*, referring to an organic brain syndrome, in the case of a problem of psychological function involving thought and emotion, the correct translation is 'delusion.'

The gist of Durkheim's general statement on religion is that there must be some *reality* (the subject of Durkheim's book) in relation to which religion, a *distortion of reality* (a delusion), takes on meaning and objective (in contrast to subjective) value. To Durkheim that underlying reality was society, while for Freud it was historical reality, reflecting both the phylogenetic and ontogenetic, or personal, past.

Significantly, both Freud and Durkheim felt the need to attenuate the blunt statement that religion is delusion, Durkheim saying 'a sort of delusion,' 'in a sense,' though insisting on it with *bien*, 'really', and Freud usually saying 'mass delusion.'

Freud formulated the relation of religion to the reality on which it is based in various ways. One is: "I believe that a large part of the mythological view of the world, which extends a long way into the most modern religions, *is nothing but psychology projected into the external world*" (1901, pp. 258-259). He set us the task of changing this "psycho-mythology" (Freud, 1897, p. 237) back into the psychology of the unconscious.

This task takes the form, for me, of interpreting specific religious concepts in terms of the psychological processes which I believe underlie (or are analogous to) them. These include the religious, mythical notions of immortality (Lutzky, 2008), deification of reproductive organs (Lutzky, 1998), Kabbalistic *tikkun* (Lutzky, 1989), the relation of deity and bonding (Lutzky, 1995) and the sacred (Lutzky, 1991, 1993, 2003). Religious constructs emerge as transformations or applications of psychological processes, or as analogous to them.

Mourning and Immortality

Many scholars have linked religion to the problem of mortality. The earliest evidence of religion is found in ritual burial which suggests that there were beliefs about an 'afterlife.' To the philosopher Ludwig Feuerbach, the tomb is the birthplace of the gods. Yet a question poses itself. Whose mortality is at issue, that of self or other, i.e., is the problem of mortality essentially existential or relational? From Freud's perspective, since one's own death is unimaginable, but the death of a stranger is not problematic, the true problem of death arises with the death of a loved one, in which the two positions are merged (Freud, 1915). To the philosopher Emmanuel Lévinas as well, the death of the other is a more primary issue than the death of the self; "to be or not to be" is "probably not the question *par excellence*" (Lévinas, 1986, p. 40). Thus from the perspective suggested here (Lutzky, 2008), the fundamental problem which death poses is not existential (the end of one's own existence), but relational (the loss of a loved one). In this case, death is an aspect of the problem of loss or separation, which occurs with the natural developmental process as well. The process of dealing with loss is mourning, which may take place both in ritual and in the intrapsychic world.

Whereas it would seem that ultimately the response to loss must be to accept the separation it involves, some psychoanalytic thinkers believe that separation is not truly possible on the psychological level. Freud said we can never really renounce anything, but rather seek substitutes for a lost object (Freud, 1908). D. W. Winnicott believed that psychologically, separation is an impossibility (Winnicott, 1971). For Winnicott, as the child develops from merger with the mother to the capacity to see the mother as a separate person, what emerges, rather than actual separation is "an infinite area of separation" or "a potential space" (Winnicott, 1971, p. 126). Potential space is a variant of Winnicott's (1951) concept of transitional experience, which includes the transitional object and phenomenon, and which is his most original and most significant contribution to psychoanalytic theory. Separation is replaced by transitional experience, an intermediate area between the sense of the other as being created by the self (subjective), and the sense of the other as existing in reality (objective). Thus, although transitional experience is a way-station on a (maturational) path leading from the former position (the other as part of self) to the latter one (the other as separate from self), paradoxically, the two relations to the object may also occur at the same time. The classical transitional object is experienced both as created by the self (and thus, since part of self, eternally present) and as given by reality (and thus, since other than self, potentially absent). For Winnicott, transitional experience is not limited to childhood, but exists throughout life as an intense experience and the core of creative living, and which is manifested in artistic and scientific creativity, in the imaginative life and in religion (thus considered a creative phenomenon) and, consequently, as the "location of cultural experience" (Winnicott, 1967, p. 121). Winnicott stated that potential space is "sacred" for the individual (1967, p. 121).

It is interesting to compare two models of mourning. One is the French anthropologist Robert Hertz's (1907) study of death symbolism, the other Freud's and others' psychoanalytic thought on mourning. First, both see the defining characteristic of mourning as the merger (symbolic or psychological) of the subject with the lost object, in which the absence and (felt) presence of the lost object are experienced at the same time. Second, both approaches consider the mourning process resolved as that merger is transformed. And third, the absence and (felt) presence of the object are ultimately experienced as existing on different levels, with the departed acquiring a new, permanent status, the bereaved possibly developing an enriched self, and hence a qualitatively different relation developing between the two.

Hertz, a member of the sociological school of Emile Durkheim, is considered the most important theoretician of death as a process of transition, the passage of the deceased from one status to another, from one world to another. Hertz based his analysis on the example of the ritual of 'double burial' found worldwide (an example is the Jewish ritual of the unveiling of the tombstone a year after the burial, considered a vestige of the rite). His model is significant for understanding interpretations of death as passage or transition even in the absence of the double burial ritual itself. Death as transition involves three parties, the corpse, the 'soul' of the deceased, and the mourners.

The corpse is afflicted with 'death pollution,' which arouses dread and leads to a ban or taboo on contact with it. The impurity (pollution) of the deceased is attributed to their transitional position, as they are suspended between two worlds, of the living and of the dead, existing in both statuses which are mixed within them. In the typical double burial ritual, there is first an initial, temporary, burial of the corpse. After death the soul too goes through a transitional period, existing on the margins of the two worlds, possibly threatening the bereaved in anger at its exclusion from the world of the living. The third term is the bereaved, required to participate in the death rites.

Hertz describes the entry into, transformation of, and exit from the bereaved's ritual status of mourning. The bereaved go through the same transition as do the body and soul of the deceased. The ban on contact with the deceased is extended to the bereaved, thus preventing the death pollution from spreading by contagion to others in the community. Segregated by the ban on them, the bereaved interrupt involvement in their everyday lives, and are bound to the deceased through the shared death impurity. Mary Douglas (1966) has described the function of ritual impurity as the establishment of boundaries. The ban binds deceased and bereaved and temporarily reestablishes the group of kin threatened with loss of its identity, while it protects the rest of the community from the threat posed by the death of a member. Thus the ban on the mourners, fusing their ritual status with that of the deceased, creates an obligatory participation of the mourners in the state of being of the departed one. According to Hertz, the ban placed on the ritual mourners is what constitutes "compulsory institutional mourning" and is its defining characteristic. Institutional mourning is "the direct consequence in the living of the actual state of the deceased" (Hertz, 1907, pp. 50-51), i.e., symbolic death. Paradoxically, the initial impact of loss through death is to intensify the relation of the living and the dead, rather than to separate them. The merged ritual statuses of deceased and mourner corresponds to transitional experience as described by Winnicott. For the mourner, the deceased is part of self and therefore present, at the same time that it is, in reality, separate from self and gone.

The socially determined transitional period of the ban effects changes in all three parties. The body disintegrates, leaving only the bones, the soul becomes pacified, and the bereaved ritual mourner sheds the polluted status and gradually prepares to take leave of the departed kin and return to everyday life, which may entail a change in social status. The relation between mourners and deceased may also be transformed.

At the end of the mourning period in the double burial ritual, the bones are disinterred and ritually purified, which alters the ritual status of the deceased, making them worthy to enter the company of their ancestors and to be reburied among them. Special rites are performed which also alter the ritual status of the soul. Then, because of the ritual action of the living, the soul may leave this world definitively and, as a 'shade,' enter the world of the afterlife to join the immortal community of ancestors. Thus in this model, ritual integrates the soul of the departed into the cosmos of the bereaved mourner. These rituals performed on the body and soul of the deceased also end the ritual mourning period, changing the status of the living, as the ban on them is lifted, and they take leave of their relative. The rite which frees the deceased to join the immortal society of ancestors parallels that which permits the bereaved kin to rejoin the society of the living, often to assume new and more mature transformed roles. To quote Hertz, the rite concluding the period of ritual mourning "is one and the same act of liberation applied to two different categories of persons" (Hertz, 1907, p. 64).

As the deceased and bereaved separate to join (or rejoin) their respective communities, a new, even obligatory relation may be established between them. The relation to the now immortal ancestor often becomes a permanent, even ritualized part of the life of the bereaved, including, for example, prayers, food offerings and anniversary celebrations.

How do the features of the ritual mourning process compare with psychoanalytic understanding of mourning? Whereas the former involves three parties, the latter involves the inner object world of the subject. Here as well, we can think in terms of entry into, transformation of, and exit from the state of mourning.

Freud noted two related initial features of entry into intrapsychic mourning. One is the withdrawal of interest from everyday life, which distances the mourner from his or her world. The other is an inward focus, an absorption in the internal world, appearing to center on the (internal) object and/or on the relation to it. These indicate that psychic work is going on, which he termed "the work of mourning" (Freud, 1917, p. 245).

Since Freud's early formulations, the essential feature of mourning is seen as an unconscious return to a lower level of subject-object differentiation, which is carried out in the service of the ego without sacrificing reality testing, usually conceptualized as 'identification,' a process in which the subject takes on qualities of the lost object, transforming itself to resemble the object. Identification is considered one of the processes which initially constituted the subject, and later, as a regressive response to loss, reconstitutes the subject. This regressive identification, confounding self and other but yet acknowledging the reality (the loss) of the other, bears significant similarity to transitional experience and processes.

Early on, Freud believed that mourning was governed by reality testing (Freud, 1926, p. 172) and that the work of mourning would come to an end when the subject gave up its "attachment to the object which has been abolished" (Freud, 1917, p. 255). At this time, Freud saw the process of identification (in which "the shadow of the object fell upon the ego" (Freud, 1917, p. 249) as occurring only in melancholia, a pathological form of mourning (Freud, 1917). Karl Abraham (1927), in contrast, suggested that temporary identification played a consoling role in mourning as well as in melancholia, with the distinction that the normal mourner never loses consciousness of the reality of the loss. Freud himself later saw regressive identification as the essential means for dealing with object loss, i.e., "If one has lost a love-object, the most obvious reaction is to identify oneself with it, to replace it from within, as it were, by identification" (Freud, 1940, p. 193).

The subject and its relation to the lost object are gradually transformed. Freud, Abraham, and Fenichel ultimately came to think that introjection of and identification with the lost object, though being the conditions for renunciation of the object, were nonetheless temporary. In this view, "[m]ourning consists of two acts, the first being the establishment of an introjection, the second the loosening of the binding to the introjected object" (Fenichel, 1945, p. 394). Recently, the work of mourning has been thought to continue until the lost object, with whom the subject has become identified, is integrated into the subject's psychic structure.

According to Roy Schafer, Freud had "implied a relation between identification and the object's psychic immortality" (1968, pp. 226-227). For Schafer, "the transitional work of mourning" (1968, p. 117) transforms the original, introjected object into an identification. From then on, the object is preserved by being integrated into the mourner's "subjective self and systemic organization" (1968, p. 235). This then permits exiting of the mourning period.

The comparison of ritual and psychoanalytic models of mourning reveals the defining characteristic of mourning to be an initial intensification of the relation between deceased and bereaved. On the ritual level, the ban on the kin (the sine qua non of ritual mourning, and its defining characteristic) separates them from their community, creating a temporary, mandatory intensification of involvement with the deceased—an identification with each other through merger of their ritual statuses, as both are suspended between life and death. On the intrapsychic level, the bereaved at first withdraw from the world and focus on the lost object, which intensifies the bond through subjective merger of identities (or of internal representations of self and other), conceptualized as (regressive) identification. Unconscious identification with the lost object is generally held to be the defining characteristic of the intrapsychic mourning process. The merger of the symbolic ritual statuses of bereaved and deceased, on the one hand, and of the unconscious intrapsychic representations of subject and object, on the other, accompanied by the bereaved's acknowledgement of the other's absence in reality, describe a transitional phenomenon.

The mourning process is exited or ended when the deceased has become integrated into the bereaved's universe (cosmos or psyche), and the bereaved has changed to accommodate the new reality. In ritual death symbolism there is both recognition of the permanent absence of the deceased from the everyday life of community and belief in the permanent presence of the deceased on another level of experience, in the afterworld. In psychoanalytic thought, at the close of the mourning period the lost object may be felt to be permanently absent from everyday life and yet be permanently present in a new way within the psychic system of the subject. At the end of the mourning period, on both ritual and intrapsychic levels, the lost object has achieved immortality.

On the ritual level, when the bereaved are freed from mourning they reenter, possibly with altered, more mature social roles, a changed community. On the intrapsychic level, integration of the object into the subject's inner world and psychic structure may affect change. Thus, on both ritual and intrapsychic levels, the regressive passage through transitional self-object dedifferentiation (or to a lower level of differentiation) may result in a transformed and potentially enriched self. The new status of both the deceased and bereaved dictates a transformed relation between them. On the ritual level, there may be a permanent, ritualized relation between the two. On the intrapsychic level, the lost object may function as inspiration or comfort, and/or aspects of his or her personality may become part of the one left behind.

In conclusion, whereas thinking about the relation between religion and mortality usually centers on existential issues (i.e., the death of the self) here it has centered on the relational issues involved in feelings about the death of the other. Mourning exists in the context of the psychological impossibility of separation and of the transitional process (the betwixt and between of bereaved and deceased, of subject and object) which takes its place. The transitional work of mourning transforms the culturally constructed soul of the deceased and the psychologically constructed internal object, thereby establishing the immortal status of the departed one. It may also create the religious category of immortality.

The characteristics of transitional phenomena resemble some religious features (or are congruent with religious categories). D. W. Winnicott sees transitional experience (potential space) as the locus of creativity and culture, including religion, and as being sacred. It is the combined features of the transitional nature of the mourning response to the problem of death, on the one hand, and the sacredness of the transitional domain, on the other, which underlie the relation between religion and the problem of mortality. The work of mourning on a psychological level transforms the 'shadow' of the object in the internal object world of the bereaved, as ritual action transforms the soul of the deceased into a 'shade' in the afterworld. Thus the mourning process, intrapsychically and ritually, transforms the 'shadow' and creates the 'shade,' the immortal twin heirs of the departed one.

Ritual Purity and Impurity

In studying the concepts of ritual purity and impurity it is interesting to ask whether the processes, dynamics and structures underlying them can be compared or identified with intrapsychic processes (Lutzky, 1994).

The concepts of ritual purity and impurity (the latter also known as pollution, contamination, or defilement) appear to be virtually universal, with purity rules and purification rites probably found in all cultures. Although to a modern Western mind it might seem that they refer either to physical or ethical states of being, anthropologists understand the concepts to be symbolic, referring to ritual status. The dimension of purity-impurity determines one's fitness to enter into communication with the pure sacred, embodied, for example, in gods, ancestors, spirits or totem, and it affects the right to approach their dwelling places, for example, altar, shrine or temple. A state of pollution or impurity cuts one off from relation with the pure sacred. A higher than ordinary level of purity is required of those in close contact with the pure sacred, for example, priests, divine kings or chiefs. Pollution and purification are inseparable categories, two sides of the same coin. But while most cultures clearly specify conditions and acts which are polluting, purity itself is not well defined. It is essentially a state of being which is free of impurity. Latin *purus*, means 'without blemish' or 'unmixed.'

Perhaps the most significant quality of pollution is its contagion. It spreads from one person to another like an infection, transmitted by direct contact or simply by proximity. Contact with a polluted person is itself polluting, although usually to a lesser degree. The essential aim of pollution rules is to prohibit physical contact (Douglas, 1968, p. 340). The community maintains its distance from those who are polluted for fear of defilement, and a polluted person keeps distance both from the community and from the pure sacred places and objects, for fear of defiling them. This distance is maintained until the polluted person has undergone ritual purification. There may even be relational pollution, so that regardless of physical contact, pollution spreads through the kin group in cases of birth or death impurity; the more closely related, the more polluted one becomes. Pollution can also be transmitted symbolically, so that an individual's polluting act can, without contact and from a distance, render the sanctuary impure. Contagion renders pollution extremely dangerous, because by logical extension, if all members of a community have been rendered impure, its relation to the pure, sacred realm may be completely disrupted (e.g., there would be no one to carry out sacrifice or other cultic activity required by the deity.)

Ritual pollution falls into many categories. The first includes acts which might be considered crimes against the society, such as murder and incest (and in Judaism, idolatry). A second includes physical states which may even be involuntary and necessary, such as death, birth and menstruation (which cross-culturally, tends to be one of the most highly polluting conditions). A third affects the sanctuary and its appurtenances. And a fourth involves social hierarchy and gender hierarchy: certain classes or castes (untouchables) being impure by definition, and the female sex being impure either by definition, or during specific times of the reproductive cycle.

To maintain the necessary level of purity there are first, rules for avoiding pollution, i.e., abstention, separation and seclusion, whose aim is to minimize contacts with polluting persons, objects, or places (this is seen in the use of menstrual huts, in the isolation of cultic personnel, and in the use of the veil). Then, when pollution does occur, purification rituals are carried out to remove it. And purification is required before contact with the pure sacred, and often before an important activity, such as war, to ensure a correct relationship with the powers involved, and guarantee success.

Sociologists and anthropologists study pollution from the point of view of its social implications. Psychologists, philosophers and theologians analyze the content of a pollution category (e.g., menstruation), to understand its universality. For example, psychoanalysis often interprets pollution beliefs as projections or symbolizations of repressed instincts or anxieties.

In her classical anthropological study of concepts of purity, pollution and taboo, Mary Douglas (1966) set forward a comprehensive theory of the widespread phenomenon of rules of pollution avoidance and purification. The gist of her argument is captured by the Greek term for pollution, *miasma*, whose root meaning is impairment of the form or integrity of something.

In order to understand pollution, Douglas used the evocative metaphor of dirt, which she defined as 'matter out of place.' She felt that the existence of dirt implies first, that there is order, and second, a disturbance of that order. "Where there is dirt there is system. Dirt is the by-product of a systematic ordering and classification of matter, in so far as ordering involves rejecting inappropriate elements. This idea of dirt takes us straight into the field of symbolism and promises a link-up with more obviously symbolic systems of purity" (Douglas, 1966, p. 35). Douglas believed that the way people react to dirt is consistent with the way they react to ambiguity or anomaly, that is, to anything that obscures order. These are anxiety-provoking, and stimulate the tendency to avoidance.

She felt that ritual pollution plays a role "in reference to a total structure of thought whose key-stone, boundaries, margins and internal lines are held in relation by rituals of separation" (Douglas, 1966, p. 41). "Not only marginal social states, but all margins, the edges of all boundaries which are used in ordering the social experience, are treated as dangerous and polluting" (Douglas, 1968, p. 340). Transitional states are dangerous, because they are neither one thing nor another, but are undefinable. What the pollution powers punish is the symbolic breaking apart of whatever should be joined together, or the joining together of things that should be kept separate. Douglas suggested that we find pollution dangers mainly in social structures in which there is clear definition of the cosmic or social structural lines, and where there is a felt need to maintain them. "A polluting person is always in the wrong. He has developed some wrong condition or simply crossed some line which should not have been crossed and this displacement unleashes danger for someone" (Douglas, 1966, p. 113).

Douglas asked how pollution beliefs relate to the sacred realm itself. She took to task those earlier anthropologists who proposed that pure and impure were two varieties of the sacred. She considered that holiness means completeness, not confusing the different classes of things, but keeping distinct the categories of creation. Pollution laws, including food laws such as *kashrut*, forbidding the mixing of categories or the acceptance of anomaly or marginality, all function to preserve the sacred order of the universe. Identifying the sacred with the social order, and then further defining pollution as anything which threatens that order, Douglas's theory necessarily rejects the subsuming of both ritual purity and ritual impurity within the category of the sacred. In response to critiques, however, she has modified her theory in the direction of earlier anthropology.

The argument for the existence of a fundamental ambiguity in the sacred, which includes both pure and impure, was strongly put forward by Emile Durkheim, and was followed by Mircea Eliade and others. Durkheim described religious forces as being of two kinds: benevolent ones, which guard the physical and moral order, and give life and health; and malevolent, impure powers, which create disorder, death and sickness, and provoke sacrilege. Contact between them is forbidden, and highly defiling. However, although pure and impure are contrasted and distanced from each other, there is at the same time a close kinship between them. They are not two separate classes, but rather two types of the same class. What the pure and impure have in common are: 1) they have the same relation to the profane or common, to which they are forbidden and untouchable; 2) they are both contagious. The sacred, like the impure, is infectious; a common thing which comes into contact with the sacred becomes 'sanctified,' and therefore can be no longer used for common purposes. Usually this sanctity can be purified simply, by washing, but sometimes it is indelible, and the object has to be destroyed; 3) transformation from one to the other is possible: the impure can change into pure (e.g., soul of a dead man is polluting up to a certain point, then becomes sacred, his bones may become relics; a pure, purifying agent can itself become impure). There are thus inequalities and incompatibilities between sacred things, which do not however affect the essential sacredness.

Issues of purity-impurity and purification-pollution (though known by other names) may play a role in the construction and maintenance of system, order, and boundary in the individual psyche, just as they do in the social system. Conversely, these processes also create categories of anomaly, ambiguity, and marginality. Two psychoanalytic concepts more or less explicitly involve the issues of pollution or purification, and permit us to get a sense of the extent to which these religious concepts may have things in common with psychological functions, content, and mechanisms. The two concepts are the purified pleasure ego and the transitional object.

One psychoanalytic use of the concept of purification refers to an early stage in the construction of ego boundaries. The failure of the primitive attempt to be rid of painful stimuli by simply hallucinating them away leads to a reorganization of the ego. In the stage that Freud has called the purified pleasure ego, all that is pleasurable is held to be ego, and all that is unpleasurable or painful to be non-ego. This is realized by introjection of aspects of the external world which are sources of pleasure, and projection outwards of whatever is a cause of unpleasure within. Here then, "What is bad, what is alien to the ego and what is external are, to begin with, identical" (Freud, 1925, p. 237). This purification process modifies ego boundaries and contents.

The purified pleasure ego is a model of an intrapsychic structure which resembles the social structure created and maintained on the basis of purity-impurity ideology. This immature ego structure is created by exclusion, through projection, of that which does not conform to its organizing principle (which in this case is pleasure). Anything which is unpleasure then becomes an anomaly. Further, the use of projection as it is found in phobia, which subsequently permits avoidance behavior or flight, suggests the extreme avoidance of whatever has been excluded from the system as incompatible with it.

Winnicott's concept of transitional phenomena may be an example of a psychoanalytic concept which bears similarities to the religious category of pollution. The transitional object or phenomenon represents a type of experience which Winnicott considered to be a form of illusion, the aim of which is to provide comfort during the difficult process of achieving separation from the maternal matrix. At first, the object world is experienced subjectively, and felt to be omnipotently created by the subject. This immature level of experience slowly yields its place to the growing capacity to relate to the object in terms of the object's own, objective qualities, acknowledging that the object exists in reality, independent of the needs and feeling of the infant. The classical transitional object is experienced as both created by the self and given in reality. Transitional experience is a way-station on a path leading from the sense that the object is created by the self to the realization that the object is real and separate. Transitional objects and experiences manifest the ambiguity and mixing of categories observed in pollution studies. The transitional object is a privileged one, inviolable, not to be treated as any common object, and may not be altered by the unauthorized, even if it is soiled, or it will lose its emotional power.

Winnicott tells us that the capacity for transitional experience remains after the disinvestment in the transitional object itself, and is diffused throughout experience as a resting place from the stress of reality testing, becoming the basis for cultural, and particularly religious experience. The transitional object, characterized as it is by ambiguity, has some of the qualities of sacredness (inviolability), although it is also close to pollution (i.e., the mixing of categories).

While Douglas felt it was incorrect to confuse sacredness with uncleanness, she did acknowledge that "religions often sacralise the very unclean things which have been rejected with abhorrence." She asked how dirt, "which is normally destructive, sometimes becomes creative" (Douglas, 1966, p. 159).

Douglas noted that formlessness is an apt symbol of beginning and of growth as it is of decay (Douglas, 1966, p. 161). The concept of transitional experience resembles the concept of the pollution of ambiguous states. Generally seen as underlying creativity and culture, it is an example of the creative function of ambiguity (or pollution).

Mechanisms of exclusion and avoidance of that which is incompatible with or confounds a given structure, and ambiguous states of being, both of which are found in society in the symbolic system of purity-impurity, have intrapsychic counterparts. Psychic structures and processes, including the early formation of the purified pleasure ego which creates 'unpleasure' as incompatible with the system, and of transitional experience, which confounds two modes of relating to the world, are examples of the creation of purity or of impurity in psychic functioning. We are reminded by Douglas and others, that pollution (i.e., the mixing of categories, the marginal, the anomalous), can be creative, and that if a system, whether social or psychological, risks being shattered by the integration of pollution, it may also find itself to be renewed and strengthened in that way.

Reparation and Tikkun

Freud saw the Greek myth of Oedipus as a cultural representation of the essential unconscious conflict in neurosis, and named the psychic complex for the myth, the Oedipus Complex. It was not only Greek culture that was capable of giving expression to unconscious Oedipal psychodynamics, since in Freud's view the same issue was expressed in other major works of Western literature, such as Shakespeare's Hamlet. Has Jewish culture also given artistic expression to unconscious psychodynamics? Let us explore the notion that Melanie Klein's concept of 'reparation' is analogous to the mythical Kabbalistic concept of *tikkun*, also meaning 'reparation' (Lutzky, 1989).

The traditional Freudian analysis of religion (as of the psyche) deals with the dynamics of a relatively constructed (Oedipal) subject, working out solutions to conflicts within the triangular structure of the family, centering on the father. The issues are then projected onto a cosmic screen. Freud's theory focuses on the concept of God, which he saw as the illusory fulfillment of a childhood wish for the continued protection of a paternal authority figure. Object relations theory, in contrast, analyzes the dynamics of the earlier initial construction of the subject within the dyadic relation to the mother. It emphasizes the evolution of relatedness, that is, of attachment and detachment (between subject and object) and of splitting and integration (within both subject and object), mainly analyzing the relationship between subject and object as it has been internalized by the subject. This approach should permit analysis of certain issues in religion, namely, those of structure and fragmentation, which are perhaps less readily accessible to the classical Freudian approach. Two main issues arise. How do aspects of the early dyadic relation to the mother (rather than those of the triadic relation including the father) motivate or influence a cultural and religious issue? Is the very process of the construction of ego/self and internal object world at all representable in cultural and religious phenomena?

Her highly original concept of reparation is considered Klein's most important contribution to psychoanalytic theory. Reparation involves fantasies of repairing the internal object which has been damaged by fantasized aggression, and therefore helps in surmounting the anxiety and guilt of the depressive position. It creates the sense of security which depends on the sense that the internal object is whole and perfect. The Kabbalistic myth of *tikkun* (which has been translated into English as restoration, restitution or reparation) is a myth of the cosmos fragmenting during creation. It is humanity's task to return the cosmos to wholeness and perfection.

The Kabbalistic myth of *tikkun* and the Kleinian concept of reparation are both metaphors of creation, fragmentation and re-creation, of the mystical cosmos on the one hand, and of the internal object world on the other. Kabbalistic tikkun may express on the mythical, religious level, the psychodynamics that the Kleinian concept of reparation identifies on the level of the individual psyche.

The myth of *tikkun* has existed in Jewish mystical thought since the second century CE. The version of *tikkun* discussed here (Scholem, 1941) is the work of the 16th century Kabbalist Isaac Luria. This myth, created not long after the expulsion of the Jews from Spain, expressed and gave meaning to the experience of exile and the fragmentation of existence. The people's longing to end the exile was understood to be the expression of the desire for *tikkun*: re-creating the original harmony and overcoming the separation from God. In the Lurianic myth three cosmic events are described: *tsimtsum* (God's self-limitation); *shevirat ha-kelim* (the breaking of the vessels); and *tikkun* (reparation of the defect in existence caused by the breaking of the vessels). About *tsimtsum*, Luria claimed that before God could create the world from nothing, he first had to create nothing. God created that 'nothing' through *tsimtsum*, contraction, in which he contracted himself into a smaller space. Creation could then be 'emanated' or projected into that space. God then created vessels to catch and hold the light emanating from the eyes of the first created being, because this light was in 'points' (chaos) and not in beams (structure), i.e., in disorganized, fragmented form. But the light streaming from the eyes was too powerful, and the vessels shattered under the force of the impact. The forces of chaos caused the breaking of the vessels, and scattered holy sparks of light throughout creation. They remain there, locked in the broken shards of the vessels (the shells of evil), until humanity frees them. In Lurianic interpretation, the breaking caused the 'exile of the Shekhinah,' which is the feminine, maternal aspect of God, an integral part of God and yet separate from him. The breaking of the vessels is the first defect in existence although it is also intrinsic to it. It is the deepest meaning of the experience of exile (Scholem, 1941). Existence has remained ever since in a state of being broken and scattered. The catastrophe which is the breaking of the vessels thus transformed the process of creation into one of re-creation, the recreation of all of existence. *Tikkun* signifies the freeing and raising up of the imprisoned sparks to their rightful level, repairing the broken vessels, unifying God through the return of the Shekhinah, and unifying man's soul as well.

As Scholem says (1941, p. 286) "Through the *Tikkun* [man] breaks the exile, the historical exile . . . and that inner exile in which all creation groans."

Kleinian theory furnishes many parallels to this myth. For Klein, the existence of the death instinct, and the annihilation anxiety and fear of disintegration which it provokes, is the first problem for the infantile psyche. The death instinct is partly deflected by being projected onto the first object, the breast, which then becomes a persecutory object. The death instinct is also partly transformed into aggression, which is then directed against the 'bad' breast. As further protection against the 'bad' persecutory object, libido is projected into the 'good' breast, and love directed toward it. These part-objects are then internalized, the better to control them. The resulting intrapsychic situation is the paranoid-schizoid position, where the object is split into 'good' and 'bad' objects, and the major anxiety is the persecutory fear of being destroyed.

With development and maturation, the split objects become integrated into one whole maternal object, experienced ambivalently, as having both 'good' and 'bad,' both loving and persecutory, features. This is a move toward greater reality testing, since now the object is experienced objectively, that is, in terms of its own qualities (whole), rather than subjectively, in terms of the feelings of the subject (split). Here the danger for the infantile psyche is not that of being destroyed, but of destroying, for if aggression is turned against the 'bad' features of the whole object, the 'good' aspect of it will be destroyed as well. Then the infantile ego feels alone and abandoned, without the vitally necessary presence of the maternal object. This intrapsychic situation Klein called the depressive position, where the major anxiety is depressive anxiety, fear of the destruction of the object, rather than of the self.

Thus existence of the internalized whole maternal object is not permanently assured. There is always danger that in anger there will be fantasized destruction of the maternal object, smashing it to fragments, and thus losing it. In that case, because of the genuine love and caring for the mother which also exists, reparative attempts take place, to restore, reconstruct, and recreate the internal (and external) maternal object. Reparation is not a defense mechanism, but a mechanism of adaptation, because it takes into account, and does not distort, reality.

The myth of *tikkun* is a metaphor of creation, fragmentation, and re-creation which expresses the same dynamics as those that underlie the Kleinian concepts of the depressive position and reparation.

Creation Both the cosmos and the object world (and simultaneously psychic structure) begin with an inner transformation, which initially structures limitation. In the Kabbalah this occurs within God, who contracts himself, while in Kleinian theory it is the power of the death instinct which is limited by its transformation into aggression. In both cases there is then projection outward (emanation in the Kabbalah, deflection in Kleinian theory) resulting in creation of the cosmos in the one case, and of the 'bad' persecutory part object in the other. This projection handles and relieves God, or the infantile psyche, of some part of its evil/aggression, and structure is achieved. In the Kabbalah, the vessels were meant to contain and overcome chaos, just as the whole internal maternal object overcomes earlier splitting in Kleinian theory.

Fragmentation But structure is not stable, and in both cases (cosmos and the internal object world) there is fragmentation and loss. In Klein's description of the infantile psyche, aggression is fantasized to be so powerful that it smashes the object to bits (Klein, 1935). In the Kabbalah the light from the first being created was so powerful that the vessels could not contain it, and it shattered them.

It is also interesting that the Kabbalistic concept of evil and the Kleinian concepts of death instinct and aggression are analogous. Here evil refers to the forces of disintegration and chaos which are part of the human condition, and the fear and pain they cause. Of all such forces, death is the most terrifying, since it threatens human relations and reveals the fragility of human life (Berger, 1967). The question of evil is at the heart of the Kabbalah (Bloom, 1975), which aimed to overcome its power (Scholem, 1960). Klein gave central importance to the death instinct (a concept received from Freud), along with the annihilation anxiety and fear of disintegration which it stimulates. Aggression also threatens disintegration, though in this case it is the disintegration of the object rather than of the self.

In the Kabbalah the result of fragmentation is loss of part of God, the Shekhinah, who goes into exile. This theme, which is related to the subject of separation and loss, is central to the Kabbalistic myth of *tikkun*. The question of loss corresponds to the Kleinian depressive position, in which fragmentation results in the loss of the loved one, both internalized and real (Klein, 1935).

The way in which the reaction to loss is expressed in the Kabbalah is in terms of longing for the return of the exiled Shekhinah. In Kleinian theory it is expressed as longing for the loved one's return—and in both cases, longing for the return of wholeness. This longing motivates the desire for *tikkun* as it does for reparation.

Both systems see a relationship between evil/aggression and the experience of fragmentation and loss. Although Klein theorized about the impersonal death instinct, it is nonetheless personal aggression which damages the object. Guilt, motivated by genuine love and concern, is an appropriate response. In contrast, in the Kabbalah mankind is responsible, not for the original chaos, but for perpetuating the states of fragmentation and exile.

Re-creation In the Kabbalah, humanity is given the task of *tikkun,* the repair of the fragmented, lost world. In psychological development, reparation is the task for the individual. *Tikkun* vanquishes the forces of evil, and reparation overcomes the effects of aggression in the internal object world. The broken vessels are restored in *tikkun*, and in reparation the object, damaged and smashed in fantasy by aggression, is put back together. *Tikkun* affects the return of the Shekhinah, while reparation brings back the lost and harmed maternal object. *Tikkun* opens the path of communion between God, now unified, and the human soul renewed, while reparation makes possible a renewed relationship between the mother and the now-integrated self. *Tikkun* ends the exile of humanity, while reparation strengthens the inner sense of home. While *tikkun* heralds the Messianic age, reparation actualizes the sense of security and wellbeing.

In the Kabbalistic myth of *tikkun* we see played out the same archaic anxieties and processes which Klein described in her concepts of the depressive position and reparation. The forces described in each deal with fragmentation and loss by creating and re-creating the internal object world as well as the mystical cosmos.

I think it is possible to say that in the same way that Greek myth expressed (or is analogous to) the unconscious dynamics of the Oedipus Complex, the Kabbalistic myth of *tikkun*, with its concepts of fragmentation and recreation of the world, expresses (or is analogous to) the unconscious psychodynamics of reparation. The experience of fragmentation underlying reparation (the breaking of the vessels, or mother symbol) is extremely difficult to bring to consciousness because it ultimately involves the issue of the integrity of the subject itself. Klein herself made a connection between the concept of reparation and religion. She (a militant atheist) said that in Heaven there will be no hate, envy or jealousy, but there will be reparation, only love within the reunited family (Grosskurth, 1986, p. 455). D.W. Winnicott (1962) astutely singled out Klein's concept of the depressive position, including reparation, as a contribution whose importance ranks with Freud's concept of the Oedipus complex.

Grünbaum acknowledged that he made the choice to identify religion with theism, belief in God, which permitted him to evaluate Freud's major psychological and philosophical contributions to a theory of religion, by using his tools as a philosopher and powerful thinker. At the same time, he recognized that other subjects can be included in the concept of religion. The work described here takes as a model Freud's early paper, "Obsessive Actions and Religious Practices" (1907). There he develops a comparison between a religious and a psychoanalytic category, ritual and obsessive (or rather in today's vocabulary, compulsive) behavior, concluding that they are analogous, though suggesting that they are in fact the same process in two different contexts.

I believe that the interpretations offered here demonstrate that it is possible to understand some religious phenomena, taken in isolation, as reflecting, analogous to, or perhaps even the result of psychological issues, structures, and processes. The idea of immortality, on both the religious and intrapsychic levels, may be the result of mourning as a transitional process. Ritual purity and impurity may be analogous to psychological boundary issues involving expulsion or fusion. A millennial mystical concept such as *tikkun* can closely resemble an original psychoanalytic notion such as reparation. The close study of religious concepts, structures and processes often reveals their deep interpenetration with psychological constructs.

References

Abraham, K. (1927). *Selected Papers of Karl Abraham, MD*. D. Bryan & A. Strachey. (Trans.). London: Maresfield Library, 1988.

Berger, P.L. (1967). *The Sacred Canopy*. New York: Anchor Books.

Bloom, H. (1975). *Kabbalah and Criticism*. New York: The Seabury Press.

Douglas, M. (1966). *Purity and Danger: An Analysis of the Concepts of Pollution and Taboo.* London: Ark, 1984.

Douglas, M. (1968). Pollution. In *International Encyclopedia of the Social Sciences*. New York: Free Press, Macmillan.

Durkheim, E. (1912). *Les formes élémentaires de la vie religieuse.* Paris: PUF, 1960/1990. 2nd edition.

Durkheim, E. (1915). *The Elementary Forms of the Religious Life.* J. W. Swain (Trans.). London: George Allen & Unwin, 2nd edition, 1976/1982.

Durkheim, E. (1995). *The Elementary Forms of Religious Life.* K. E. Fields (Trans.). New York: The Free Press.

Fenichel, O. (1945). *The Psychoanalytic Theory of Neurosis.* New York: Norton.

Freud, S. (1897). *The Origins of Psychoanalysis: Letters to Wilhelm Fliess, Drafts and Notes: 1887-1902.* Marie Bonaparte, Anna Freud, and Ernst Kris (Eds.). New York: Basic Books, 1954.

Freud, S. (1901). The Psychopathology of Everyday Life. *The Standard Edition of the Complete Psychological Works of Sigmund Freud, 6*, vii-296. London: Hogarth Press.

Freud, S. (1907). Obsessive actions and religious practices. *The Standard Edition of the Complete Psychological Works of Sigmund Freud, 9*, 15-28. London: Hogarth Press.

Freud, S. (1908). Creative writers and day-dreaming. *The Standard Edition of the Complete Psychological Works of Sigmund Freud, 9*, 141-154. London: Hogarth Press.

Freud, S. (1915). Thoughts for the times on war and death. *The Standard Edition of the Complete Psychological Works of Sigmund Freud, 14,* 273-300. London: Hogarth Press.

Freud, S. (1917). Mourning and melancholia. *The Standard Edition of the Complete Psychological Works of Sigmund Freud, 14*, 237-258. London: Hogarth Press.

Freud, S. (1925). Negation. *The Standard Edition of the Complete Psychological Works of Sigmund Freud, 19*, 233-240. London: Hogarth Press.

Freud, S. (1940/1938). An Outline of Psycho-Analysis. *The Standard Edition of the Complete Psychological Works of Sigmund Freud, 23*, 139-208, London: Hogarth Press.

Grosskurth, P. (1986). *Melanie Klein.* London: Hodder & Stoughton

Hertz, R. (1907/1960). A contribution to the study of the collective representation of death. In *Death and the Right Hand.* R. and C. Needham (Trans.). Glencoe, IL: The Free Press.

Klein, M. (1935). A contribution to the psychogenesis of manic-depressive states. In *Contributions to Psycho-Analysis.* London: Hogarth Press, 1950.

Lévinas, E. (1986). Bad conscience and the inexorable. In R. A. Cohen (Ed.). *Face to Face with Lévinas.* Albany, NY: SUNY Press.

Lutzky, H. (1989). Reparation and tikkun: A comparison of the Kleinian and Kabbalistic concepts. *International Review of Psycho-Analysis, 16*, 449-58.

Lutzky, H. (1991). The sacred and the maternal object: An application of Fairbairn's theory to religion. In *Psychoanalytic Reflections on Current Issues.* H. Siegel et al. (Eds.), 25-44. New York: New York University Press.

Lutzky, H. (1993). On a concept underlying Indo-European terms for the sacred. *Journal of Indo-European Studies, 21,* #3/4, 283-301.

Lutzky, H. (1995). Deity and the social bond: Robertson Smith and the psychoanalytic theory of religion. In *William Robertson Smith: Essays in Reassessment.* William Johnstone (Ed.). Sheffield: Sheffield Academic Press, 320-30.

Lutzky, H. (1997). *Délire*: Delirium or delusion? *Durkheimian Studies/Etudes Durk-*

heimiennes, New Series *3,* 15-16.
Lutzky, H. (1998). Shadday as a goddess epithet. *Vetus Testamentum*, *48,* 15-36.
Lutzky, H. (1999). Translating Durkheim: An afterword on the translation of *délire*, *Durkheimian Studies/Etudes Durkheimiennes*, New Series *5,* 61-62.
Lutzky, H. (2003). Desire as a constitutive element of the sacred. *Archive for the Psychology of Religion/Archiv für Religionspsychologie, 25*, 62-70.
Lutzky, H. (2008). Mourning and immortality: Ritual and psychoanalysis compared. In *Mourning Religion: Modernity, Meaning, Psychoanalysis*. W. B. Parsons, D. Jonte-Pace and S. E. Henking (Eds.). Charlottesville, VA: University of Virginia Press, 141-157.
Pickering, W. S. F. (1999) Postscript on the translation of *délire. Durkheimian Studies/ Etudes Durkheimiennes.* New Series *5.*
Schafer, R. (1968). *Aspects of Internalization*. Madison, CT: International Universities Press, 1990.
Scholem, G. (1941). *Major Trends in Jewish Mysticism*. New York: Schocken.
Scholem, G. (1960). On *the Kabbalah and Its Symbolism*. New York: Schocken.
Winnicott, D. W. (1951). Transitional objects and transitional phenomena. In *Playing and Reality*. Harmondsworth, England: Pelican, 1974.
Winnicott, D. W. (1971). The place where we live. In *Playing and Reality*. Harmondsworth, England: Pelican, 1974.
Winnicott, D. W. (1967). The location of cultural experience. In *Playing and Reality*. Harmondsworth, England: Pelican, 1974.

Chapter 7
Another Epistemic Evaluation of Freud's Oedipal Theory of Religion

Ralph W. Hood, Jr.

Grünbaum (1984, 1993) has been widely recognized for documenting the limited empirical support for classical Freudian theory in terms of both findings and methods. A cornerstone of Grünbaum's critique is his assertion that Freud never abandoned his commitment to psychoanalysis as a *natural science* (Grünbaum, 1984, 1987), and thus, Freud's methods and findings should be judged as *natural science* claims. At the same time, Grünbaum rejects the idea that the value of Freudian theory is in the creation of a new hermeneutical method applicable to psychology as a distinct human science, as proposed by Ricouer (1970) and Habermas (1971). In the lead chapter for this volume, Grünbaum focuses upon the epistemic warrant for Freud's theory of religion. In simple terms, does the evidence warrant the acceptance of Freud's explanation of religion as a delusion (and hence false) rather than simply an illusion (focused only upon psychological motivations for holding religious beliefs)?

In this chapter I will focus upon four areas in which I have substantial agreement with Grünbaum but with caveats that moderate the harshness of his basic conclusions. The areas in which the harshness are moderated are (1) Freud's assumed commitment to natural science methodologies and metaphysics; (2) the analysis of the psychological *motivations* for religious beliefs as opposed to the epistemological warrant for the *content* of religious beliefs which came to be viewed by Freud as delusions; (3) empirical research focused upon the Catholic doctrine of the Virgin Birth; a subject that Grünbaum notes is surprisingly ignored by believing Catholic commentators on Freud's theory of religion (e.g., Küng, 1979; Meissner, 1984); and finally, (4) the application of classical Freudian theory to understanding the serpent handlers of the southeastern United States. While this is not addressed by Grünbaum it is relevant to his concern with Freud's phylogenetic theory, completed in *Moses and monotheism* which makes only one reference to serpents (Freud, 1939, p. 36). In choosing these four areas in which to dialogue with Grünbaum the subtext is always an assessment of the value of classical Freudian theory for the contemporary psychology of religion. My position is that it remains considerable.

Ought the Psychology of Religion be a Natural Science?

It is difficult to date when psychology emerged as a discipline. If Robinson (1995) would argue that the conceptual options for psychology are rooted in a distant past, many others would argue that psychology began when it identified with natural science assumptions associated with Wundt and his experimental laboratory founded toward the end of the nineteenth century in Leipzig, Germany. As Robinson (1995, p. 281) notes, "the essential attitude of the experimental psychologist today may be said to have originated in the Leipzig laboratory." However, Robinson also reminds us that Wundt's interest in folk psychology, or precisely the kind of cultural and historical anthropology that Grünbaum cites as the weakest of the two distinctively psychoanalytic arguments of Freud's critique of religion (the phylogenetic or ethno-psychological argument) was obviously not only inimical to experimental methods but, more crucially, was "not explicable in the language of natural science" (Robinson, 1995, p. 280).

Since its inception psychology has never been able to agree upon natural science assumptions as sufficient warrant for its knowledge claims. Robinson (1995) reminds us that psychology was seduced by a metaphor it took as defining natural science—a mechanistic approach that treated the proper object of psychology as simply matter's quantified motion. In a word, psychology became materialistic. It is well noted that Freud's effort in his *Project for a scientific psychology* intended to provide a model of psychology as a natural science meaning "to represent psychical processes as quantitatively determinate states of specifiable material particles" (Freud, 1895/1950, p. 295). This admittedly premature, unfinished, and unpublished (in Freud's lifetime) work was written in a few weeks and played no part in Freud's mature if ever changing theory of psychoanalysis. Thus, while Freud may have desired that psychology be a natural science, his permanent contribution to psychology is not neurophysiological speculations, but his distinctive psychoanalytic psychology, one that Grünbaum (1984) notes the lack of empirical support for in natural scientific terms.

In one of his latest writings on psychology and religion (in reaction to the emergence of Bolshevism and his critique of Marxism) Freud stated, "Strictly speaking there are only *two* sciences, psychology pure and applied and natural science" (Freud, 1933, p. 179, emphasis mine).

It is instructive to remember that as Freud was developing his psychology another psychologist of note, William James, was struggling with psychology and the limits of what it could illuminate about religion from a natural science perspective. As I have argued elsewhere (Hood, 2008) James' most influential work for psychologists of religion, *The Varieties of Religious Experience* (1902/1985) followed upon his disappointment with his other great work, *The Principles of Psychology* (James, 1890/1981). In that text James had tried to see how far psychology could advance if conceived purely as a natural science. While claiming to avoid metaphysics, reviewers quickly pointed out how metaphysical his work was. James' own abridgement of the *Principles*, his *Psychology: The Briefer Course* (James, 1892) left out much of the metaphysical discussions of the *Principles* and became a model for contemporary psychology textbooks in which data are presented as if their evidential warrant came from experimentally established and empirically verified natural science methods from which the content of psychology as a natural science supposedly emerges. However, his own summary of the value of this restricted psychology was cautious:

> . . . at present psychology is in the condition of physics before Galileo and the laws of motion, of chemistry before Lavoisier and the notion that mass is preserved in all reactions. The Galileo and the Lavoisier of psychology will be famous men indeed when they come, as come they someday surely will, or past successes are no index to the future. When they do come, however, the necessities of the case will make them 'metaphysical.' Meanwhile the best way in which we can facilitate their advent is to understand how great the darkness in which we grope is, and never to forget that *the natural science assumptions with which we started are provisional and reversible things* (James, 1892, p. 468, emphasis mine).

In the *Varieties,* like Freud, James focused upon careful phenomenological descriptions of experience and produced explanations that are more hermeneutical than causal. In this sense, both Freud and James produced lasting psychologies that focus upon both the motives for belief as well as the epistemological warrant for the content of belief with, as we will note, different conclusions.

If James was self-consciously aware of the limits of natural science with respect to psychological questions that are accentuated in the psychology of religion, Meissner (1984) has noted the same for Freud in his analysis of the Freud/Pfister correspondence. Pfister had raised the issue of Freud's rhetorical use of "science" as both an effort to establish the legitimacy of psychoanalysis and a rather naïve commitment to a particular metaphysics. James did the same in his critique of Freud. He is reported by Ernest Jones, one of Freud's earliest biographers, to have said "The future of psychology is yours" (Richardson, 2006, p. 514). However, this is less likely to be correct in light of his letter to Ms. Calkins of September 19, 1909. There James expressed a more cautious appreciation of Freud and psychoanalysis:

> I strongly suspect Freud, with his dream-theory, of being a regular *hallucinė.* But I hope that he and his disciples will push it to its limits, as undoubtedly it covers some facts, and will add to our understanding of "functional" psychology, which is the real psychology (Perry, 1935/1974, p. 123).

Likewise, in the *Varieties*, in a less thinly veiled reference to Freud, James echoed what has become a standard critique of classical Freudian theory—the refusal to abandon or limit the pansexual motivation *for* and explanation *of* the content of certain religious beliefs. James rejected the claim that religious belief was "perverted sexuality" (James, 1902/1985, p. 18).

> The plain truth is that to interpret religion one must in the end look at the immediate content of the religious consciousness. The moment one doe this, one sees how wholly disconnected it is in the main from the content of sexual consciousness (James, 1902/1985, p. 19).

James goes on to conclude as he had in the abridgement of the *Principles* that the real issue as to the natural science presumptions of psychology were metaphysical. "The whole theory has lost its point in evaporating into a vague general assertion of the dependence *somehow* of the mind upon the body" (James, 1902/1985, p. 19, emphasis in original).

The James comments above parallel advances in psychoanalytic theory. Contemporary psychoanalysts argue that Freud's Oedipal theory of religion is at best limited or more likely false (Pruyser, 1973; Shafranske, 1985). The movement to object relations theory, and a cultural psychology that argues for an epistemological stance that avoids the natural science warrants for truth claims (Belzen and Uleyn, 1992; Pruyser, 1973; Winnicott, 1971) are issues Grünbaum rightfully minimizes as his discussion of Freud's theory forces a consideration of both its ontogenetic and phylogenetic claims, involving the epistemological warrant for the content of religious beliefs and not simply psychological motivations for holding religious beliefs. Thus, the distinction between illusion and delusion must be acknowledged. If James was more willing than Freud to abandon a commitment to psychology as a natural science, perhaps it was because he needed less of a warrant to justify his interest in religion. Grünbaum may be correct in arguing that the epistemological warrant for Freud's Oedipal theory is weak (an issue we shall return to below). However, he is surely correct in noting that while Freud may have been personally motivated to deny the truth claims of religion, he did not think that psychoanalytic insight into illusions would suffice to justify rejection of religion. Only religion as delusion, not as illusion, could do this. James, on the other hand, sought the truth within religion and thus unlike Freud who thought science could refute the truth claims of religion by focus upon its phylogenetic past, James thought his descriptive methods linked to his commitment to functionalism could show the truth claims of religion to be in the future, as its fruits were harvested. However, both Freud and James were careful to separate the motivational claims for belief from the truth content of beliefs. So with Grünbaum I wish to address these two issues but with a more interrelated discussion producing conclusions that moderate Grünbaum's own.

Ontogenetic and Phylogenetic Issues in Freud's Theory of Religion

In his *New Introductory Lectures on Psychoanalysis* Freud noted that "Religion is an attempt to master the sensory world in which we are situated by means of a wishful world we have developed within us as a result of biological and psychological necessity. But religion cannot achieve this" (Freud, 1933, p. 168). It is Freud's argument about the necessary failure of religion's central truth claim that must be addressed in light of Freud's atheism. In the light of reason religion must fail as the God to which it appeals is illuminated as a product of delusion. To defend this argument both Freud's ontogenetic and phylogenetic explanations of religion (those that Grünbaum see as Freud's uniquely psychoanalytic explanations) must be addressed in turn. Here, we accept Grünbaum's equation of religion with theism and focus upon the Abrahamic faiths where God is in some profound sense personal and often imaged or described in masculine terms. In addressing the truth claims of religion I shall refer to a thesis I have developed more fully elsewhere in addressing feminist critiques of Freud's abandonment of the seduction theory (Hood, 1997) and in truth claims relevant to Freud's theory of religion (Hood, 1992). The issue to be addressed is not simply the motivational basis for belief in a personal God, but the metaphysical issue of whether or not psychoanalysis can be used to provide epistemological warrants for the denial that such a belief is justified, whatever psychological comfort it may provide to the believer. Even delusions that sooth the soul remain false.

Freud's Abandonment of the Seduction Theory

The epistemological issue we confront is illuminated by the contrast between Peter Gay, the noted biographer of Freud, and Elaine Westerlund, a leading proponent of what we shall term the feminist critique of Freud. Gay, incredulous of the range and sweep of Freud's seduction theory stated, "What is astonishing is not that Freud eventually abandoned the seduction theory, but that he adopted it in the first place" (1988, p. 91). On the other hand, Westerlund argued that Freud never privately abandoned the seduction theory and his public disavowal was a betrayal of women insofar as "Freud was seduced into and seduced others into protecting the sexual offender, and betrayed the sexual victim" (1986, p. 308). In other words, the debate is over the historical reality of sexual events, not simply their psychological reconstruction or fantasized construction in memory. Historical truth is part of the epistemological warrant by which the material truth referenced in narrative is evaluated (Spence, 1982). Whatever else the psychological value of narrative truth (and it is considerable), historical reality matters.

Masson's (1984) work remains the most controversial assault on Freud's abandonment of the seduction theory widely recognized as an essential move in the creation of psychoanalysis. In an early paper on *The aetiology of hysteria*, Freud laid the groundwork for the critical move by stating, "You will readily admit that it would be a good thing to have a second method of arriving at the aetiology of hysteria, one in which we should feel less dependent on the assertions of patients themselves" (Freud, 1896, p. 191). The movement away from the acceptance of patient's claims of actual sexual abuse led to Freud's own minimization of historical truth in favor of narrative truth (Spence, 1982). Both Masson and Westerlund argued that Freud was intimately familiar with the reality of childhood sexual abuse, including Freud's likely witnessing of autopsies of actual sexually victimized children in the Paris morgue (Masson, 1984). Westerlund (1986) also emphasizes that Freud must have known of actual sexual abuse of children and that Freud protected peers known to have sexually abused patients and non-patients alike. Examples she cites include Sandor Ferenczi's sexual intimacy with his step-daughter and Ernest Jones' sexual activity with young girls. Finally, both Masson and Westerlund note that it was common, not rare, for the first generation of psychoanalysis to have sexual relations with their clients and to protect one another from public awareness of this fact. In this context it is worthy of note that both Masson and Westerlund assert that Freud was explicitly involved in the deliberate historical distortion of facts in several of his case studies which he later admitted. For instance, he modified the case histories of both Katrina (Freud, 1895/1955, case 4, pp. 125-134) and Rosalia (Freud, 1895/1955 case 5, pp. 135-181) which he admitted in footnotes added at a later date (Freud, 1895/1955, p. 134 for Katrina and p. 170 for Rosalia). Thus, psychoanalysts protected males known to be guilty of sexual abuse, most commonly fathers. While one can argue this was a matter of professional discretion, both Masson (1984) and Westerlund (1986) see this as an instance of a distinctive male *Weltanschauung* created by psychoanalysis to favor fantasy over reality—or narrated truth over historical truth. This despite Freud's claim that psychoanalysis did not have a *Weltanschauung* as broad and satisfying as a religion but must rest content within the more limited one of science (Freud, 1933).

It is in the shift from narrated to historical truth that moves Freud from his ontogenetic to his phylogenetic explanation of religion. Freud's psychogenetic theory of religion focuses upon the motivation for belief and as such gives desire a central role. Illusion and historical truth are orthogonal, illusion may be true, but in the grand scheme of things this is unlikely, especially insofar as religion is not merely an "intellectual misdemeanor" (Freud, 1927, p. 32) associated with philosophical concepts. Freud is interested in a vulgar and lived religion, of a God and a son-God with belief claims that neither history, nor science, nor reason can support. Freud was terse in his consideration of Vaihinger's philosophy, which anticipated Winnicott's (1971) expanded notion of illusion. Vaihinger, (1924/1968) had developed the law of ideational shifts integral to his philosophy of "As if." Accepting that beliefs we know to be false might nevertheless have practical utility, he argued for a dynamic relation between dogmas, doubt, and hypotheses in which what once was dogma is unmasked as fiction via hypothesis testing. About religion Vaihinger wrote:

> Myths, similes, even the conscious fictions of the founders of religions either become dogmas to the founders themselves, or to the adherents among the people, and rarely pass through the stage of hypothesis. On the other hand, during the decline and break-up of a religion all three stages stand out very clearly. At first all religion consists in general dogmas (the dogma itself has developed from a hypothesis or fiction). Then doubt appears and the idea becomes hypothesis. As doubt grows stronger, there are some who reject the idea entirely, while others maintain it either as a public or private fiction (Vaihinger, 1924/1968, p. 129).

Freud used his own historical narrative (truthfully!) to provide and explicit rejection of Vaihinger (and by inference of transitional claims to protect religion as a cultural psychology immune from scientific falsification).

> I am reminded of one of my children who was distinguished at an early age by a peculiarly marked matter-of-factness. When the children were being told a fairy story and were listening to it with rapt attention, he would come up and ask: "Is that a true story?" When he was told it was not, he would turn away with a look of disdain. We may expect that people will soon behave in the same way toward the fairy tales of religion in spite of the advocacy of "As if" (Freud, 1927, p. 29).

It is clear that as Grünbaum wisely emphasizes Freud did not make the error of using the fact that religion is an illusion as an epistemological warrant to deny the truth claims of religion. The critical move for Freud was in accepting the challenge to deny the claims of religion if unmasked as delusional falsifications of history. In Freud's most maligned and last public work on religion he stated:

> I have never doubted that religious phenomena are only to be understood on the pattern of individual neurotic systems familiar to us—as the return of long since forgotten, important events in the primeval history of the human family—and that they have to thank precisely this origin for their compulsive character, and that, accordingly, they are effective in human beings by the force of the *historical truth* of their content (Freud, 1939, p. 58, emphasis mine).

Delusion: Idiosyncratic and Shared

The importance of Freud's phylogenetic view of religion is that it is to his claim that religion is a delusion and hence false. To compliment Grünbaum's discussion of Freud's view I want to address both the definitional stance with respect to delusion and the concern that Freud's historical truth of religion is embedded in Lamarckian theory.

First, with respect to delusion, Grünbaum relies upon various editions of the Oxford *Psychiatric Dictionary* definition to the effect that delusions must be idiosyncratic and not shared. Freud's phylogenetic theory requires the existence of mass delusions even though, "No one, needless to say, who shares a delusion ever recognizes it as such" (Freud, 1930, p. 81). However, as he had earlier noted, as opposed to illusions, "In the case of delusions we emphasize as being essential their being in contradiction with reality" (Freud, 1927, p. 31). Religion is a cultural phenomenon but as such is not protected from also being delusional.

The radical nature of Freud's phylogenetic theory or religion ought not to be underestimated. Recent efforts to modify clinical understandings of those who adhere to delusionary beliefs follow political correctness in arguing that rather than being idiosyncratic individual neuroses and hence a caricature of religion, are actually mass-delusions and a protective umbrella from the harsh reality of God's non-existence (Freud, 1907, 1930).

Psychologists who would protect religious claims from falsification reject Freud's claim that delusionary beliefs can be shared and still be false. This applies even to hallucinatory experiences, as the recent history of modifications in the American Psychiatric Association's *Diagnostic and Statistical Manual of Mental Disorders* (DSM) shows. Hallucinations can interact with delusions in Freud's phylogenetic theory of religion, yet each remains indicative of pathology *even when culturally supported.* However, the last several revisions of DSM have cautioned against identifying hallucinations as pathological if there is normative support for these practices. This was made especially clear in DSM-III-R:

> When an experience is entirely normative for a particular culture—e.g., hallucinating the voice of a deceased in the first few weeks of bereavement in various North American Indian groups, or trance and possession states occurring in culturally approved ritual contexts in much of the non-Western world—it should not be regarded as pathological (American Psychiatric Association, 1987, p. xxvi).

In DSM-IV, a hallucination is defined only as "a sensory perception that has the compelling sense of reality of a true perception but that occurs without external stimulation of the relevant sensory organ" (American Psychiatric Association, 1994, p. 767); it is not automatically deemed to be an indication of mental illness. The most recent edition of this manual (DSMIV-TR) simply cautions that "a clinician who is unfamiliar with the nuances of an individual's cultural frame of reference may incorrectly judge as psychopathology those normal variations in behavior, belief, or experience that are particular to the individual's culture" (American Psychiatric Association, 2000, p. xxxiv).

This move toward a non-critical cultural psychology allows that at best psychiatric theory must adhere to cultural conventions in the identification of not just delusions, but even hallucinations. The belief content of religion is protected from criticism if the concept of mass-delusion is denied.

Freud's suggestion that religion saves individuals from creating their own idiosyncratic caricatures of religion easily identified as delusional (Freud, 1907) is paralleled by William James' insight that the relationship between individual experience and collective shared experience is empirically important:

> A genuine first-hand experience . . . is bound to be a heterodoxy to its witness, the prophet appearing as a mere lonely madman. If his doctrine proves contagious enough to spread to any others, it becomes a definite and labeled heresy. But if it then still prove contagious enough to triumph over persecution, it become itself an orthodoxy; and when religion has become an orthodoxy, its day of inwardness is over; the spring is dry; the faithful live at second hand and stone the prophets in their turn (James, 1901/1985, p. 270).

Both Freud and James distinguish idiosyncratic beliefs and experiences from culturally shared ones. Empirically, the process by which one creates idiosyncratic beliefs as a caricature of religion versus acquired, shared, beliefs or a culturally acknowledged religion are important issues for the psychology of religion, but one that cannot be meaningfully addressed if the content of culturally shared beliefs is immune from a critical assessment of their truth value.

Empirical Evidence for Freud's Phylogenetic Theory Reconsidered

Grünbaum is aware that the truth of Freud's of religion largely hinges on the phylogenetic theory of religion, but finds it considerably weakened by its apparent reliance upon Lamarckian evolutionary theory. He cites Freud's statement in *Moses and Monotheism* (1939, p. 101) in this volume (Chapter 1, p. 15) with his own emphasis added in brackets "men have always known (in this special [Lamarckian] way) that they once possessed a primal father and killed him." Freud's reference is to a phylogenetic transmitted knowledge that apparently requires the inheritance of acquired characteristics. Grünbaum notes that the theory itself is intellectually comprehensible but weakly supported if it relies upon Lamarckian theory. However, a reconsideration of Freud's phylogenetic speculation within the confines of Darwinian theory is possible.

Freud's phylogenetic theory is embedded in the provocative thesis that there can be mass-delusion in the sense of culturally shared religious belief that is nevertheless false.

> If the development of civilization has such a far-reaching similarity to the development of the individual and if it employs the same methods, may we not be justified in reaching the diagnosis that, under the influence of cultural urges, some civilizations, or some epochs of civilization—possibly the whole of mankind—have become 'neurotic'?" (Freud, 1930, p. 144).

The notion that the Oedipal drama individually experienced recapitulates an event in evolutionary history that resulted in hominization was proposed by Freud as evidence for the delusionary nature of religion. Humankind killed its real biological father, not the God-man Jesus. This is the material truth distorted in various ways in the historical narratives of the two of the Abrahamic faiths. Christians, believers in the son-God, acknowledge the primal murder with Paul's doctrine of original sin, leaving only Jews who believe in the father-God to bear the burden of their denial that they murdered God (Freud, 1930).

Badcock (1980) renewed academic interest in Freud's primal horde speculations by relying upon species who share many common adaptive features with humans even if they are less genetically similar to humans than other species as the great apes, chimpanzee, and gorilla, Evolutionists have focused upon the gelada baboon (*Theropithecus gelada*) as particularly relevant to Freud's primal horde speculations (Crook, 1966; Jolly, 1970).

While more genetically distant from humans that the great apes, chimpanzee or gorilla, humans share with geladas precisely those adaptive features that differentiate them most from their more genetically similar relatives. The shift to a focus on adaptive features (for instance geladas almost exclusively live in open country and are terrestrial as opposed to forest dwellers who spend at least part of their life in trees) allows for what Jolly (1970, p. 12) calls directional equivalence for gelada and basal hominids. Crook (1966, p. 241) documented that geladas live as one male breeding units, with several females, admits roaming bands of interactive young males. This is thus an empirical exemplar for a real historical primal horde postulated by Freud. The basic sex-driven aggression by which the gelada maintains its one male breeding unit is associated with male conflict in attempting to overthrow the dominant male in order to be able to breed. However, as Freud speculated, hordes of non-breeding males learn to survive via hunting and if they establish deferred obedience (incest taboo) by remorse for having killed the dominant male (father), Freud's evolutionary hypothesis is given empirical support (Badcock, 1980, 1990). . Furthermore, it can be demonstrated on non-Lamarckian grounds if we assume that this process of selection corresponds to instincts in animals. Thus, natural selection can account for a Darwinian interpretation that allows what Freud needs most to support his phylogenetic theory, a bridge over the "gulf between individual and group psychology" (Freud, 1939, p. 100).

That the bridge is not a Lamarckian archaic memory trace, but a Darwinian instinctive tendency adds all the more to the epistemological warrant for Freud's claim that the specific contents of religious beliefs are delusional markers of real historical events. Thus, Freud concludes, "We too believe the pious solution [monotheism] contains the truth—the *historical* truth not the *material* truth" (Freud, 1939, p. 129, emphasis in original). Of course, here Freud emphasizes the narrated historical distortion of the material truth. Earlier he had noted that the many riddles of the universe reveal themselves slowly to science, but with respect to religion Freud believed the riddle had been solved by "the only road which can lead us to knowledge of reality outside ourselves" (Freud, 1927, p. 31). If Grünbaum is right that Freud's phylogenetic theory is the weakest link in his rejection of the truth claims of religion, it is nevertheless his strongest claim to an understanding of religion's origin.

The above summary of Badcock's evidence for classical Freudian theory is directly relevant to Grünbaum's syllogistic model for the epistemological warrant for Freud's phylogenetic hypothesis. It does not mean the controversial theory is true, but it does mean that the hypothesis of a primal horde and its crucial role in hominization has some empirical support and thus Grünbaum's criticism of this aspect of Freud's theory is at least somewhat mitigated. Badcock (1986, 1990) has marshaled considerable additional evidence, all within the framework of Darwinian evolutionary theory for Freud's phylogenetic theory. Jones had anticipated this in his reply to the Lamarckian underpinnings of Freud's phylogenetic theory, "Nevertheless there are alternative possibilities, e.g., along Darwinian lines, which would preserve the essence of his conclusions (Jones, 1957, p. 369). One hastens to add that there certainly are counter claims to Freud's evolutionary speculations. To cite but one example, DeMause (1991) argues for the universality of incestuous behaviors, not of an incest taboo, as demanded by Freudian theory. *"It is incest itself, not the absence of incest—that has been universal for most people in most places at most times*" (1991, p. 125, emphasis in original). However, the point here is not an evaluation of the empirical evidence but the fact that classical Freudian theory, and especially the phylogenetic theory of religion, is at least partly a matter of empirical evidence. Historical truth matters, as the feminist critique of Freud, noted above, reminds us. While narrative truth is worthy of psychological illumination, Grünbaum is correct to note that Freud never succumbed to the temptation to deny the epistemological warrant for the content of religious belief by uncovering the psychological motivations for holding such beliefs. This is why the original title for Freud's last work on religion was abandoned. He did not write, *The Man Moses, an Historical Novel* as first intended (Jones, 1957, p. 207). Instead he proposed a theory of monotheism, unmasked as perhaps humankind's grandest and most enduring delusion. Freud's theory may be wrong but if it is, it is because it is an empirical claim to truth that can be falsified and not simply an illusion expanded into shared cultural beliefs incapable of falsification simply because they are shared.

An Indirect Empirical Test of Oedipal Theory

Insofar as the epistemological warrant for Freudian theory is partly based upon empirical evidence, Grünbaum (1984) has elsewhere provided what has become a standard critique. However, with respect to Freud's specific theory of religion there are interesting empirical studies focusing upon the Virgin Birth, which, as Grünbaum notes, has been surprisingly neglected by such apologists as Meissner and Küng.

Carroll (1986) has presented a provocative theory of the psychological origins of the cult of the Virgin Mary that is based upon classical Freudian theory. Carroll assumes the Freudian theory provides a means to illuminate the particular content of religious beliefs as they emerged in history, in this case the sudden emergence of the cult of the Virgin Mary in the fifth century with the concurrent emphasis of the passion and suffering of Christ. Not only is Carroll's work valuable in demonstrating the hermeneutical power of Freudian theory to illuminate the specific content of religious beliefs, but it is empirically testable. Carroll has provided some empirical tests, using historical data that support classical Freudian theory (Carroll, 1986; Hood, Hill, & Spilka, 2009). Consistent with Grünbaum's claim that there needs to be additional warrant for Freud's theory we devised an empirical study to test Carroll's theory of the origin of the cult of the Virgin Mary, interpreted in terms of classical Oedipal theory.

Carroll derives his theory of the origin of the cult of the Virgin Mary from classical Freudian theory. First, he noted that the Catholic doctrine includes three interrelated beliefs; (1) Mary was sinless; (2) *viriginitus in partu* (her maidenhead was never ruptured) and (3) *viriginitus post partum* (she was a lifelong virgin). While not all aspects of this are official Catholic dogma, nevertheless in the popular mind Mary unlike almost any other mother in religious myth is perpetually virgin, devoid of sexuality. The Freudians suspect denial and defense against an erotic attraction—of son to mother.

A second intriguing aspect of Carroll's theory is the empirical fact that commitment to the cult of Mary is strongest in countries characterized by a machismo complex, a culturally endorsed fierce male domination and sexual exploitation of women. Finally, Carroll provides historical and ethnographic data to show that in areas where both the cult of Mary and the machismo complex are common, males tend to come from father-ineffective families. These three "data points" are easily illuminated by accepting Freud's Oedipal theory, applied only to males.

If we accept that males are sexually attracted to their mothers and wish the death of their fathers both in terms of the ontogenetic and phylogenetic hypotheses of Freud we can make two empirical hypotheses regarding motivation to accept the cultural content of religious beliefs associated with the cult of the Virgin Mary. First, males strongly attracted to their mothers but with strong erotic repressions will be attracted to the cult of the Virgin Mary. Second, behaviors and beliefs associated with this cult follow from the Oedipal dynamic: the machismo complex is a substitute for maternal repression as displaced sexuality; the denial of sexuality to Mary is a defense for sexuality attraction; the attraction to the passion and suffering of Christ is unconscious guilt and punishment for taboo desire as well as pleasure in the suffering and death of the father. All of this emerges historically in patterns predictable from classical Freudian theory. The essentials of the theory can also be empirically tested and support Carroll's thesis, and thus also classical Freudian Oedipal theory.

Hood, Morris, and Watson (1991) deliberately selected non-Catholic believers to see if the pattern and content of the Cult of Mary outlined by Carroll could be empirically supported. Using art works we first established quantitative rankings of crucifixes/cross as to the degree of representation of a *suffering* Christ. (The cross was a base level control). We selected four crucifixes and one cross, easily ranked in order of degree of suffering (cross = lowest).

After much pilot work we then selected five artistically ambivalent figures of the Virgin Mary. The ambivalent we sought was a Mary that was equally erotic and nurturing. Thus we excluded representation of Mary and the Christ child with an erect penis. [Ironically an artistic confirmation of Freudian Oedipal views at least at the ontogenetic level (see Steinberg, 1983)]. We selected five reproductions of which for our purpose one was the "target" picture, Jean Mirailhet's *La Vierge de miséricorde* (Our lady of mercy). This fifteenth century painting is commonly acknowledged as being in the tradition of Mary as *Mother Church* (Barraclough, 1981, pp. 12-13). Mary is represented with her opening her cape, with figures protected under it. Her open cape reveals what to Freudian eyes is an almost perfect likeness of a circumcised penis. A similar fifteenth century *Mother Church* painting by Piero della Franscesa (*Mother of Mercy*) reveals a harsher Mary, with an open cape that is not an obvious penis shape. It was rated low on both the erotic and nurturing scales. Only Mirailhet's painting, rated as equally erotic and nurturing fit Carroll's criteria of ambivalence. (Not incidentally, our procedures also indicate that Freudian claims to sexual symbolism can be indirectly empirically assessed).

The actual study was simple—we selected believing but non-Catholic males. They were assessed on a measure that allowed us to determine their degree of maternal bonding. In the crucial part of this study for our present purposes each participant was taken into a room with the crucifixes/cross randomly on the wall. Each was to select the item that most indicated what Christ meant to them. Next, they turned to another wall in which the five reproductions of the Virgin were randomly mounted. They then were asked to select the painting that indicated what Mary most meant to them.

The results of appropriate data analyses indicated support for Carroll's thesis. Simply put, males strongly bonded to their mothers picked the ambivalent Virgin and the crucifix with the most suffering Christ. Thus, males minimally familiar with Catholic tradition, having the Oedipal dynamic associated with classical Freudian theory are attracted to religious representations historically embedded in a faith tradition whose belief content makes psychological sense, and is supported by delusions that are not simply idiosyncratic but shared as culturally accepted apparitions (Carroll, 1986). Mary may not have been a Virgin in historical truth, but she must be in narrative truth. Empirical research can suggest why it is that the content of religious belief remains as it does despite little independent empirical or epistemological warrant. As Freud claimed, mass delusions, cultural psychology, and the capacity for neurosis and even psychoses may be one and the same (Brown, 1959; Freud, 1930, 1939).

Contemporary Serpent Handlers of the Southeastern United States

It is interesting that Freud's exploration of the psychology of the two Moses ignores their historical and symbolic connection to serpents. Only in a brief line does Freud refer to the second Moses of the wandering Jews to whom tradition attributes the erection of a brazen serpent as a God of healing (Freud, 1939, p. 36). This is curious, given that classical Oedipal theory can be used to illuminate both the belief in and practice of what La Barre (1969) has explored as a pathological religious sub-culture—the serpent handling sects of the southeastern United States. La Barre was an anthropologist, trained in classical psychoanalysis. While our own work on the serpent-handling sects is largely an empirical and conceptual counter to La Barre's (Hood, 2005; Hood & Williamson, 2008), our concern here is to note that classical Oedipal theory is both hermeneutically illuminating and has empirically testable components that are relevant to the belief content and to the ritual that follows from it.

Freud's allusion to the brazen serpent as a God of healing is likened to the legend of Asklepios which La Barre (1969, p. 70) notes was a physician-God, slain by Zeus because he was so successful in healing that Zeus's brother, Hades, was concerned with the removal of so many souls from the underworld. Zeus's remorse led him to restore Asklepios to life. Asklepios' rod came to symbolize healing and regeneration, a single serpent wrapped around it. The issue of the symbolic nature of serpents is crucial to understanding the contemporary serpent handling sects of the southeastern United States.

While snakes have symbolic signification in almost every culture of the world, they are polysemic (Mundkur, 1983). Be that as it may, the relationship between serpent and phallus is the most likely contended for a universal symbol (Jones, 1961), so much so that La Barre has asked, "Where is the snake *not* a phallic symbol?" (1969, p. 74). However, as a phallic symbol the serpent is associated with the Oedipal drama in ways supportive of Freud's phylogenetic theory of religion.

La Barre is one of the few anthropologists to see current value in Freud's theory of the origin of monotheism. He cites examples (e.g., Exodus 4: 3 and 7: 9-11) in support of his conclusion that power over serpents was the special métier of the Hebrews in Egypt [Freud's first Moses] (La Barre, 1969). Likewise, Freud's Moses of the Exodus obeyed God, reminding us of the physician-God Asklepios' own handling of serpents:

> And the LORD said unto Moses, Make thee a fiery serpent, and set it upon a pole: and it shall come to pass, that every one that is bitten, when he looketh upon it, shall live. And Moses made a serpent of brass, and put it upon a pole, and it came to pass, that if a serpent had bitten any man, when he beheld the serpent of brass, he lived (Numbers 21: 7-8).

Even if we ignore La Barre's claim that Moses was a snake shaman we cannot ignore his insight that the serpent is an integral symbol not only of regeneration in healing but resurrection from death. The serpent's shedding of his skin has often been linked psychologically with immortality, and La Barre sees the origin of circumcision in an imitation of this process. As La Barre (1969, p. 80) diagrams it: "Snake : immortal : sheds skin :: phallus : immortal : circumcision." Circumcision is, of course, for Freud symbolic castration, and is linked in the Oedipal drama to remorseful obedience to the slain father and the acceptance of the incest taboo integral to the process of hominization. Thus, the serpent as symbolic castration is integral to worship in monotheism, including not simply those who worship the father but also those who worship the son. La Barre (1969, p. 84) reminds of John 3: 14-15 "And as Moses lifted up the serpent in the wilderness, even so must the Son of man be lifted up That whosoever believeth in him should not perish, but have eternal life." Thus, among those who worship the Son the serpent is a phallocentric symbol of rebellion and delayed obedience. Campbell (1974, p. 296) has a photograph of a sixteenth century German coin in which the crucified Christ is on one side; the other side has a serpent coiled around the cross. Likewise, Marshall (2001) makes reference to the crucifixion with respect to "our serpent of salvation."

A symbolic understanding of castration is neither a rational explanation for the practice nor a sufficient epistemological warrant for belief either in circumcision nor, as we shall see, for the handling of serpents. However, as La Barre notes with respect to rationalist explanations of circumcision "The fault with such rationalist explanations is that they *are* rational" (1969, p. 79, emphasis in original). Freud's phylogenetic theory of religion illuminates what for many has eluded rationalist but not psychoanalytic explanation. It is an explanation rooted in what is an archaic belief, if not practice. For as La Barre (1969, p. 69) notes, "The immediate ancestor of snake symbolism in the American Southeast is Semitic, specifically Biblical."

If there is a foundational text for serpent handling it is in the literal acceptance of Mark: 16: 17-18:

> And these signs shall follow them that believe; In my name shall they cast out devils; they shall speak with new tongues; They shall take up serpents; and if they drink any deadly thing, it shall not hurt them; they shall lay hands on the sick, and they shall recover.

Associated with the early Pentecostal churches, our focus here will be upon the implementation of only one of these signs, handling serpents. How are we to understand this practice, given that those who handle snakes risk bites, maiming, and death (Hood, 1998; Hood & Williamson, 2008)?

If Freud was delighted with the dualism of two Moses, biblical scholars recognize two authors of the gospel of Mark. Critical studies reveal a second author who completed the abrupt ending of Mark at 16:8 in the early part of the second century. This "longer Mark" was accepted as canonical by the Catholic Church and was never excluded from any Protestant Bible (Kelhoffer, 2000; Thomas & Alexander, 2003). Furthermore, as Kelhoffer (2000, pp. 346-388) has carefully documented, it was precisely because non-Christian religious movements were gaining status by handling serpents in the context of numerous references to serpents in Greco-Roman culture that the unknown author of the "longer Mark" included handling serpents as one of the signs that the followers of Jesus could also accomplish. However, there is no historical evidence that the early followers of Jesus handled serpents nor are there artistic representations of Christians handling serpents in the long tradition of Christian art. This, despite the last verse in the gospel of Mark which states, "And they went forth, and preached everywhere, the Lord working with them, and confirming the word with signs following" (Mark 16, 20). However, it is my contention that early followers of Jesus handled and representations of handling were likely and the empirical task is to document this. However, this is not our concern here.

Kelhoffer (2000, p. 416) notes that while there is no evidence that early Christians handled serpents, the twentieth century praxis of handling serpents received its legitimate justification from the longer Mark. We have documented this history elsewhere (Hood, 1998, 2005; Hood & Williamson, 2008). Here we merely wish to note that handlers believe that they must be obedient to their God, and he demands the handling of serpents simply as an act of obedience. To accept this belief flies in the face of reason that would protect one from explicit danger. Yet insofar as this practice began to be modeled in the first part of the nineteenth century (perhaps for the first time; perhaps a practice recovered from an ancient tradition) allowed a cultural tradition to emerge (or re-emerge). Yet not everyone will take from a sacred text a clearly stated belief, especially one that involves the handling of deadly serpents. We suggest that only those with a powerful attraction to the symbolic meaning of the serpent are likely to be attracted to the belief that commands handling and to express that belief in practice. Freud's Oedipal theory is precisely capable of illuminating such practices. A psychodynamic interpretation of serpent handling may not exhaust its meaning as a cultural expression of religious belief but it does provide evidence in support of Freud's phylogenetic theory of religion. Handling can be viewed an overt expression of the Oedipal drama and the return of the repressed (Hood and Kimbrough, 1995). As La Barre (1969, p. 76) has noted,

> The transmission of this symbolism [snake phallus] from the ancient Hebrews to the snake–handlers is here direct, demonstrable, and plainly cultural–historical. No great mystery about cultural continuity can arise for anyone cognizant of the constant and intense preoccupation with the ancient cultural documents themselves, in the Bible-reading belt of the southeastern United States. As heirs of European culture and its past, these folks are sometimes poverty-stricken indeed, but they have the Book. The value of a sacred text understood in terms of its plain meaning does permit archaic knowledge to survive in the "Book" and for that which is repressed to return under appropriate circumstances.

The serpent handlers of the contemporary southeastern United States elevate not only the serpent but their own selves, as the illusion that they do not die is overshadowed by the delusion that in handling serpents they are but being obedient to a God whose historical truth they narrate through a glass darkly.

Conclusion

Grünbaum has provided a useful return to the question of the scientific merit of Freudian theory in general and its explanatory value for understanding religion in particular. The four areas we have explored have highlighted the continued relevance of classical Freudian theory. First, in recognizing that despite the rejection of Freudian theory as *science,* the issue of what constitutes science is driven home by the failure of both James and Freud to express human psychology in the more narrow confines of efficient causation. Thus, both Freud and James shared a vision of a science that had to be opened to metaphysical revisions especially in terms of what "natural" science might mean with respect to psychology. Likewise, both sought the truth in any religious claims, one by what it masked of the past, the other by what fruits it might yield in the future. Yet for both, truth mattered.

Second, Freud's phylogenetic theory is not as weak as Grünbaum suggests, especially if one advances a Darwinian rather than a Lamarckian understanding of archaic memory trace in terms of instinctual dispositions that can be inherited. It is the phylogenetic view that makes the ontogenetic Oedipal drama so powerful and a possible empirically testable theory of religion.

Empirical tests can be devised that are germane to the content of religious belief and our example in support of Carroll's historical work show that classical Oedipal theory can be empirically tested on par with any other psychological theory. As I read Grünbaum's early criticism of psychoanalysis (1984), the issue is that there is insufficient empirical evidence for psychoanalytic claims, but not that such evidence could not be forthcoming.

Finally, the contemporary serpent handlers provide a test case for Freud's view that actual historical truth matters. Delusion not illusion provides the unique psychoanalytic critique of religion and thus, *"tant pis"* for religion (Freud, 1927, p. 37). If Freud had the courage to deny the material reality of any and all gods, even of God, it was because he clearly provided a theory in which delusion unmasked that low value of any warrant for the evidence that the Gods exist other than as distortion of an historical truth his science could not deny. Freud was keenly aware of the scientific criticism of his phylogenetic theory and of Robertson Smith's work which he heavily relied upon in *Totem and Taboo* (1913, p. 139) and is re-affirmed in *Moses and Monotheism* (1939, p. 130-132). Still he was not persuaded to change, and perhaps we can quote with Badcock (1980) what he said of the critics of his libido theory, "He who knows how to wait need make no concessions" (Freud, 1921, p. 91). If he is right in the latter he may also be right on the former. As Jones stated the case with respect to *Moses and Monotheism*,

> Freud first thought of his Moses theory as an interesting historical romance, but the more he reflected on it the more probable did it seem. He did not conceal the hypothetical elements in it, so difficult to substantiate, but we can hardly fail to regard it as a brilliant example of the imaginative intuition, and Freud's intuitions was more often right than wrong (Jones, 1957, p. 374).

In time intuitions have a way of becoming testable as what constitutes natural science expands. James and Freud tested the limits of natural science, each suggested that in James' terse phrasing of the truth in religious experience, there was something he simply identified as "MORE" (James, 1902/1895, p. 401). Furthermore, he went on to ask the relevant question Freud also addressed, "Is such a 'more' merely our own notion, or does it really exist?" (James, 1902/1985, p. 401). If James was suspicious of Freud's reductionist understanding of religious experience his appreciation of the role of the subliminal was not far from Freud's. As Browning noted, "Since the subliminal for him [James] can also be a place of forgotten memories and obscurely motivated passions, it would have been only a small step for James to reach the classical Freudian position" (1980, p. 261). One cannot imagine James endorsing Freud's phylogenetic theory as an answer, but one can believe he would applaud Freud's persistence in asking the right question. If Freud's phylogenetic theory is not the proper answer it awaits a better empirical alternative. The refutation of Freud's phylogenetic thesis must be empirical. And this can be accomplished only if social scientists do not avoid asking the right questions. As one American transcendentalist said, "Be it life or death, we crave only reality" (Thoreau, 1854/1939, p. 103).

References

American Psychiatric Association (1987). *Diagnostic and Statistical Manual of Mental Disorders* (3rd ed., rev.), Washington, DC: American Psychiatric Association.

American Psychiatric Association (1994). *Diagnostic and Statistical Manual of Mental Disorders* (4th ed.), Washington, DC: American Psychiatric Association.

American Psychiatric Association (2000). *Diagnostic and Statistical Manual of Mental Disorders* (4th ed. rev.), Washington, DC: American Psychiatric Association.

Badcock, C. R. (1980). *The Psychoanalysis of Culture*. Oxford: Basil Blackwell.

Badcock, C. R. (1986). *The Problem of Altruism: Freudian-Darwinian Solutions*. Oxford: Basil Blackwell.

Badcock, C. R. (1990). *Oedipus in Evolution: A New Theory of Sex*. Oxford: Basil Blackwell.

Barraclough, G. (1981). *The Christian World: A Social and Cultural History*. London: Thames & Hudson, Ltd.

Belzen, J. A. & Uleyn, A. J. R. (1992). What is real? Speculation on Hood's implicit epistemology and theology. *The International Journal for the Psychology of Religion*, 2, 165-170.

Brown, N. (1959) *Life Against Death: The Psychoanalytic Meaning of History*. Middletown, CT: Wesleyan University Press.

Browning, D. S. (1980). *Pluralism and Personality: William James and Some Contemporary Cultures of Psychology*. Cranbury, NJ: Associated University Presses.

Campbell, J. (1974). *The Mythic Image*. Princeton, NJ: Princeton University Press.

Carroll, M. P. (1986). *The Cult of the Virgin Mary*. Princeton, NJ: Princeton University Press.

Crook, J. H. (1966). Gelada baboon head structure and movement. *Symposium of the Zoological Society of London*, 18, 237-258.

DeMause, L. (1991). The universality of incest. *Journal of Psychohistory*, *19*, 123-164.

Freud, S. (1895/1950). Project for a scientific psychology. *The Standard Edition of the Complete Psychological Works of Sigmund Freud*, 1, 295-397. London: The Hogarth Press.

Freud, S. (1895/1955). Case histories. *The Standard Edition of the Complete Psychological Works of Sigmund Freud*, 2, Case 4, Katrina. 125-134; Case 5, Fraülein Elisabeth von R., 135-181. London: The Hogarth Press.

Freud, S. (1896). The aetiology of hysteria. *The Standard Edition of the Complete Psychological Works of Sigmund Freud*, *3*, 187-222. London: The Hogarth Press.

Freud, S. (1907). Obsessive actions and religious practices. *The Standard Edition of the Complete Psychological Works of Sigmund Freud*, *9*, 15-27. London: The Hogarth Press.

Freud, S. (1913) Totem and taboo. *The Standard Edition of the Complete Psychological Works of Sigmund Freud, 13*, xiii—162. London: The Hogarth Press.
Freud, S. (1921). Group psychology and the analysis of the ego. *The Standard Edition of the Complete Psychological Works of Sigmund Freud, 18*, 69-143. London: The Hogarth Press.
Freud, S. (1927). The future of an illusion. *The Standard Edition of the Complete Psychological Works of Sigmund Freud, 21*, 1-56. London: The Hogarth Press.
Freud, S. (1930). Civilization and its discontents. *The Standard Edition of the Complete Psychological Works of Sigmund Freud, 21*, 59-145. London: The Hogarth Press.
Freud. S. (1933) New introductory lectures on psychoanalysis. *The Standard Edition of the Complete Psychological Works of Sigmund Freud, 22*, 3-182. London: The Hogarth Press.
Freud, S. (1939). Moses and monotheism: Three essays. *The Standard Edition of the Complete Psychological Works of Sigmund Freud, 23*, 1-137. London: The Hogarth Press.
Gay, P. (1988). *Freud: A Life for Our Time*. New York: Doubleday.
Grünbaum, A. (1984). *The Foundations of Psychoanalysis: A Philosophical Critique*. Berkeley, CA: University of California Press.
Grünbaum, A. (1993). *Validation in the Clinical Theory of Psychoanalysis: A Study in the Philosophy of Psychoanalysis*. Madison, CT: International Universities Press.
Habermas, J. (1971). *Knowledge and Human Interests*. Boston: Beacon Press.
Hood, R. W., Jr. (1992). Mysticism, Reality, Illusion and the Freudian Critique of Religion. *The International Journal for the Psychology of Religion, 2*, 141-159.
Hood, R. W. Jr. (1997). Psychoanalysis and fundamentalism: Lessons from a feminist critique of Freud. In J. L. Jacobs & D. Capps (eds.), *Religion, Society, and Psychoanalysis* (pp. 42-57). Boulder, CO: Westview Press.
Hood, R. W. Jr. (1998). When the spirit maims and kills: Social psychological considerations of the history of serpent handling and the narrative of handlers. Invited paper, *The International Journal for the Psychology of Religion, 8,* 7 1-96
Hood, R. W. Jr. (Ed.) (2005). *Handling Serpents: Pastor Jimmy Morrow's Narrative History of His Appalachian Jesus' Name Tradition*. Mercer, Georgia: Mercer University Press.
Hood, R. W. Jr. (2008).Theoretical Fruits from the Empirical Study of Mysticism: A Jamesian Perspective. *Journal für Psychologie*, Jg., Ausgabe 3.
Hood, R. W. & Kimbrough, D. (1995). Serpent–handling holiness sects: Theoretical considerations. *Journal for the Scientific Study of Religion, 34*, 311-322.
Hood, R. W. Jr. & Williamson, P. W. (2008). *Them That Believe: The Power and Meaning of the Christian Serpent–Handling Tradition*. Berkeley: University of California Press.
Hood, R. W., Jr., Morris, R. J., & Watson, P. J. (1991). Male Commitment to the Cult of the Virgin Mary and the Passion of Christ as a Function of Early Maternal Bonding. *The International Journal for the Psychology of Religion, 1*, 221-231.
Hood, R. W. Jr., Hill, P. C., & Spilka, B. (2009). *The Psychology of Religion: An Empirical Approach* (4th ed.). New York: Guilford.
James, W. (1892). *Psychology: The Briefer Course*. New York: Henry Holt.
James, W. (1890/1981). *The Principles of Psychology*. Cambridge, MA: Harvard University Press.
James, W. (1902/1985). *The Varieties of Religious Experience. A Study in Human Nature*. Cambridge, MA: Harvard University Press.
Jolly, C. (1970). The seed-eaters: A new model of hominid differentiation based on a baboon analogy. *Man*, 5, 5-25.

Jones, E. (1957). *The Life and Work of Sigmund Freud, Vol. 3, The Last Phase*. New York: Basic Books.

Jones, E. (1961). *Papers on Psycho-Analysis* (5th ed.). Boston: Beacon Press.

Kelhoffer, J. A. (2000). *Miracle and Mission: The Authentication of Missionaries and Their Message in the Longer Ending of Mark*. Tübingen: Mohr Siebeck.

Küng, H. (1979). *Freud and the Problem of God*. New Haven: Yale University Press.

Marshall, R. F. (2001). Our serpent of salvation: The offense of Jesus in John's Gospel. *Word & World*, XXI, 385-393.

Masson, J. (1984). *The Assault on Truth: Freud's Suppression of the Seduction Theory*. New York: Farrar, Strauss, and Giroux.

Meissner, W. W. (1984). *Psychoanalysis and Religious Experience*. New Haven: Yale University Press.

Mundkur, B. (1983). *The Cult of the Serpent*. Albany: State University of New York Press.

Perry, W. (1935/1974). *The Thought and Character of William James*, Vol. 2. Westport, CT: Greenwood Press.

Pruyser, P. W. (1973). Sigmund Freud and his legacy: Psychoanalytic psychology of religion. In C. Y. Glock & P. E. Hammond (Eds.), *Beyond the Classics? Essays in the Scientific Study of Religion* (pp. 243-290). New York: Harper & Row.

Richardson, R. D. (2006). *William James: In the Maelstrom of American Modernism*. Boston: Houghton Mifflin.

Ricouer, P. (1970). *Freud and Philosophy*. New Haven: Yale University Press.

Robinson, D. N. (1995). *An Intellectual History of Psychology* (3rd ed.). Madison, WI: University of Wisconsin Press.

Shafranske, E. P. (1985). Freudian theory and religious experience. In R. W. Hood, Jr. (Ed.), *Handbook of Religious Experience* (pp., 200-230). Birmingham, AL: Religious Education Press.

Spence, D. P. (1982) *Narrative Truth and Historical Truth: Meaning and Interpretation in Psychoanalysis* New York: W. W. Norton.

Steinberg, L. (1983). *The Sexuality of Christ in Renaissance Art and in Modern Oblivion*. New York: Pantheon.

Thomas, J. C., & Alexander, K. E. (2003). 'And the signs are following:' Mark 16: 9-20–A journey into Pentecostal hermeneutics." *Journal of Pentecostal Theology, 11,* 147-170.

Thoreau, H. D. (1854/1939). *Walden or Life in the Woods*. New York: The Heritage Press.

Vaihinger, H. (1924/1968). *The Philosophy "As if": A System of the Theoretical, Practical, and Religious Fictions of Mankind*. New York: Barnes & Noble.

Westerlund, E. (1986). Freud on sexual trauma: An historical of seduction and betrayal. *Psychology of Women Quarterly*, *10*, 197-310.

Winnicott, W.W. (1971). *Playing and Reality*. New York: Basic Books.

Chapter 8

Mapping the Imagination: Heroes, Gods, and Oedipal Triumphs

Benjamin Beit-Hallahmi

Grünbaum (this volume) reviews two kinds of Freudian explanations for religious beliefs, one based on the mechanisms that create psychopathology, and the other based on universal childhood experiences. His critical judgment is summed up as "*A fortiori*, the psychoanalytic ontogeny of theism still lacks evidential warrant, with the possible exception of the psychogenesis of the doctrine of the Virgin Birth of Jesus" (p. 13). As to Freud's phylogeny of religion, it is rightly rejected by Grünbaum as totally lacking any supportive evidence.

Grünbaum's analysis of Freud's ideas weighs carefully every claim against theism and for atheism. He is extremely even-handed, but is an atheist just like Freud. I am puzzled by Grünbaum's references to "Mary" and "Joseph," two mythological figures, as if they were real people and claims could be made about their lives. Here he followed Freud's well-known error of treating "Moses" as part of history, rather than of mythology. These two puzzling cases demonstrate the power of cultural traditions. Neither Freud nor Grünbaum would treat Krishna, Isis, or Zeus this way.

As I read the work of Freud and his disciples, my concerns are slightly different than those of Grünbaum. To me, dismissing supernaturalism does not require any academic buttressing, and I see no need to defend it. The burden of proof is on those who promote supernaturalism, as representatives of the 60,000 religions in this world come before us to make their case. I have listened to some of the claims (not of all 60,000) and found them unconvincing (I have actually described the beliefs of about 1,800 religions; Beit-Hallahmi, 1998). A representative of religion number 49,565 may yet be able to convince me tomorrow, but from all I have heard so far, my conclusion is that supernaturalist claims are just so many fairy tales. I don't think we should spend a lot of time looking at the evidence for fairies or for Little Red Riding Hood (Farrell, 1955). After all, religionists find the claims of all 59,999 religions other than their own to be totally ridiculous, after spending much less time and effort on considering them than the average atheist.

Freud never wrote about the connection between his being an atheist to his daily work, but, according to one testimony, in 1905 said: "I remain what is known as an old-fashioned, honourable atheist, trying to help people by helping them to gain insight into themselves" (Goetz, 1975, p. 142). Grünbaum reminds us that Freud became an atheist as an adolescent in the 1870s, and was quite outspoken about it. He was quite representative of his generation of European intellectuals, and especially of European Jews (cf. Beit-Hallahmi, 2002). As a young man (and throughout his life), he refused to take part in any religious rituals, and did his best to avoid the Jewish wedding ceremony required by law to make his marriage official in Austria. Grünbaum notes that only in 1901 did Freud start offering psychological explanations for religion. As I discuss psychoanalytic interpretations, I would like to separate the dismissal of supernaturalism from the task of proposing psychological explanations for religious ideas.

The Religious Mindscape

Religious believers, who number in the billions and comprise most of humanity, share the supernaturalist assumption, which affirms the existence of greater and lesser spirits inhabiting an invisible world, affecting our universe, and demanding our attention and worship (Cf. Argyle & Beit-Hallahmi, 1975; Beit-Hallahmi, 1989; Beit-Hallahmi & Argyle, 1997). We know that particular religions become the focus of social identity, and are tied to claims of uniqueness, superiority, and competition with other groups, which promote identical claims.

Religious ideas have had a long history. There are indications of religious acts during the Middle Paleolithic period, between 100,000 and 40,000 years ago. The evidence includes burial sites and remains of animal worship, with massive investment of resources in activities and artifacts which have no bearing on survival, at a time when all human communities were in danger of extinction. Archeologists suggest that only ideas about communicating with the spirit world can explain these acts and such an investment (Kaufman, 1999). While artifacts and customs have changed since the Stone Age, the basic belief in the spirit world has not. The young religions we know best, crystallized during the past five millennia, are proud to proclaim their antiquity and their unchanging nature, and they do indeed reflect ideas that have not changed in 100,000 years. Written creeds are a recent invention, and the theology of the past millennium is already a response to growing secularization. Today, we are used to religions that offer us comprehensive, persuasive, and pleasing conceptions of the universe and our place in it. As Freud mockingly laments: "How comprehensive, exhaustive, and final are the doctrines of the believers compared with the labored, poor, and patchy attempts at explanation which are the best we can produce!" (1939, p. 157).

The plausibility, legitimacy, and coherence of belief systems are created by culture and socialization, as individual minds assimilate cultural givens. Religious beliefs, like other aspects of culture, are acquired through social learning, and the ontogenesis of any individual's belief system is no mystery. People learn religion at the local level, exposed to one of 60,000 possibilities, as soon as they are capable of learning. Religious indoctrination, done informally, starts in early childhood, through exposition, modeling, and narration. Religious beliefs are accessible and attractive to all, especially children, and can be taught informally by any parent anywhere. Most adult believers have learned all they know about their religion as children, and most children naturally and simply accept what they are told and enjoy taking part in rituals which reinforce religious teachings. Individual religious identity is, in the vast majority of cases, totally predictable in terms of culture and intergenerational continuity. Adult beliefs and publicly displayed commitments are tied to the accidents of birth, geography, and history. In 99 percent of the cases, young humans are successfully taught to accept the tenets of whatever faith their parents hold. (Converts from one religion to another are a small minority within the worlds billions of believers, and their conversions reflect social learning as well.)

Religious believers don't think in terms of basic tenets or abstractions. Children and adults learn specific religious beliefs through exposure to many stories, especially triumphal narratives which tell us about contacts between the world of the spirits and human heroes who are close to the gods. For the believers, a myth is a true report of real and important events, proving the power and mercy of the gods, and any interpretation follows from that assumption. Faith is sustained by narratives of past glories and promises of future triumphs.

Religious assertions quite explicitly aim at going above and beyond nature, which necessarily means moving to the realm of human fantasy, guided by desire, and the religious imagination is a triumph over reality, most clearly expressed in the denial of death. Victory over nature and over our natural limitations is the fantasy with which religious discourse starts, and miracle narratives remind us that the limitations of nature could be indeed overcome by the power of the spirits. Miracle narratives assure us that even if the universe is not totally benign, benevolent forces are active on our side and will intervene on our behalf, if we only obey their commands. Such narratives are always naturalistic claims (Beit-Hallahmi, 2001) presented as evidence for the power of spirits and the power of those connected or obedient to them.

Impossible and improbable narratives constitute proof that those who speak for the world of the spirits are indeed in direct contact with it, and that the great spirits do intervene in mundane reality to reward those of faith and devotion.

Moreover, they serve to persuade us not of the reality of the world of the spirits in general, but of the superiority of one particular belief system and one particular claim to authority. Common miracle narratives are part of the great plot, a texture of compensations and consolations leading up to the promise of triumph. They buttress and provide evidence for the validity of particular religious assertions. Religious and political groups, and their leaders, wish to establish a unique identity and superiority in relation to competing entities. In a religious context, superiority is claimed by reporting contacts with the spirit world, proven through earthly miracles and triumphs.

Freud described the mechanics of creating popular narrative fictions, which " . . . were the imaginary satisfactions of unconscious wishes, just as dreams are . . . But they differed from the asocial, narcissistic products of dreaming in that they were calculated to arouse sympathetic interest in other people and were able to evoke and satisfy the same unconscious wishes in them too" (Freud, 1925-1926, pp. 64-65). Fantasies which go beyond individual dreams or daydreams must be received by an audience in the same way any work of art achieves its place in culture; not through deliberation, but through individual creativity and through conscious and unconscious psychological processing.

In the creation of religious beliefs and narratives, the artists hide behind divine authorities or mythical prophets and revelations, but the resulting mythologies offer us anthropocentric fantasies accessible to all. The creators of cultural fantasies, like any artist, can engineer any solution to human problems, just as we can travel anywhere in our daydreams.. Wishes are our only guide, and so we may invent a spiritual pregnancy or a pregnancy with no father in any form.

To say that miracles are stories of events beyond human comprehension is to miss their essential psychological and cultural function. On the contrary, the stories must be, and are, comprehensible and accessible. Components of cultural traditions are not often questioned or critically examined, especially when they are gratifying or non-threatening. The audience for religious narratives does not consider the pros and cons of their being possible or plausible.

Psychological theories of religion assume that because of universal mechanisms and dispositions, we are ready to accept and create general claims about the spirit world, and some specific fantasies about the denizens of that world in interaction with humans. Beyond explanations of the general readiness for religion in general, we need to account for the appearance of specific beliefs. One question that transcends the realm of religion and relates to all aspects of culture is that of particular narratives about gods, saints, and heroes that humans become attached to. A salient cultural or universal fantasy raises the question of its special power over a substantial number of individual minds.

When Grünbaum examines psychoanalytic explanations for specific religious doctrines, such as the doctrines surrounding the Virgin Birth, he concludes that Freud's notion of repressed Oedipal conflicts is much more plausible than any conscious explanations offered to justify them: "Psychologically, the doctrine of the virgin birth provides a golden, sublime opportunity to fulfill the wish to dissociate motherhood from sexuality. In the second place, if the hypothesized role of the Holy Ghost in Mary's pregnancy was only to render Jesus' conception miraculous, would it not be more credible that God the father created his own son directly *ex nihilo*—as he had done with photons, for example—rather than that the asexual story of the five Gospels is true? Hence let us proceed on the basis of our prior motivational interpretation" (Grünbaum, this volume, pp. 28-29). In this chapter, I will try to follow more closely the possible motivational meanings of virgin birth narratives. Exploring further the meaning of this fantasy, which has been canonized in Christianity, I will look at related ideas in other cultures.

Miraculous and Asexual Conception Narratives

The Virgin Birth doctrine is just one among thousands of miracle narratives, found worldwide, which report the involvement of spirits, angels, and gods in human procreation. These accounts have to do with the conception and birth of gods. The irregular ways in which heroes are born in religious mythology show some degree of regularity.

Conception Difficulties and Divine Intervention

The notion of difficulties in conception and birth, which are resolved thanks to spirit intervention, is extremely common, and religious people everywhere use it in describing their own lives. Mythological stories describe explicit messages from great spirits and actual visits by angels, either in response to human prayers or through surprising acts by supernatural agents. This plot is found several times in the Old Testament, as a barren woman gives birth to a hero thanks to divine intervention.

The three generations of the Israelite mythological founding family were similarly afflicted and blessed. A childless woman (Genesis 18:1-15; 21:1-2), Rebekah, Isaac's wife, was barren until the Lord responded to Isaac's prayers (Genesis 25:21). In the third generation it was the barren Rachel, Jacob's second wife, who eventually gave birth to Joseph and Benjamin (Genesis 30:22-24; 35:17-18).

The story of Samson, the Old Testament hero, starts with a divine intervention (Judges 13). His (unnamed) mother was barren. His father Manoah could not impregnate her. Then an angel of the Lord came to annunciate the conception and birth of a redeemer. Following a second encounter with the angel, the woman conceives and Samson is born. This particular birth narrative has been interpreted by scholars as reflecting the idea of divine paternity (Mobley, 2006).

Stories of barren women having children through divine intervention reflect human realities and literary craft. The reality is that childless women have been socially excluded and inferior. Some narratives describing this reality are literary masterpieces (1 Samuel 1). Our heart goes out to Hannah, and we cannot fail but be impressed by her husband Elkanah, loving and devoted, just as we cannot fail to rejoice in Hannah's triumph, as she became a mother, producing a mythical prophet.

Divine Paternity of Heroes

Stories about the superhuman children of the gods abound, and in most of them conception is due to sexual intercourse between gods and human females. Here is one from Genesis (6: 1-4, 6):

> And it came to pass, when men began to multiply on the face of the earth, and daughters were born unto them, That the sons of God saw the daughters of men that they were fair; and they took them wives of all which they chose. There were giants in the earth in those days; and also after that, when the sons of God came in unto the daughters of men, and they bare children to them, the same became mighty men which were of old, men of renown.

This reads like a synopsis of hundreds of Greek narratives describing sexual intercourse between gods and women and its progeny, but we find it in the Old Testament.

One of these "men of renown" was Herakles (or Hercules to the Romans), who was the greatest hero to the ancient Greeks. His story began when Zeus decided to find the perfect woman in order to have a perfect son. The woman was Alcmene, wife of Amphitryon. This myth was possibly meant to teach us how humans can reach immortality and divine status. This involves first being a descendant of the gods, then performing miracles, and then dying a particularly horrifying death (Nagy, 1997). Thus, the myth of Herakles reads like an early version of the Jesus myth, without the virgin birth.

Divine Paternity of Kings

Not only mythical heroes, but some real historical figures had stories of divine paternity attached to them. The idea of the divine ruler, fathered by gods is widespread, from Europe to Japan. Asserting divine paternity or divine sanction incurs clear political advantages, and so we may regard such claims, when made by living kings, to be manipulative and self-serving. In ancient Greece, Alexander the Great was believed to be the son of Zeus. In Egypt, the king was described as son of one of the leading gods, who had intercourse with the king's mother. Until the end of World War II, the Japanese emperor was officially considered divine, a descendant of Amaterasu, the Shinto Sun goddess.

In ancient Egypt, narratives of the divine paternity of kings often described their mothers as virgins. Mutemua was a virgin queen, who gave birth to the Pharaoh Amenkept (or Amenophis) III, the builder of the great temple of Luxor. On the temple walls we see depictions of the god Kneph impregnating the virgin spiritually by holding a cross, the symbol of life, to her mouth. Among Roman emperors, Augustus was reputed to be the spiritual son of Apollo, conceived when his mother spent a night in the god's temple.

Divine paternity was also ascribed to historical men of great wisdom and reputation. Pythagoras, Socrates, and Plato were among those who won such honors (Hägg & Rousseau, 2000). Of Plato it was related that his mother Perictione was a virgin who conceived him immaculately to the god Apollo. Apollo himself revealed the circumstances of this conception to Ariston, the affianced husband of the virgin.

Virgin Birth of the Gods

The birth stories of greater and lesser gods in all cultures contain specific references to virgin mothers. Dionysus, the Grecian God, was said to be the son of Zeus and the virgin goddess Persephone. In India, the ten avatars of Vishnu, of whom the best known are Rama and Krishna, are believed to have been the outcome of virgin births.

Miraculously Inseminated Virgins

One story about Mithras, the Persian god worshipped all over the Roman empire, describes him as being born of Anahita, an Immaculate Virgin Mother. Anahita conceived Mithras from the seed of Zoroaster (Zarathustra) preserved in the waters of Lake Hamun in the Persian province of Sistan. Fantasies about the eternally potent ejaculate play a prominent role in a related eschatological tradition. Followers of Zoroaster believe that their future saviors, the three Saosyants, will be conceived inside a fifteen-year-old virgin's womb, by Zoroaster's own semen, preserved in a lake, where she would go swimming. So these three saviors will be Zoroaster's biological sons (Boyce, 2000).

Zoroastrian traditions had influenced younger religions formed in West Asia, and the Zoroastrian story of the three saviors later became a Jewish legend. A medieval collection of legends known as the Alphabet of Ben Sira contains the story of three ancient sages who were born of virgins and grew up to be true saints and great scholars. All three were the product of stray semen, ejaculated at a bathhouse, which then entered their mother's body. Only one of them knew who his father was. That was Ben Sira, the legendary author of the deuterocanonical book *Ecclesiasticus*, or Sirach. His father, according to the story, was none other than the mythological prophet Jeremiah, who was forced by evil men to masturbate in the bath, and thus impregnated his own daughter, who later visited the same bathhouse. Because of the special circumstances of his birth, Ben Sira was not considered a bastard son of incest. This narrative, has been treated with disdain by rabbinical authorities, but is still quoted by rabbis today in the context of rulings about artificial insemination (Rosner, 2001).

Divine Fathers and Human Virgins

Numerous narratives describe the gods coming down to earth in pursuit of human virgins. One of the best known was Danae, a virgin impregnated by Zeus through a shower of gold, which led to the birth of Perseus, a well-known Oedipal hero. Justin Martyr, the second-century Church Father wrote that this narrative had been "another forgery of that treacherous serpent" (Slusser, 2003, p. 110), invented by the Devil, who, knowing that Jesus would be born to a virgin, produced the early miracle to bewilder the believers.

Divine Asexual Conception

Some birth narratives describe a conception by gods without any physical contact. In some cases, the mother is not a virgin, but conception is asexual or purely "spiritual." In a traditional narrative found among the Aztecs, the goddess Coatlicue gave birth to the twin gods Quetzalcoatl and Xolotl after being impregnated by a ball of feathers. She was not a virgin at the time, and had given birth to 400 other children.

One Hindu tradition describes Krishna as conceived following a "mental transmission" which traveled from the mind of his father Vasudeva to the womb of his mother Devaki. Apis, the sacred bull of Memphis, was believed to have been begotten by a deity descending as a ray of moonlight on a lucky cow.

There are several accounts of the virgin birth of Buddha. One describes Maya, an immaculate virgin who conceived him through divine inspiration. Another version relates how he was conceived by his mother's dreaming of a white elephant, without intercourse, and the delivery was out of her side. Another tells of Maya having been carried away by spirits to the Himalayas, where she underwent ceremonial purifications at the hands of four queens. The Bodhisattva then appeared to her, and walked round her three times. Then the Buddha (the incarnate Bodhisattva) entered her womb.

> Zoroaster, the mythological founder of the ancient Iranian religion, was believed to have been born of the fifteen-year-old virgin Dughdova who conceived after she had been visited by a shaft of light, or a ray of divine reason. As an infant, Zoroaster miraculously escaped several attempts on his life, and was protected by animals, including a she-wolf that nursed him (Nigosian, 1993).

The she-wolf brings us to Romulus and Remus, the mythological founders of Rome, who were the children of the god Mars, and a Vestal virgin. According to some traditions Mars seduced Rhea Sylvia, the Vestal virgin, in a dream, leading to the conception of the twins (Staples, 1997).

Parthenogenesis

Several miracle narratives do not include any father. The Egyptian sun-god, Ra, was said to have been born of a virgin mother, Net (or Neith), and to have had no father. Horus, in some accounts, was said to be the parthenogenetic child of the Virgin Mother, Isis. One story about the birth of Ganesha relates how the goddess Parvati, while bathing, created a boy out of the dirt of her body and assigned to guard her bathroom door. When her husband, the god Shiva, returned, he was surprised to find this stranger at the door, and knocked off the boy's head. Parvati broke down in grief, and Shiva attached an elephant's head to the boy's body.

Complete Self-Creation

We have at least one story of a god's birth out of a rock (deus saxigenus). Mithras was born on December 25, when he came out of a rock, fully grown and armed. Later on, Mithras would shoot an arrow into a rock, producing water. The idea of a lifeless rock which gives birth (*petra genetrix*) appears remarkable. Producing water out of rocks seems only slightly less so. In the Old Testament, Moses is described as producing water out of rocks by striking them (Exodus 17:1-6; Numbers 20:1-13).

Modern Miracle Narratives

The British prophetess Joanna Southcott (1750-1814), who still inspires admirers, announced in 1814 that she would soon give birth to a divine child named Shiloh. Joanna, sixty-four at the time, was never pregnant, and died soon thereafter (Balleine, 1956).

Among the Branch Davidians, known because of the 1993 Waco tragedy, there were rumors of a miracle pregnancy. Vernon Wayne Howell (1960-1993), later known as David Koresh, joined the Branch Davidians in 1981. He became the lover of Lois Roden, a woman in her seventies, who was then the prophetess. Claims about her being pregnant by her young lover, who was in his twenties, were circulating, as evidence of messianic powers and events. She died in 1986, and Koresh became the prophet (Tabor and Gallagher, 1995).

Waiting for "Spiritual Procreation"

Ideas about asexual procreation are not only tied to ancient myths. One modern Hindu movement, Brahma Kumaris, promises the world that the future holds in store spiritual procreation, without any physical contact. This is an international Hindu revival movement, founded in 1937 in Karachi by Dada Lekh Raj (1877-

1969), a wealthy diamond merchant, who started having visions at the age of 60, and adopted the name of Prajapita Brahma. Sexual activity is proscribed, and the sexes are strictly separated. Most active members of the group are celibate women, and the leadership is exclusively female. The group's belief system proclaims pacifism and love, but at the same time predicts a nuclear war which would wipe out all of the world's population, except for the Brahma Kumaris membership. Following this cataclysm, a new era will begin, one of peace and prosperity. Procreation will take place spiritually, and that is why sex is already superfluous.

Approaching Interpretation

Asexual procreation ideas have always been found in the human imagination, part of the cultural baggage in every culture. Because the natural process of conception and birth is so familiar to humans, any claims to exceptionality in this context are easily noted and appreciated. The stories we have encountered make sense only because the audience knows what conception means and how children are born. Only because of that is the story awe-inspiring. If all were born in such ways, the miracle narrative would lose its power (cf. Spiro, 1968).

Miraculous birth narratives generate awe and submission, as we realize that they signify what is beyond the reach of ordinary humans. We cannot have these miracles in our own lives, but we can attach ourselves to the heroes, saints, and gods who will protect us. Widely shared fantasies must be gratifying in some way, and our hunch is that they offer a solution to an experienced problem. Normal birth is experienced as less than desirable, and the idea of an immaculate, asexual conception seems to hold a universal attraction, as in many of the narratives the message is one of evading carnality, and avoiding conception or birth through the vagina. A "spiritual" procreation, with asexual conception and birth, without bodily contact and body fluids, seems ideal. A spiritual conception and a virgin mother are offered as the best combination. Being impregnated by semen without intercourse is almost as good as a purely spiritual conception, and when virgins are impregnated by uterus-homing ejaculate, we are told that the children they bear are destined for greatness. The modern Brahma Kumaris version is a continuation of a stream of seemingly eternal fantasies.

The extraordinary prevalence of these fantasies, and the readiness or eagerness to embrace them at all times and all cultures mean that such ideas are universally attractive. Even if not most central in any given tradition, these stories continue to circulate and are considered plausible. Even when such stories are relatively marginal in a particular culture, we know about them because they have been transmitted and institutionalized in some way.

Oedipal Templates

The constellation of both positive and negative wishes directed at parents, according to Freud (1915-1916), is thought to be expressed in a well-known narrative formula, in which miraculous salvation from death is followed by bloody struggles and triumph often precedes tragedy. Freud's ideas about the prevalence of the Oedipal have been criticized first because he collected his data, such as they were, from neurotics, and those neurotics came only from European culture (e.g., Horney, 1939), but Johnson and Price-Williams (1996) found Oedipal themes to be globally ubiquitous, and Brown (1991), in his list of human universals, included religion, mythology, and the "Oedipus complex." Kluckhohn (1959) presented a survey of global mythology, with the following themes found in all cultures: creation, flood, slaying of monsters, incest, sibling rivalry, castration (*vagina dentata*), Oedipal stories, and hero myths. Ubiquitous themes in myths were said to ". . . result from recurrent reactions of the human psyche to situations and stimuli of the same general order" (p. 268).

Freud defines the Oedipal matrix of the hero as follows:

> A hero is a man who stands up manfully against his father and in the end victoriously overcomes him. The myth in question traces this struggle back to the very dawn of the hero's life, by having him born against his father's will and saved in spite of his father's evil intentions (Freud, 1939, p. 9).

We can claim evidence of Oedipality by finding predicted regularities in the materials, and the concordance of certain motifs appearing together in consistent patterns. The typical configuration combines an irregular, miraculous, birth with violent intergenerational conflict and the hero's choice of the wrong love object. The asexual birth may be a triumphal way of starting life, but it is followed by mortal dangers. The father is pushed aside, but he is still a force. The Ganesha story is a prime example of Oedipality, with no virgin mother but with parthenogenesis, eliminating the father completely. Ganesha was conceived without any male involvement, but the non-father still wants to kill the rival (Hershman, 1974).

An Oedipal triumph is defined as the elimination of the love rival or the reduction of the rival to an inferior position (Akhtar, 2009; Palombo, 1994). An Oedipal winner is somebody who is greater than his father, completely independent of his father, or eliminates his father physically. Miracle birth narratives such as the Virgin Birth express one version of a decisive Oedipal triumph. Only gods and some divine humans are entitled to such a fate. Philosophers and kings sometimes may gain this honor, signifying greatness.

Thus, in Greek mythology, Cronos, who castrated his father Uranus and married his sister Rhea, was told that his son would defeat him. He swallowed his first five children. The sixth, Zeus, was saved miraculously, raised by nymphs on Crete, and came back to defeat his father. Later on, Zeus himself received a similar warning about his children by his wife Metis, and so turned her into a fly and swallowed her. This led to Athena being born fully grown out of his head. In the Mahabrata, the story of Krishna's birth starts with a prophecy, in which king Kamsa is warned that his sister Devaki's future son will kill him. Kamsa killed the first six of Devaki's children. The seventh baby, Krishna, is saved by being smuggled to the home of foster parents. Eventually, Krishna returns, kills his uncle Kamsa, and has intercourse with his aunt Kubja (Campbell, 1981).

One story of Oedipal triumph and tragedy has led to one of the greatest dramatic texts in history, *Oedipus Tyrannos* by Sophocles, and has been presented countless times in numerous traditions. In the Middle Ages, the *Oedipus Tyrannos* narrative was attached to the mythological figure of Judas Iscariot. Medieval legends related how Judas killed his father and married his mother. It was after discovering his terrible crime that Judas met Jesus and entered Christian mythology in search of absolution (Freemantle, 1950: Schendler, 1954). The story apparently appeared in Europe in the eleventh century, and it is suggested that the Crusades and anti-Semitism, as well as heightened concern about incest taboos, played a role in its popularity (Yarom, 1993). Jewish medieval legends attached this narrative to the Old Testament mythical figure of Joshua (Reider, 1960).

Oedipal triumph narratives have been surveyed systematically since the nineteenth century. The beginning of what might be called cultural studies in the nineteenth century, with the work of such scholars as E.B. Tylor (1832-1917) and Johann Georg von Hahn (1811-1869), led to published observations on the commonalities in many hero myths. Rank (1914), after looking at thirty-four myths from the Mediterranean basin and West Asia, offered a general formula, or "standard saga," which could be found in innumerable mythological stories and fits such well-known cases as those of Krishna, Moses, Isaac, Oedipus, and Jesus. The mythological hero is the son of royal parents, born in a difficult birth (often after a long period of childlessness), prophesied to be a danger to the safety of his father, who banishes him (often by putting him in a basket and setting it afloat). The child is then saved by poor people or animals, and only upon maturity does he discover his real parents. He eventually gains the love and recognition of his people, achieves fame and greatness, and wreaks vengeance on his father, fulfilling the prophecy.

According to Rank, one origin of this plot is what Freud called the 'family romance' (Freud's [1909] account of the family romance was first published as an integral part of the Rank 1914 text). Young children, disappointed with their actual parents, imagine that they had been adopted or kidnapped, and that their real parents were richer, more powerful, or more loving, than the shabby substitutes they live with. The family romance plot eliminates the immediate reality of the parents, while another common fantasy gets rid of the parents altogether. Many classic children's stories tell the story of an abandoned, orphaned or outcast child, like Peter Pan, David Copperfield, Oliver Twist, Huck Finn, Tom Sawyer, or Heidi. Orphans like Harry Potter are prevalent in folktales, fairy tales, and popular literature (Gordon and Sherr, 1974).

All human attachments carry costs, and some are painful. The fantasy of avoiding painful ones is only natural. The story of Mithras coming out of a rock expresses a narcissistic fantasy of self-sufficiency and superiority. This is the most extreme rejection of parents, who are no longer necessary for procreation. The family romance may have to do not only with physical parentage, but also with developing unique and creative individuality (Greenacre, 1958). An artist may claim that he had no father and did not need one, because "I am my own father." A case in point is the psychoanalyst and artist Erik Erikson, who grew up as Erik Homburger, but then changed his name, around the age of forty, to Erikson, becoming Erik son of Erik (Erikson, 1970; Falk, 1975-76).

The family romance fantasy is the source of the double parenting motif in the hero myth, while other motifs can easily be identified as Oedipal, involving conflict, competition, and violence. Rank's model was expanded into the life of the hero template by Raglan (1936), who came up with a list of twenty-two elements which are part of the hero myth of all cultures:

1. The hero's mother is a royal virgin
2. His father is a king, and
3. Often a near relative of his mother, but
4. The circumstances of his conception are unusual, and
5. He is also reputed to be the son of a god.
6. At birth an attempt is made, usually by his father or his maternal grandfather to kill him, but
7. He is spirited away, and
8. Reared by foster-parents in a far country.
9. We are told nothing of his childhood, but
10. On reaching manhood he returns or goes to his future Kingdom.
11. After a victory over the king and/or a giant, dragon, or wild beast,
12. He marries a princess, often the daughter of his predecessor and
13. And becomes king.
14. For a time he reigns uneventfully and
15. Prescribes laws, but
16. Later he loses favor with the gods and/or his subjects, and
17. Is driven from the throne and city, after which
18. He meets with a mysterious death,
19. Often at the top of a hill,
20. His children, if any do not succeed him.
21. His body is not buried, but nevertheless
22. He has one or more holy sepulchers.

We should note that in Raglan's template, the mother's virginity is the starting point of the hero's mythical biography. Not all hero narratives include all twenty-two elements, but if we examine the traditions concerning Krishna, Moses, Romulus, Perseus, Jesus, Herakles, and Buddha, we find that at least fifteen elements are present. In the case of Krishna, the best match, twenty-one are present.

Why does the myth of the hero include Oedipal elements? Heroes are known and admired for slaying monsters, saving their people from disasters, sometimes killing their fathers, uncles, and other relatives and non-kin in struggles over succession. Being born to a virgin or committing incest seems to us less vital to the hero biographical formula, but in reality hero myths are likely to include such elements, thus pointing to the attraction of what might only be called Oedipal templates.

The idea of an irregular birth does not appear as a discrete event, but as a component in a biography, describing the life of a hero, king, or god. Such biographies glorify and create attachment and devotion by reporting the exceptional events of one life. Most components of the biography are exceptional, and the birth story is one of them. But birth mode does not depend on the hero, and he is not responsible for this miracle.

When we attribute divine paternity or a miraculous conception to a human hero, it is evidence for inherent superiority. If the man is superhuman in his earthly achievements, he just cannot be a mere mortal in starting life through a normal birth, out of an actual vagina.

Local versions of miracle birth themes may reflect specific cultural and historical factors. Narratives easily turn into identity markers and political symbols, and then reflect struggles about real power, authority and legitimacy. Traditions, formed in part by in group fantasies, develop quickly, just like group identities.

Sociological and anthropological interpretations see myth as symbolizing, reflecting, and strengthening social structures or as attempting to gain social advantages. Obeysekere (1981) offered an alternative explanation to the double parenting motif in " . . . the hero must be born of royal parents to be legitimate: yet he must *also* be born of ordinary people to be popular" (p. 49). While this interpretation assumes the masses' need for someone just like them, Freud has proposed an opposite functional explanation:

> It can also be used to provide for our hero a patent of nobility to elevate him to a higher social rank. Thus Cyrus is for the Medes an alien conqueror; by way of the exposure myth he becomes the grandson of their king. A similar trait occurs in the myth of Romulus: if such a man ever lived he must have been an unknown adventurer, an upstart; the myth makes him a descendant of, and heir to, the royal house of Alba Longa (Freud, 1939, p. 11).

It may be that local variations found in prevalent narratives mirror variations in family structure and dynamics (Obeyesekere, 1990). Leach (1966) offers a structuralist hypothesis to account for the Christian Virgin Birth myth, as reflecting an extremely patriarchal society, in which there is a large gap between the rulers and the ruled. These suggested explanations (cf. Levi-Strauss, 1963) cannot easily account for the great variety of miracle birth stories.

How Are These Narratives Religious?

Oedipal winner narratives are not inherently religious, and are not consciously associated with other claims about the supernatural world and communications with it. Their conscious function is to glorify gods and heroes and attract believers. The narratives we are discussing here are created and then gain currency because of a conscious message and additional unconscious gratifications.

For the believers, the message in the miracle birth narratives is exceptionality, divinity, uniqueness, and superiority. This is consciously presented as miraculous, characterized by interventions and communications coming from the spirit world. The canonized denial of conception, pregnancy, and normal birth is an assertion of uniqueness and superiority. The miraculous or immaculate birth is a stunning miracle. The psychoanalytic consensus has been that these fantasies express the denial of sexual intercourse between one's parents, and this is the only kind of intercourse one is really concerned about.

Claiming divine paternity implies strong and close contact with great spirits. How and why would a virgin birth add to other claims of superiority for kings, gods, and heroes? Victory over earthly paternity is decisive evidence of superiority, much stronger than other kinds of proof. A resurrection from death is a greater miracle than a virgin birth, but bypassing normal paternity is still a victory over nature and fate. The message in many of the narratives is that having been conceived without sexual intercourse and being born without passing through the vagina is the ideal way to start life, but only a few heroes and gods have experienced this privileged route.

Religious Oedipal victories are tied to immortality and divinity, and a few heroes can escape both birth and death. Religious fantasies provide us with a parallel for pure birth without sex, and that is pure death without decay (cf. Himmelfarb, 1993). There are two myth figures in the Old Testament, and three in the New Testament who, according to standard Jewish and Christian interpretation, are reported to have ascended to heaven: Enoch (Genesis 5:24), Elijah (2 Kings 2:1-12), Jesus (Luke 24:51; Acts 1:9), Paul (2 Corinthians 12:2-4), and John (Revelation 4:1). At both ends of the life cycle, purity is evidence of power and superiority, granted to only a few who deserve immortality and divinity.

The Oedipal template is relevant not only to mythology, but to some rituals. Genital mutilation, part of initiation rites which affect about 20 percent of humanity, are consciously interpreted in various cultures as completing the process of gaining a full sexual identity. We have to recall that the mutilation is performed by father-figures, and for females, mother-figures (Bettelheim, 1954). In Judaism it is highly recommended that the father perform the circumcision on his son.

Oedipal Triumph and Christianity

Jones (1951b, p. 416) proposed that "The story of religion is a never ending attempt to overcome the Oedipus complex and to achieve peace of mind, through atonement with the father." This generalization seems directly relevant to Christian traditions. Jones (1951a) stated that Christian mythology was capable of integrating the basic family system of mother, father, and son, while Judaism concentrated on the father, and other traditions focused only on the mother or the son. Later developments in Christianity in the direction of developing the Holy

Ghost as the third person in the trinity were, according to Jones, mere attempts to deny the son's incestuous desires, and the father's role in procreation.

The centrality of Oedipal triumph in Christian mythology and the Oedipality of belief formation in individual believers has been discussed for almost a century. The specific Oedipal solution offered by the new religion has been suggested by Freud (1913, 1939) as an explanation for its historical victory over Judaism and its continuing attractiveness. Moxon (1931) already stated that the belief in the virgin mother has clear Oedipal origins, and Ingham (1992) noted that Freud's reading of Oedipal impulses in religious traditions actually ignored the Jesus-Mary relationship, in favor of emphasizing father-son competition.

Fromm (1964) proposed that Christianity was an Oedipal rebellion and a victory over the father-god. Dundes (1981) pointed out that unlike other Oedipal heroes, Jesus does not kill his father, but rather submits to him. However, by becoming one with his father, Jesus achieves the Oedipal ideal of becoming his own begetter. Simo (1983) stated that when comparing the myth of Jesus with the prototypical Oedipus story, Jesus is the Oedipal winner, because of his reward in the form of eternal life in Heaven, at the side of his mother, following a symbolic father murder. He murdered his father symbolically, through the Virgin Birth, which minimizes the role of the father, and the total marginality of Joseph, the earthly father.

Research on individual believers in the Christian sphere of culture has shown some support for the idea that Oedipality is involved in determining deity images. In a study of 4,660 French Catholic children, parental references to God were found to increase in both girls and boys between the ages of nine and fifteen. The image of God in boys was more often connected to the maternal image of the Virgin Mary and less often to the image of Jesus, while the opposite was true for girls (Deconchy, 1968). Larsen and Knapp (1964) found that the deity image as rated by females was more benevolent, while males rated it as more punitive. This was interpreted as supporting the Oedipal origins of the deity image.

The Purity Ideal and Miraculous Births

In Judaic and Christian traditions, both mortality and physical procreation were the consequences of the Fall, and the physical aspects of birth were treated with abhorrence (Paert, 2003). According to the Old Testament rules of purity, childbirth is followed by ritual pollution (Leviticus 12). In the case of a son, a woman is impure for seven days, and she can enter the sanctuary after forty days, while having a daughter leads to fourteen days of impurity, and being able to enter the sanctuary after eighty days. Brown (1988) described sexual renunciation as a central element in the history of early Christianity, but this contrast is not unique to Western traditions and an idealization of chastity can be found everywhere, just as women in India are considered impure following a birth, and in all cultures it is believed that "the female body performs all the 'dirty' work of life" (Hershman, 1974, p. 284). One solution to the inherent sinfulness of sex is to limit it to procreation within marriage, which has been embraced by numerous traditions (Greslé-Favier, 2009).

Being born without sex seems to a common fantasy, if not a universal ideal, expressed in a variety of creative solution to the challenge of sexual procreation. Is it possible that this ideal is simply a result of a general aversion to sex, and the horror of an unclean anatomy, and not anything we could define as Oedipal?

The thought of vaginal conception and delivery bring to mind contamination by bodily fluids, and bypassing the birth canal is preferred. We find many expressions of the abhorrence of normal procreation, and a preference for asexual, "spiritual" way of coming into this world. Mother's genitals are dirty, which is common enough feeling: ". . . for this is no way to be born, to be copulated and masturbated for nine months by the membrane, the yawning membrane which toothlessly devours, as the UPANISHADS say, and I know that I was born in a different way . . ." (Artaud, 1963, p. 83). When writing this in 1945, Antonin Artaud was hospitalized in a psychiatric hospital, diagnosed as a schizophrenic. We realize that his insane ideas are quite close to those of many supposedly sane individuals, who entertain the fantasies we are discussing here.

We know that children experience conscious revulsion at the thought of their parents having sex as they discover the facts of procreation. "My parents didn't do it" is a common reaction, and there is nothing pathological about it. Here is a recollection taken from *Facebook*:

> "Derrick: Sex is when a man puts his . . . in a woman's . . .
> Leigh: Oh no, that can't be true, that's disgusting.
> Derrick: It is true I promise, all adults do it—even your parents.
> Leigh: Oh no, my parents don't do that . . . they're religious.
> I went home and told my mother and she killed herself laughing and then regaled all her friends with the story of Leigh and Derrick's conversation about the facts of life."

The anatomical proximity of procreation and elimination, and especially the proximity of vagina and anus in women, has been noted with disappointment and revulsion by men. Echoing Swift (Brown, 1959), Yeats notes masculine complaints, but counters with a woman's voice:

> "A woman can be proud and stiff
> When on love intent;
> But Love has pitched his mansion in
> The place of excrement;
> For nothing can be sole or whole
> That has not been rent" (1957, p. 513).

Kubie (1937), in a classical survey of fantasies about our filthy bodies, stated that ". . . in general a prominent or out-jutting part of the body carries a presumption of cleanliness, whereas a cavity, or cleft, or hole, or pit in the body carries the presumption of dirt" (p. 395), and "In reality the reactions of men and women to the body of woman are dominated by this retreat from 'dirt'-laden clefts and apertures. We have found this to be true in women as well as men" (p. 396), so that a woman may suffer from "an obsessive conviction that she has one aperture too many, and that a dirty one" (p. 398).

Kubie's claims are supported by recent research. Herbenick (2009) found that men had more positive attitudes about women's genitals than women. The female genitals may be perceived as disgusting, but semen is just as revolting as female secretions, according to Miller (1997), thus involving all procreation in revulsion. "Both the penis and the vagina tend, however, to share in this inhibiting sense of filth; and out of this is derived a system of unconscious ideas shared by men and women alike: The vagina is dirty. Therefore it is worthy only of dirty objects. Anything which enters it either is dirty to begin with or becomes dirty on penetration. All body secretions are dirty. Both vaginal mucus and the semen of the male are dirty. Intercourse therefore consists of being filled full of dirt and of being smeared with dirt. Neither the impressive ceremonials of the wedding service nor the exhilaration of deep infatuation can effectively lift the taboos which fantasies such as these represent and enforce" (Kubie, 1937, pp. 422-423).

Female genitals are not only devalued, but also feared (Beit-Hallahmi, 1985). This is part of a complex of denial and hostility towards women, which finds many expressions in mythology. The reality of birth by females is denied in Genesis and in hundreds of other traditions when a male deity is the creator of humanity in the first birth, and when Eve is created from Adam's (spare?) rib. Male initiation rites in traditional cultures include a rebirth, which is a birth from the father, nullifying birth from a woman and creating a complete masculine identification (Reik, 1958). Freud's analysis of the phenomenon of aversion to the genitals related it to Oedipal issues. He suggested that the common view of sex as something dirty has to do with the connection between the genitals and excrement, but it can only be a significant factor in behavior because of fantasies about incestuous object-choice. When Freud first noted this phenomenon, he states that ". . . the genitals act as a reminder of excremental functions" (Freud, 1905, p. 40), and adds, "It is scarcely possible to exaggerate the pathogenic significance of the comprehensive tie uniting the sexual and the excremental, a tie which is at the basis of a very large number of hysterical phobias" (p. 41). Later on, Freud states that "The excremental is all too intimately and inseparably bound up with the sexual; the position of the genitals—inter urinas et faeces nascimur [we are born between urine and feces]—remains the decisive and unchangeable factor . . ." (1912, 11, p. 189).

Most humans manage to overcome their inhibitions, at least to the extent of having sexual intercourse, but in some individuals, and possibly in many, unconscious anxiety about object choice is the cause of psychopathology, according to one of Freud's more startling statements: ". . . anyone who is to be really free and happy in love must have surmounted his respect for women and have come to terms with the idea of incest with his mother or sister. Anyone who subjects himself to a serious self-examination on the subject of this requirement will be sure to find that he regards the sexual act basically as something degrading, which defiles and pollutes not only the body. The origin of this low opinion, which he will certainly not willingly acknowledge, must be looked for in the period of his youth in which the sensual current in him was already strongly developed but its satisfaction with an object outside the family was almost as completely prohibited as it was with an incestuous one" (1912, 11, p. 186).

In *Civilization and Its Discontents*, Freud notes again that " . . . all neurotics, and many others besides, take exception to the fact that 'inter urinas et faeces nascimur'" (Freud, 1930, p. 106). This aversion in adult men means immaturity, as it is typical of "all neurotics," and reflects a failure to overcome Oedipal anxieties. It leads some men to a devaluation of any love object, while those who have mastered such anxieties are able to perform sexually and to enjoy what they do without undue inhibitions.

Even if we don't accept Freud's ideas about Oedipality or his observations on the sexual theories of children (1908), we cannot deny the confusion and anxiety experienced by children as they learn the complicated realities of procreation and kinship. Children's confusion, ambivalence, and anxiety may be expressed directly in "My parents didn't do that." As adults, we consciously dismiss these sentiments, as we all supposedly know well the "facts of life," but sex is forever tied to anxiety and conflict. Our readiness to entertain or take seriously stories about birth without sex is just one indication of the survival of childhood confusions and anxieties in so many adults. Birth is a mystery, and so is the human family, and fantasies about other options of avoiding parental sexuality, conception, and parentage easily arise. Heroes always escape from their parents and return triumphant, and we all share these exploits. We cannot escape, but we can identify with them and try to keep close to them.

Every individual child, when faced with the problem of internalizing the meaning of family roles, experiences inevitable confusion about such things as the difference between a mother and a wife. Mother is first perceived as mothering the whole family, including father, and getting the incest taboo right is much harder. The universal anxiety about sex and object choice is reflected in narratives of confused and hidden identities, where parents are not parents and sons are not sons. Oedipal fantasies, as expressed in the stories we find in every culture, are about escaping the inescapable: Bypassing birth, parenting, and the family.

Miracle birth narratives may reflect a desire for purity and an aversion to sex, but if this were the most important or exclusive motivation, we would find discrete birth narratives expressing this wish. In reality, as we have seen, the asexual birth narrative appears always within a wider plot, which is clearly Oedipal. As significant as the purity ideal may be, it appears together with other motifs, part of the predictable conflict template, and bypassing parental intercourse in birth is followed by threats from fathers, grandfathers, uncles, or kings (as in the cases of Jesus and Krishna). The miracle birth motif is the opening for a story that not only starts, but also ends with an Oedipal triumph. It seems that childhood confusion about sex and parents, and the desire for purity are easily channeled to the unifying Oedipal template.

The Oedipal Paradox

Which is a worse crime, knowingly killing an innocent child or unknowingly killing one's father? "In the story of Oedipus—as it has been told to us in the Greek myth—the primitive fact is not parricide and incest, but rather the criminal parental couple who has condemned the newborn Oedipus to death. Thus it could be said—adhering to the myth—that Oedipus experienced in his cradle the infanticidal intention of his parents, united against him in the combined parental figure" (Fornari, 1974, p. 240).

How should we read the *Oedipus Tyrannos* plot, or the story of Krishna? The question has given rise to both intuitive and counter-intuitive interpretations. This well-known plot combines miracles, triumph, and tragedy. What all versions convey is the biography of a hero who is first and foremost a victim, a helpless baby miraculously saved from death. The straightforward reading involves the audience in celebrating victories and mourning failures, through identification with the hero, who is an unwitting slave to fate. This starts with birth in the absence of love, when the baby is facing a death threat from his parents, kin, or others in positions of authority. The starting point of the plot is the experience of helplessness, which truly reflects the beginning of life, when we feel terrified, overwhelmed, and immobilized, at the mercy of parents and caretakers.

The perception of the child as the victim in the family situation is an essential component of universal Oedipal mythology. We all identify with the child victim; Oedipus, Moses, Krishna, Jesus, or Ganesha, and we experience the stories as they are told from the victim's point of view. Our intuitive feeling may be that these popular stories reflect children's insecurity about parental love. After almost being killed as a baby, as an adult the hero is a victim of predestination. He cannot be in control, and can at best cope with unfolding events (Fortes, 1959).

Freud, in his counterintuitive reading, turns the story on its head, suggesting that this narrative is a denial and a cover-up. The family, locus of love and devotion, is actually a battlefield, but the source of threatened and actual violence in the story is the child, and not the parents (Freud, 1909). The hostility towards the father is projected on him in the myths. The child is not a victim of cruel, blind fate, but a would-be perpetrator, full of criminal schemes. Our identification with the victim is in reality identification with the schemer's hidden designs. The many narratives in which the hero is a parricide or patricide seems to support Freud's view, and the spontaneous admiration for patricide has been admirably portrayed in the *Playboy of the Western World* (Synge, 1998).

Hero myths are about rebelling against the father and against all authority, power, and legitimacy, and for a rearrangement of power relations. The father is both the one who wields actual power and the symbol of all authority for the child. If the hero is a child threatened with death by his parents (or other family members), who then takes revenge on them, it is a clear accusation against family and authority, and a subversive incitement against parental, and especially paternal, authority. It tells us that parental love is far from being unconditional, and then that punishment for the crimes of parricide and incest is far from predestined, and relies on desperate human efforts.

The *Oedipus Tyrannos* template is one of rebellion against the family and paternity, as evidenced first by the two sets of parents, and then by the horrifying presence of parricide and incest. It undermines the conventions and norms of culture and family by telling a story of the ultimate crime. Transgression is exposed and punished only after the unthinkable became a reality and horrifying crimes have been committed. But most Oedipal winners, in most cultures, like Zeus and Krishna, remain unpunished and triumphant, celebrated in countless festivals around the world. Greek culture initially had offered a complete triumph version of the *Oedipus Tyrannos* story. Dodds (1973) reported that in the *Oedipus Tyrannos* plot as told in Homeric times, there is no tragic ending, as "in the story Homer knew he continues to reign in Thebes after his guilt is discovered, and is eventually killed in battle and buried with royal honors. It was apparently a later mainland myth, the *Thebans*, that created the Sophoclean 'man of sorrows'" (p. 36).

All narratives of alternative paternity are subversive of paternity and family. All versions of Oedipal triumph fantasies, in which human fathers are demoted in favor of divine fathers, spiritual conceptions, or no conceptions at all, are subversions of paternal authority and legitimacy. It is the dethronement of the Oedipal father. Any enactment of Oedipal triumph undermines authority (even when followed by punishment) as it begins with the idea that true parental love is far from universal.

Miracle birth fantasies revolve around the role of the father, and aim at showing how the earthly father or an earthly father is rather superfluous. It seems that we can arrange narratives in an ascending order of paternal exclusion, and gradations in the disassociation from sexuality, which start with hints about the father's inadequacy, as expressed in some Old Testament narratives, through a limited, but physical, role for the father as the sperm donor, to "spiritual conception" and then a total absence of any father in any role. Old Testament narratives about the miracles that saved barren women from inferiority and exclusion really convey the theme of fathers who are weak and pushed aside. Infertility is often blamed on the husband, and a barren wife raises doubts about her husband's virility and potency. All these narratives convey a message of or contesting aternity (and very rarely maternity). All virgin birth fantasies, as well as other asexual procreation narratives and the 'family romance' themes, carry a similar message of doing without a father, who is reduced, replaced and eliminated. This clearly undermines the status of all earthly fathers, and there is no other kind. The message to all fathers is that we can do without them.

How did such a subversive story become part of our universal heritage? If we assume that some kind of cultural leadership is in control, and decides on investing resources in particular fantasies, we may wonder why the enacting of Oedipal triumph is supported by so many cultural establishments. Those in positions of power are naturally older males, the fathers of the community, and fathers to their families, and still we observe them allowing these subversive narratives to become part of collective consciousness. These fathers celebrate the myths that convey not only subversion, but enmity, as rebels are glorified and celebrated.

Popular explanations of culture assume that traditions are preserved when they aid the survival of the established order. We are all both fathers and sons, parents and children. It is possible that our experiences as children take primacy, and even as adults we view life from a child's perspective. We identify with the hero, who kills his father, while we also consciously want to believe that we are victims, not wishing to destroy and subvert the family and the social order. The universal celebration of Oedipal winners indicates that Oedipality is stronger than other forces in creating cultural products.

Believing in the Virgin Birth

Islam accepts the Christian notion of the Virgin Birth as a great miracle, refers to Jesus as Issa Bin-Maryam (Jesus son of Mary), but rejects the belief in his divinity, and so belief in the Virgin Birth of the mythological Jesus is a basic tenet of faith in for the majority of Christians and for all faithful Moslems . The appearance of Protestantism did not mean a rejection of the notion, proclaimed anew by Martin Luther and John Calvin, and held by conservative Protestants ever since (Machen, 1930/1958). This means that in the twenty-first century, this idea may be taken seriously by hundreds of millions, and there is nothing esoteric about it.

In the early twentieth century, United States Fundamentalism has been defined (and self-defined) as guided by complete faith in the five *fundamentals*: the inerrancy of the Bible, the virgin birth of Jesus, the supernatural atonement, the physical resurrection of Jesus, and the authenticity of the Gospel miracles. Another version of the "five points" included: The divine inspiration of the Bible, the depravity of man, redemption through the blood of Christ, the true church as a body composed of all believers, and the coming of Christ to establish his reign. Even when conservative Protestants do not include the Virgin Birth among their essential tenets, their belief in it follows from the notion of inerrant scripture. Polls in the United States show that the Virgin Birth idea is more likely to be believed by Protestants, because of their tradition of Biblical literalism.

The reality of United States culture in the twenty-first century is that the belief in the Virgin Birth is more popular than the belief in the value of the theory of evolution. This was noted in 2003 on The Feast of the Assumption of Mary, celebrated on August 15, which commemorates the death of the Virgin Mother and her bodily assumption to Heaven. "So here's a fact appropriate for the day: Americans are three times as likely to believe in the Virgin Birth of Jesus (83 percent) as in evolution (28 percent)" (Kristof, 2003, p. A24).

We cannot assume that the reason for such a high level of support for Virgin Birth idea has to do with cultural dynamics, beyond an overall high level of religiosity. The United States population expresses support for most tenets of Christianity, like the population of Poland and unlike the population of France or Britain, but even in Britain one-third of the population believes in the Virgin Birth. There are complex historical reasons for the unique pattern of religiosity in the

United States, and other (or related) ones for the high level of belief in secular conspiracy theories (Goertzel, 1994).

But what does this level of public commitment mean? When we observe religious adults, their adherence to a particular system may reflect social learning and conformity around an operationalized identity. For hundreds of millions, such an identity is tied to low ego-involvement, rather than a preoccupation with religious ideas. Individuals vary in the psychic investments they make in various beliefs and rituals, and the meaning of particular beliefs for individual believers should be carefully assessed. Their publicly observed support may be only a matter of an automatic loyalty to the group and an automatic response to an identity marker (Beit-Hallahmi, 1989). In the majority of cases, individual attachment to traditional narratives can be explained by social learning. It is likely that most believers in received narratives of miraculous births today are simply expressing loyalty to tradition and identity, without real ego-involvement. We need to explore the individual dynamics of attachment to particular stories. How invested are individual believers in particular beliefs and rituals in terms of their own psychic and material resources? We do find indications in some cases of a real psychic investment in the Virgin Birth icon. Thus, when the literary critic Terry Eagleton makes his case for Christianity and fantasizes about an apparition that would astound non-believers, what comes to his mind is "the Virgin Mary ... clutching the baby Jesus" (Eagleton, 2009, p. 132).

The question of whether an individual's attachment to the Virgin Birth doctrine in Christianity is correlated with his level of Oedipal concern could be measured in a variety of ways. Hood (this volume) presents one method of testing such questions experimentally. Further research into the individual psychodynamics of attachment to Oedipal narratives should follow Hood's exemplary work.

We cannot go back in time to the first appearance of Oedipal triumph narratives, but the research done today can reliably assess the psychological processes that have been involved. In this way, some a-historical motivations may be uncovered.

Conclusion

What has been unique about classical psychoanalytic efforts is the focus on the actual content of beliefs and rituals, and the actual behavior of concrete believers and communities (Beit-Hallahmi, 1996; Faber, 2002).

Its approach to the study of religious beliefs and practices has been much closer to the experiences of the majority of humanity than of most psychologists and sociologists, who seem to avoid dealing with the substance of religion, such as beliefs in the Virgin Birth or the Eucharist.

Oedipal triumph narratives raise two issues. First, why are they so attractive, and second, why have such subversive stories been allowed to survive? The observations presented here seem to indicate that some classical Freudian ideas, more than 100 years old, appear still more than relevant and better than adequate. The red thread we find in all narratives is powerful urge to save mother and keep her away from the dirty paternal penis. Being impregnated by a divine penis is better, as it does not involve the temporal father. Being impregnated without any physical contact is best. Psychological approaches other than classical psychoanalysis simply have nothing to say about virgin birth narratives or other religious beliefs.

The classical psychoanalytic way of looking at religion has been that of viewing religious beliefs, practices, and narratives as created in the context of childhood, metaphorically and literally. Religion isn't just something we learn as children; it is created by the childish mind, reflecting infantile anxieties and wishes, and our confused understanding of the human family, especially paternity. The way childhood and the family are experienced is echoed in fantasies of divine families and human family relations with the spirit world. This is a permanent area in the map of the human imagination.

References

Akhtar, S. (2009). *Comprehensive Dictionary of Psychoanalysis*. London: Karnac Books.

Argyle, M. and Beit-Hallahmi, B. (1975). *The Social Psychology of Religion*. London and Boston: Routledge & Kegan Paul.

Artaud, A. (1963). *Artaud Anthology*. San Francisco: City Lights Publishers.

Balleine, G.R. (1956). *Past Finding Out: The Tragic Story of Joanna Southcott and Her Successors*. New York: Macmillan.

Beit-Hallahmi, B. (1985). Dangers of the vagina. *British Journal of Medical Psychology, 58*, 351-356.

Beit-Hallahmi, B. (1989). *Prolegomena to the Psychological Study of Religion*. Lewisburg, PA: Bucknell University Press.

Beit-Hallahmi, B. (1996). *Psychoanalytic Studies of Religion: Critical Assessment and Annotated Bibliography*. Westport, CT: Greenwood Press,

Beit-Hallahmi, B., and Argyle, M. (1997). *The Psychology of Religious Behaviour, Belief, and Experience*. London and New York: Routledge.

Beit-Hallahmi, B. (1998). *The Illustrated Encyclopedia of Active New Religions*. New York: Rosen Publishing.

Beit-Hallahmi, B. (2001). Explaining religious utterances by taking seriously super-naturalist (and naturalist) claims. In G. Hon & S. Rakover (eds.) *Explanation: Philosophical Essays*. Dordrecht: Kluwer.

Beit-Hallahmi, B. (2002). Political and literary answers to 'Jewish Questions': Freud, Herzl, Joyce, Proust. In J. Bunzl & B. Beit-Hallahmi, (eds.) *Psychoanalysis, Identity, and Ideology: Critical Essays on the Israel/Palestine Case*. Boston: Kluwer.

Bettelheim, B. (1954). *Symbolic Wounds: Puberty Rites and the Envious Male*. Glencoe, IL: Free Press.

Boyce, M. (2000). *Zoroastrians: Their Religious Beliefs and Practices*. London: Routledge.

Brown, D.E. (1991). *Human Universals*. Philadelphia: Temple University Press.

Brown, N.O. (1959). *Life Against Death*. Middletown, CT: Wesleyan University Press.

Brown, P. (1988). *The Body and Society: Men, Women, and Sexual Renunciation in Early Christianity*. New York: Columbia University Press.

Campbell, J. (1981). *The Mythic Image*. Princeton: Princeton University Press.

Deconchy, J.P. (1968). God and parental images: The masculine and feminine in religious free associations. In A. Godin (Ed.) *From Cry to Word*. Brussels: Lumen-Vitae.

Dodds, E.R. (1973). *The Greeks and the Irrational.* Berkeley: University of California Press.

Dundes, A. (1981). The hero pattern and the life of Jesus. *Psychoanalytic Study of Society, 9*, 49-84.

Eagleton, T. (2009). *Reason, Faith and Revolution: Reflections on the God Debate.* New Haven, CT: Yale University Press.

Erikson, E. H. (1970). Autobiographic notes on the identity crisis. *Daedalus*, 99, 730-759.

Faber, M.D. (2002). *The Magic of Prayer: An Introduction to the Psychology of Faith.* Westport, CT: Praeger.

Falk, A. (1975-76). Identity and name changes. *Psychoanalytic Review, 62*, 647-657.

Farrell, B.A. (1955). Psychological theory and the belief in God. *International Journal of Psychoanalysis, 36*, 187-204.

Fornari, F. (1974). *The Psychoanalysis of War.* Garden City, NY: Doubleday.

Fortes, M. (1959). *Oedipus and Job in West African Religion.* Cambridge: Cambridge University Press.

Freemantle, A. (1950). The Oedipal legend in Christian hagiology. *The Psychoanalytic Quarterly, 19*, 408-409.

Freud, S. (1901). The Psychopathology of Everyday Life. *The Standard Edition of the Complete Psychological Works of Sigmund Freud*, 6, vii-296. London: Hogarth Press.

Freud, S. (1905). Fragment of an Analysis of a Case of Hysteria. *The Standard Edition of the Complete Psychological Works of Sigmund Freud*, 7, 1-122. London: Hogarth Press.

Freud, S. (1908). On the sexual theories of children. *The Standard Edition of the Complete Psychological Works of Sigmund Freud, 9,* 209–226. London: Hogarth Press.

Freud, S. (1909). Family romances. *The Standard Edition of the Complete Psychological Works of Sigmund Freud*, 9, 235-242. London: Hogarth Press.

Freud, S. (1912). On the universal tendency to debasement in the sphere of love. *The Standard Edition of the Complete Psychological Works of Sigmund Freud*, 11, 177-190. London: Hogarth Press.

Freud, S. (1913). Totem and Taboo. *The Standard Edition of the Complete Psychological Writings of Sigmund Freud*, 13, 1-164. London: Hogarth Press. Grünbaum

Freud, S. (1916-1917). Introductory Lectures on Psychoanalysis. *The Standard Edition of the Complete Psychological Writings of Sigmund Freud*, Vol. 15. London: Hogarth Press.

Freud, S. (1925-1926). An autobiographical study. *The Standard Edition of the Complete Psychological Writings of Sigmund Freud. 20*, 7-70. London: Hogarth Press.

Freud, S. (1930). Civilization and its discontents. *The Standard Edition of the Complete Psychological Writings of Sigmund Freud, 21*, 64-145. London: Hogarth Press.

Freud, S. (1939). Moses and monotheism. *The Standard Edition of the Complete Psychological Writings of Sigmund Freud*, 23, 1-138. London: Hogarth Press.

Fromm, E. (1964). The *Dogma of Christ and Other Essays on Religion, Psychology and Culture.* New York: Holt, Rinehart and Winston.

Goertzel, T.G. (1994). Belief in conspiracy theories. *Political Psychology, 15*, 733-744.

Goetz, B. (1975). That is all I have to Say about Freud: Bruno Goetz's Reminiscences of Sigmund Freud. *International Review of Psycho-Analysis*, 2, 139-143.

Gordon, K.H., Jr. and Sherr, P.C. (1974). The adolescent orphan in literature: A bibliography for the study of the adolescent. *Journal of the American Psychoanalytic Association, 22*, 537-541

Greenacre, P. (1958). The family romance of the artist. *Psychoanalytic Study of the Child, 13*, 9-36.

Greslé-Favier, C. (2009). *Raising Sexually Pure Kids: Sexual Abstinence, Conservative Christians and American Politics*. Amsterdam/New York: Rodopi.
Hägg, T. & Rousseau, P. (eds.) (2000). *Greek Biography and Panegyric in Late Antiquity*. Berkeley: University of California Press.
Herbenick, D.L. (2009). The development and validation of a scale to measure attitudes toward women's genitals. *International Journal of Sexual Health*, *21*, 153-166.
Hershman, P. (1974). Hair, sex and dirt. *Man*, 9, 274-298.
Himmelfarb, M. (1993). *Ascent to Heaven in Jewish and Christian Apocalypses*. New York: Oxford University Press.
Hood, R.W., Jr., Morris, R.J., & Watson, P.J. (1991). Male commitment to the cult of the Virgin Mary and the passion of Christ as a function of early maternal bonding. *International Journal for the Psychology of Religion, 1*, 221-231.
Horney, K. (1939). *New Ways in Psychoanalysis*. New York: Norton.
Ingham, J.M. (1992). Freud in a forest of symbols: The religious background of psychoanalytic anthropology. In David H. Spain (ed.) *Psychoanalytic Anthropology After Freud: Essays Marking The Fiftieth Anniversary Of Freud's Death*. New York: Psyche Press.
Johnson, A.W. & Price-Williams, D. (1996). *Oedipus Ubiquitous: The Family Complex in World Folk Literature*. Palo Alto, CA: Stanford University Press.
Jones, E. (1951a). A psycho-analytic study of the Holy Ghost. In *Essays in Applied Psychoanalysis*. London: The Hogarth Press and the Institute of Psychoanalysis.
Jones, E. (1951b). Psychoanalysis and the Christian religion. In E. Jones, *Essays in Applied Psychoanalysis*. Vol. 2. London: The Hogarth Press and the Institute of Psychoanalysis.
Kaufman, D. (1999). *Archaeological Perspectives on the Origins of Modern Humans*. Westport, CT: Bergin & Garvey.
Kluckhohn, C. (1959). Recurrent themes in myths and myth-making. *Daedalus*, *88*, 268-279.
Kristof, N. D. (2003). Believe it, or not. *The New York Times*, August 15, p. A 24.
Kubie, L.S. (1937). The fantasy of dirt. *Psychoanalytic Quarterly*, *6*, 388–425.
Larsen, L. & Knapp, R.H. (1964). Sex differences in symbolic conceptions of the deity. *Journal of Projective Techniques and Personality Assessment*, *28*, 303-306.
Leach, E. (1966). Virgin birth. Proceedings of the Royal Anthropological Institute of Great Britain and Ireland, 39-49.
Levi-Strauss, C. (1963). *Structural Anthropology*. New York: Basic Books,
Machen, J.G. (1930/1958). *Virgin Birth of Christ*. London: James Clarke.
Miller, W.I. (1997). *The Anatomy of Disgust*. Cambridge, MA: Harvard University Press.
Mobley, G. (2006). *Samson and the Liminal Hero in the Ancient Near East*. London: T. & T. Clark Publishers
Moxon, C. (1931). A psychoanalytic study of the Christian creed. *International Journal of Psychoanalysis*, *2*, 54-70.
Nagy, G. (1997). *The Best of the Achaeans: Concepts of the Hero in Archaic Greek Poetry*. Baltimore: The Johns Hopkins University Press.
Nigosian, S.A. (1993). *The Zoroastrian Faith: Tradition and Modern Research*. Montreal: McGill-Queen's University Press.
Obeyesekere, G. (1981). *Medusa's hair: An essay on personal symbols and religious experience,* Chicago: University of Chicago Press.
Obeyesekere, G. (1990). *The Work of Culture: Symbolic Transformation in Psychoanalysis and Anthropology*. Chicago: The University of Chicago Press.
Paert, I. (2003). *Old Believers, Religious Dissent and Gender in Russia, 1760-1850*. Manchester: Manchester University Press.
Palombo, S.R. (1994). Oedipus and the Sphinx: Triumph and Catastrophe. *Journal of the American Psychoanalytic Association*, *42*, 635-653.

Raglan, F.R. Somerset (1936). *The Hero: a Study in Tradition, Myth, and Drama.* London: Methuen.

Rank, O. (1914). *The Myth of the Birth of the Hero: A Psychological Interpretation of Mythology.* New York: Nervous and Mental Diseases Publishing Co.

Reider, N. (1960). Medieval Oedipal legends about Judas. *Psychoanalytic Quarterly, 29,* 515-527.

Reik, T. (1958). *Ritual: Psychoanalytic Studies.* New York: International Universities Press.

Rosner, F. (2001). *Biomedical Ethical Issues and Jewish Law.* Jersey City, NJ: Ktav Publishing House.

Schendler, D. (1954) Judas, Oedipus and various saints. *Psychoanalysis, 2,* 41-46.

Simo, J. (1983). On Christianity and the Oedipal winner. *Psychoanalytic Review, 70,* 321-329.

Slusser, M. (2003). *St. Justin Martyr: Dialogue with Trypho.* Washington, DC: Catholic University of America Press.

Spiro, M.E. (1968). Virgin Birth, Parthenogenesis and Physiological Paternity: An Essay in Cultural Interpretation. *Man, 3,* 242-261.

Staples, A. (1997). *From Good Goddess to Vestal Virgins: Sex and Category in Roman Religion.* London: Routledge.

Synge, J.M. (1998). *The Playboy of the Western World and Other Plays.* New York: Oxford University Press.

Tabor, J. & Gallagher, J. (1995). *Why Waco? Cults and the Battle for Religious Freedom in America.* Berkeley: University of California Press.

Yarom, N. (1993). *Body, Blood and Sexuality.* New York: Peter Lang.

Yeats, W.B. (1957). "Crazy Jane Talks with the Bishop." *The Variorum Edition of the Poems of W. B. Yeats.* New York: Macmillan.

Index

About the Contributors

Adolf Grünbaum is the Andrew Mellon Professor of Philosophy of Science, Primary Research Professor in the Department of History and Philosophy of Science, Research Professor of Psychiatry, and Chairman of the Center for Philosophy of Science, all at the University of Pittsburgh. Among his best known books are *Philosophical Problems of Space and Time* (second edition, 1973); *Modern Science and Zeno's Paradoxes* (second edition, 1968); *The Foundations of Psychoanalysis: A Philosophical Critique* (1984); and *Validation in the Clinical Theory of Psychoanalysis: A Study in the Philosophy of Psychoanalysis* (1993). He is a Fellow of the American Academy of Arts & Sciences.

David Livingstone Smith is associate professor of philosophy at the University of New England in Biddeford, Maine. He earned his Ph.D. at Kings College, University of London, where his research focused on Freud's philosophy of mind. He is the author of numerous papers and six books, including *Freud's Philosophy of the Unconscious* (Kluwer, 1999), *Why We Lie: The Evolutionary Roots of Deception and the Unconscious Mind* (St. Martin's Press, 2004) and, most recently, *The Most Dangerous Animal: Human Nature and the Origins of War* (St. Martin's Press, 2007).

Jerry S. Piven teaches in the Department of Philosophy at Case Western Reserve University, where his courses focus on philosophy of religion, existentialism, psychoanalysis, and metaphysics. He is the editor of *The Psychology of Death in Fantasy and History* (2004) and *Terrorism, Jihad, and Sacred Vengeance* (2004), and author of *Death and Delusion: A Freudian Analysis of Mortal Terror* (2004), *The Madness and Perversion of Yukio Mishima* (2004), and numerous articles on psychoanalysis, religion, and history. He has recently co-authored a book with psychiatrist Yuko Katsuta titled *Nihon No Kyoki* (Japanese Madness, 2007).

Michael P. Carroll is professor and chair in the Department of Sociology at the University of Western Ontario. He has authored seven books and numerous articles on popular religion and has often argued for the value of psychoanalysis in explaining some, but only some, of the patterns associated with popular religion. His most recent book, *American Catholics in the Protestant Imagination* (The Johns Hopkins University Press), examines a variety of unacknowledged historiographical biases that continue to structure the academic study of Catholicism.

Carlo Strenger is currently cochair of the clinical graduate program at the psychology department of Tel Aviv University and has previously held teaching appointments at the philosophy department at Hebrew University. He is a member of the Daseinsanalytisches Institut Zurich and of the Permanent Monitoring Panel on Terrorism of the World Federation of Scientists. He has written six books and numerous scientific articles, in the last decades primarily about the impact of globalization on meaning and personal identity.

Harriet Lutzky received her Ph.D. in Clinical Psychology and a Certificate in Psychotherapy and Psychoanalysis from New York University. She has been a Visiting Lecturer and Research Associate at Harvard Divinity School. Formerly Maître de Conférences at the University of Paris, she currently teaches courses on psychology and religion, and on the concept of the sacred, at New York University.

Ralph W. Hood, Jr. is professor of psychology at the University of Tennessee at Chattanooga. He is a former president of the Division of the Psychology of Religion of the American Psychological Association and a recipient of its William James, Distinguished Service, and Mentor Awards. He is a former editor of the *Journal for the Scientific Study of Religion* and a current coeditor of the *Archive for the Psychology of Religion.* He has published over 200 articles and book chapters. Among his recent books are *Them that believe: The power and meaning of contemporary Christian serpent handling* (with W. Paul Williamson), and *The Psychology of Religion: An empirical approach, 4th ed.* (with Peter Hill and Bernard Spilka).

Benjamin Beit-Hallahmi is the author, coauthor, editor, or coeditor of eighteen books and monographs on the psychology of religion, social identity, and personality development. Among his better-known publications are *The Psychology of Religious Behaviour, Belief and Experience; The Psychoanalytic Study of Religion,* and *Psychoanalysis, Identity, and Ideology.* In 1993 he was the recipient of the William James Award (Division 36 of the American Psychological Association) for his contributions to the psychology of religion. Currently, he is professor of psychology at the University of Haifa and senior research associate at the Institute for the Study of Secularism in Society and Culture, Trinity College, Hartford, CT.

Breinigsville, PA USA
20 July 2010
242125BV00001B/7/P

9 780765 707222